Voices of the Sages

Old Testament Wisdom in Dialogue

Endorsements for *Voices of the Sages*

"Brian Toews does readers of Israel's Scriptures a real service with his impressive study. He examines the third section of the Writings, that section that seems to be the "leftovers" of the Hebrew Bible after the Torah and the Prophets, and views it as an extremely important wisdom contribution to the entire canon. Creatively viewing the various books in this collection in the form of sages gathered together around a discussion of major themes of Scripture, he shows the importance of this section of the Tanak, as well as the distinctive contribution of its many voices. There are many highlights in his treatment such as the treatment of Proverbs as providing a way to live the Shema in everyday practical life, a significant female perspective (the Megillot) and the importance of marriage. There is important synthesis of themes like the kingdom of God, along with a helpful tracing of these ideas in the New Testament. Some helpful practical applications to contemporary believers round out the study. Toews has clearly sat at the feet of these sages and learned much!"

    - **Dr. Stephen Dempster**, Emeritus Professor of Religious Studies, Crandall University

"Imagine that you have been invited to a dinner featuring a dozen biblical authors of the Old Testament Writings. That is what Brian Toews does in his new book as he explores the many common themes in these familiar and not-so-familiar books of the Bible. Toews' engaging writing draws us into the discussion and gives us new insights that enrich our understanding and appreciation of this portion of the Bible that he has studied deeply and taught for thirty years."

    - **Dr. Daniel Estes**, Distinguished Professor of Old Testament, Cedarville University

"There's a seat for us at the table. Brian Toews brings us to a friendly conversation between the authors of and persons within the neglected wisdom writings of the Old Testament. In *Voices of the Sages*, David and Naomi interact with Job. Esther gets advice from the likes of Daniel, Ruth, Lady Wisdom of Proverbs, and even the Song of Songs. These and many other conversations reveal how God's wisdom works. Listening at the table has opened my ears to the wisdom conversations I need to hear. Every student and every minister of the word needs to study this book."

    - **Dr. Gary Edward Schnittjer**, Distinguished Professor of Old Testament, Cairn University

"Reading and recommending this book brings me great joy. I have had the privilege of learning from Brian Toews for almost thirty years, and the book in your hands is just a portion of the fruit of Dr. Toews' lifetime of careful scholarship and creative thinking about the Bible. I commend it to those who are new to the Old Testament, as well as to those who have spent many years meditating on the scriptures. It is engaging, edifying, and clearly written — a delight to read as you reflect on the text of scripture."

    - **Dr. Jonathan Master**, President, Greenville Presbyterian Theological Seminary

"The world of OT scholarship is ripe for this book, and I can think of no one better qualified than Brian to address the unity of the Writings. Drawing on his expertise in canonical and compositional studies, biblical theology, and intertextuality, his contribution is both readable by students, and stimulating for scholars. No conversation on the Writings will be complete without listening to his pioneering voice here."

    - **Dr. Ray Lubeck**, Professor in Bible & Theology, Jessup University-Multnomah

"*Voices of the Sages* will be the most eye-opening book about the Bible that you read this year. It is not difficult to find resources that will provide excellent content about an individual book in the Bible, but it is quite rare to find a text that links themes and ideas across so many biblical books as well as *Voices of the Sages*. Toews pulls back the curtain to reveal the hidden connections that the wisdom literature shares with other books of the Old Testament. Using what he calls con-textuality and montage, Toews offers sure guidance into the deep ties between Ruth and Proverbs, the Chronicles and the Psalter, Ecclesiastes and Song of Songs, and many others. Discovering these links will propel the reader into a richer understanding of the Hebrew Bible as a whole. The product of a lifetime of reading and studying the Bible, *Voices of the Sages* is amazingly accessible and understandable, even for those readers without Hebrew. This book will be deeply satisfying for all who study, teach and preach the Old Testament."

    - **Dr. Timothy S. Yoder**, Professor of Theological Studies, Dallas Theological Seminary

"Brian Toews has done all Christians, as students of the Old Testament, a wonderful service by providing an accessible introduction to the Old Testament that avoids overspecialization and overgeneralization. His approach to the texts as conversations between sages works well to show how the texts function within their canonical context and how we, as modern readers, can learn from Old Testament authors as sages. These authors and their texts are the masters who want us, as their disciples, to learn the deep things of God. This accessible study of the Old Testament is a generous contribution to the church and should be on the bookshelves of pastors and all laity."

- **Dr. Greg Peters**, Professor of Medieval and Spiritual Theology, Biola University

"Dr. Toews looks at how joined the Old Testament books are instead of seeing them as randomly compiled individual stories. He does this by engaging the conversational themes interconnecting the books following the particular threads of Wisdom and Kingdom in the texts. Readers of *Voices of the Sages* will learn how using the contextual order of the Writings is revealing and helpful in rightly interpreting the Word of God."

- **Dr. Mark Menga**, Communication & Cinema Studies Professor, Lancaster Bible College

"Three decades' worth of Old Testament students have experienced the Bible coming alive through Prof. Toews's careful study and engaging teaching. *Voices of the Sages* is the culmination of his thoughtful research on the Writings, the third section of the Hebrew canon. Rather than emphasizing a particular linear order of the books of the Writings, Toews creatively presents the books as linked in conversation around the central theme of wisdom, demonstrating the interconnectedness of Scripture. Academics, pastors, and lay people will appreciate this essential guide through an oft-neglected part of the Hebrew Bible."

- **Dr. Benjamin D. Giffone**, Assoc. Professor of Biblical Studies, Hindustan Bible Institute & College

"In *Voices of the Sages*, Brian Toews, a lifelong student, teacher, and scholar of the Hebrew Bible, experiments with the implications of reading and hearing the Writings-corpus as a corpus, while also allowing for each individual book to speak on its own terms. Toews pursues reading the Writings as a collection of literature that is unified by its overall message, while bringing attention to the fact that Israelites and Judean sages, at times, engage in sharp theological conversation with one another. The validity of this volume's thesis is legitimized by the way in which the Writings have been assembled in the history of their existence. The lexical, conceptual, and thematic linkages between texts pressured ancient editors to make various associations within the collection that led them to order the corpus into various canonical arrangements. Books already in conversation with one another were thus stitched together in ways that much more overtly brought these theological dialogues to light. It is here that Toews joins the sages by highlighting much of the same throughout each chapter of this thought-provoking volume."

- **Dr. Robert C. Kashow**, Adjunct Professor, Salve Regina University

"Toews has done an excellent job comparing and contrasting the various books to show how both human wisdom and divine wisdom are personified. I would heartily recommend the book to anyone seeking to grow in God's wisdom."

- **Dr. Tom Halsted**, Dean of the School of Biblical Studies, The Master's University

Voices of the Sages
Old Testament Wisdom in Dialogue

BRIAN G. TOEWS

McGahan

Voices of the Sages: Old Testament Wisdom in Dialogue

Copyright © 2024 by Brian G. Toews

All rights reserved. No part of this publication may be reproduced, stored in a retrieval system, or transmitted in any form or by any means—electronic, mechanical, photocopy, recording, or any other—except for brief quotations in printed reviews, without the prior permission of the publisher.

Cover artwork created using DALL·E, an AI program by OpenAI.

Unless otherwise indicated, all Scripture quotations are from The ESV® Bible (The Holy Bible, English Standard Version®), © 2001 by Crossway, a publishing ministry of Good News Publishers. Used by permission. All rights reserved.

McGahan Publishing House | Lynchburg, Tennessee
www.mphbooks.com

Requests for information should be sent to:
info@mphbooks.com

ISBN 978-1-951252-32-8 (Paperback)

To Brenda,
שלי אשת חיל

Contents

Preface 9

1 - Introduction: The Writings, Wisdom, and Poetry 13

2 - Chronicles: The House that Wisdom Built 33

3 - The Book of Psalms: The Wise Ascend to Zion 54

4 - Job: Human Versus Divine Wisdom .77

5 - Proverbs: Wisdom Loves Those Who Love Her 102

6 - Ruth: Woman Wisdom 132

7 - The Song of Songs: Creation's Call to Love 151

8 - Ecclesiastes: The Preacher on Wisdom 177

9 - Lamentations: Suffering and Hope .198

10 - Esther: The Absence of the Presence of the Lord 222

11 - Daniel: The Power and Wisdom of the God of Heaven . . .254

12 - Ezra-Nehemiah: Israel's Return – Wisdom and Folly 284

Afterword: Reflections for Today 312

Appendix: Conversations in *Voices of the Sages* 319

Preface

The genesis of this book was thirty years ago, as I read a few paragraphs in John Sailhamer's *Introduction to Old Testament Theology*. Sailhamer introduced me to two new ideas: reading biblical books within their textual neighborhoods and text collections/combinations as montages. This first concept, "con-textuality," is "the notion of the effect on meaning of the relative position of a biblical book within a prescribed reading order."[1] In other words, how is our understanding of a text affected by the texts we read before it, after it, or near it? Sailhamer then went on to discuss the implications of reading Ruth after Proverbs, following the Hebrew Bible book order. This idea fascinated me: I had never considered the book of Ruth as existing anywhere other than between Judges and Samuel.

Sailhamer then transitioned to a related idea: montage, a technique borrowed from film-making. Montage is "the effect of meaning which one achieves by juxtaposing two related or unrelated pieces of film."[2] When watching a montage, viewers make a whole out of individual parts. Those parts push the viewer to analyze and construct meaning from the images in the series. The famous "Rocky" montage comes to mind: at the 1:13 mark of the movie, the wordless montage of Rocky's training culminates in his running up the steps of the Philadelphia Museum of Art. Viewers naturally analyze these film shots to form unified and coherent meaning from the image collection: underdog determination, aspiration to greatness, Philly grit, etc.[3] Sailhamer argued that montage is present not only in film but also within texts and collections of texts.

---

1 John H. Sailhamer. *Introduction to Old Testament Theology: A Canonical Approach*. Grand Rapids, MI: Zondervan, 1995: 213. Although serial order comes into play, I broaden out con-textuality to reading texts with texts within the Writings irrespective of order.

2 Sailhamer, *Old Testament*, 214.

3 This montage has had such a powerful effect on viewers that every day, people run up the steps of the Philadelphia Museum of Art and raise their arms in triumph.

Sailhamer's points sparked my interest in the *Ketuvim*, also called the Writings, the third division of the Hebrew Bible after the *Torah* (Law) and the *Nebi'im* (Prophets). Combining his two ideas, I posed the question, "How does juxtaposition affect the meaning of the various books in the Writings?" I have spent the last thirty years thinking through con-textuality and montage in the Writings, particularly with respect to the collection's wisdom instruction. These ideas have resurfaced again and again in my teaching, research, and academic papers over the course of my career. *Voices of the Sages* is a compilation of my thinking thus far.

The Writings are the forgotten stepchild of the Hebrew Bible, the Tanak. Studies on the Law and Prophets abound, but most scholars view the Writings as a haphazard collection of loosely related books of various genres and themes. The individual books generate quite a bit of study, but the collection as a whole has not been seriously considered until recently. As *Voices of the Sages* will demonstrate, I propose that the Writings are a conversation-creating collection: the juxtaposition of the books forces readers to make connections between them, generating more insight. These connections are here represented as conversations between books. As the title suggests, *Voices of the Sages* personifies the texts in the Writings as sages who dialogue and argue about related topics within their pages. Each book in turn becomes the interaction's focus; the sages consider its text contextually with their text. Intentionally de-emphasizing serial order, I imagine the books as eleven sages sitting around a circular table, conversing. Depending on the topic being discussed, some sages have more to say than others. The texts speak both to their neighbors and across the table; the dialogue is an open one.

Many of the conversations in *Voices of the Sages* can be found in the academic literature. Other connections result from my own reflections. Sometimes, connections stem from an explicit textual link, such as Ruth and the Proverbs 31 woman of virtue. Other times, different texts contain a repeated line throughout, such as "the fear of the Lord." This phrase then serves as a reference point for other texts. The film world offers another illustration here: the "Field of Dreams" saying "If you build it, he will come" guides the film through its repetition within the story. Still other connections emerge from reading the Writings as montage, texts to be read up against other texts in the collection. What meaning is created when readers read Daniel, Esther, Ruth, and Proverbs off each other? *Voices of the Sages* explores all these types of connections in hopes that readers develop eyes to see further insights on their own beyond the pages of this book.

Voices of the Sages also offers a rare focus: the wisdom thread within the Writings. To this end, the sages' conversation revolves around their presentation of wisdom. The juxtaposition of the five traditional wisdom books—Psalms, Job, Proverbs, the Song of Songs, and Ecclesiastes—with the other books in the Writings highlights the latter's oft-overlooked wisdom elements. The sages' conversations thus deepen and broaden readers' understanding of wisdom beyond the classic five books into the corners of the whole collection.

Several decisions I made while writing this book are noted here. *Voices of the Sages* is intended for biblically literate but not necessarily academic readers—readability was a high priority. I assume readers are familiar with the basic content of each book in the Writings and seek to build on that foundational knowledge. *Voices of the Sages* is not a technical, academic work; instead, its tone and depth mimic a classroom discussion of learners gaining insight from one another. From time to time, I include a footnote to clarify a more obscure point, and each chapter ends with a "Further Reading" section suggesting ... a few academic works for further study.

Regarding particular language, the Hebrew name for Israel's God, *YHWH*, has been translated as Lord, following the pattern of the New Testament. When especially significant, I note that Lord refers to *YHWH*, the covenant God of Israel. Whenever possible, I avoid gendered terms, preferring "people" or "person" for Hebrew masculine nouns that carry a general meaning. When gender appears relevant, I retain specifically male and female terms. In keeping with tradition, I capitalize nouns and pronouns that refer to God or Jesus, though not in general OT references to the promised messiah. Unless otherwise noted, all biblical quotations come from the ESV, which does not capitalize nouns and pronouns referring to God.

Lastly, the subject of *Voices of the Sages* is wisdom, a highly applicational topic. However, I can only suggest general applications of this wisdom because wisdom decisions are made in the context of a person's own unique life situation.

Finally, I wish to acknowledge several people's contributions to my intellectual and spiritual life as well as the writing of this book. I am thankful for the teaching and research opportunities given to me by Cairn University over the course of my 30 years at the institution. As I have already mentioned, the late John H. Sailhamer's writings and our conversations set me on this wisdom path. My students have been a joy to teach; their engagement with me and these books has enriched and deepened my own insight. My colleague Gary E. Schnittjer has been my Old Testament conversation partner for over 25 years. I can only hope our dialogue has been as beneficial to him as these interactions have been to me; this work owes much to him and his counsel. Thank you to McGahan Publishing House for publishing this book. Finally, I want to thank my wife and editor, Brenda Mellon, PhD, my co-laborer. My ideas and her clarity have birthed what we hope is a helpful, useful, and inspiring text.

Introduction: The Writings, Wisdom, and Poetry

Voices of the Sages seeks to help readers deepen their understanding of biblical wisdom by looking at the Old Testament wisdom texts in the Writings and teasing out their connections with one another. While many books and studies already look to the wisdom texts for instruction for living, this book takes a different approach: examining these texts as if they were conversing with one another.

Much of the scholarly discussion of the Writings focuses on the order of the books and the date of their collection. Books situated next to each other prompt certain connections; for example, the neighboring books of Esther and Daniel highlight each other's similarities and dissimilarities, revealing layers of meaning and instruction for the reader. To be more specific, Esther and Daniel both negotiate a Gentile king's court with wisdom, yet they do so quite differently. The books of Job and Proverbs being back-to-back underlines the central theme of the fear of the Lord in both books while encouraging complementary perspectives regarding the Lord's dealings with the righteous and wicked.

As stated above, *Voices of the Sages* delves into conversations created by a synchronic reading of the texts in the Writings. The book of Job offers an example of this type of wisdom conversation: Job and his friends attempt to figure out Job's situation based on their own wisdom and understanding. The men of Hezekiah must have had similar conversations over their task of collecting the proverbs of Solomon (Prov 25:1), discussing which ones to include and exclude. Yet another example is the dialogue necessary to choosing wisdom when faced with competing or contradictory advice, such as in Proverbs 24:4-5: "Do not answer a fool according to his folly" and "Answer a fool according to his folly." How can both proverbs be wise? As all who seek wisdom have experienced, meditation, reflection, and discernment characterize the wisdom endeavor. Though an individual activity (Ps 1:2), the pursuit of wisdom also allows and encourages communal dialogue and conversation. *Voices of the Sages* imagines a group of texts able to speak, seated around a table, discussing their content, their meaning, their difficult points, their tensions, and their resolutions. While questions of book order matter and will be discussed later in this introduction, reading the Wisdom texts with less attention on their sequence and more attention on their thematic intersections offers helpful and unpublished insight into biblical wisdom. Consequently, *Voices of the Sages* examines the Writings in a circular arrangement as opposed to a line, opening each text to its relationship with all the others, regardless of printed order.

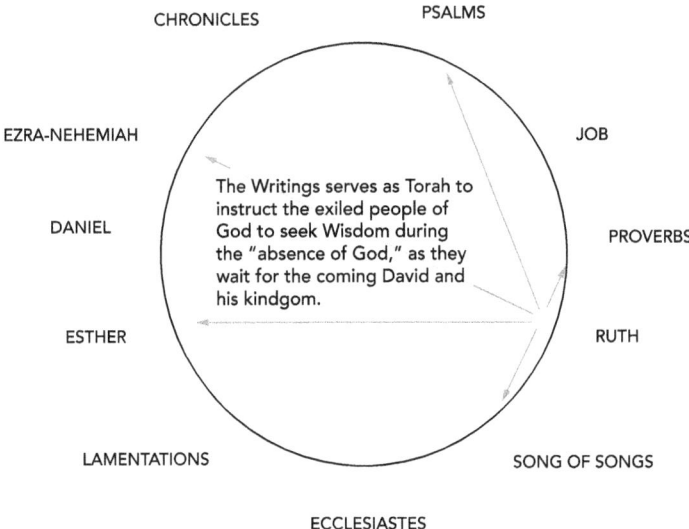

The above diagram sketches this text's treatment of the book of Ruth in Chapter 6: after acknowledging the helpful connections between Ruth, Proverbs, and the Song, *Voices of the Sages* broadens the conversation to include the "voices" of the books of Esther, Ezra-Nehemiah, and Psalms as well.

To engage these texts well, a few preliminary topics need attention. This introduction therefore explains four foundational elements for this wisdom conversation: a basic definition of wisdom, a brief discussion of the history of the Writings, a thematic overview of the Writings, and a short primer on how to read Hebrew poetry.

What is Wisdom?

Scholar Robert Gordis calls the Writings "the repository of wisdom" of the Hebrew Scriptures.[4] But what is wisdom? This section explores the idea of wisdom and how wisdom is characterized in the Old Testament, giving the reader some depth and breadth with which to think about these texts.

One of the ways to better understand the meaning of a word is to look at its word-field: words with similar meanings in the same context. When considered together, the words within a given word-field play off of each other, offering nuances to enhance the reader's understanding of the passage as a whole. The Hebrew word for wisdom, *hokmah*, is typically translated "wisdom" or "skill," as seen below in context in Proverbs 1:2-7. The underlined words form the wisdom word-field.

1:2 To know wisdom and instruction,

To understand words of insight,

3 To receive instruction in wise dealing,

In righteousness, justice, and equity;

4 To give prudence to the simple,

Knowledge and discretion to the youth—

5 Let the wise hear and increase in learning,

And the one who understands obtain guidance,

---

[4] As early as 1971, Robert Gordis stated, "It may be noted that the third section of the Bible, called *Ketubim*, the Sacred Writings or Hagiographa, is not a miscellaneous collection, but, on the contrary, has an underlying unity. Basically, it is the repository of Wisdom." *Poets, Prophets, and Sages: Essays in Biblical Interpretation.* Bloomington, IN: Indiana Univ Press, 1971: 33. Julius Steinberg has offered another more recent justification for a wisdom perspective of the Writings in *Die Ketuvim: Ihr Aufbau und Ihre Botschaft.* Hamburg; Philo, 2006: 484.

6   To <u>understand</u> a proverb and a saying,

       The words of the wise and their riddles.

7   The fear of the Lord is the beginning of <u>knowledge</u>;

       Fools despise <u>wisdom</u> and <u>instruction</u>.

The list below offers an expanded English definition of each word in the wisdom word-field, showing the nuances in this passage:

- Instruction (*musar*) – discipline, correction, rebuke, instruction
- To understand (*bin*) – understand, discern, consider
- Insight (from *bin*) – insight, discernment, understanding
- To deal wisely (*sakal*) – to prosper, to have success, to be prudent, to have insight, to consider
- Righteousness (*sedeq*) – what is right or correct
- Justice (*mishpat*) – justice, judgment, just decision
- Equity (*mesar*) – equity, uprightness, fairness
- Prudence (*'ormah*) – shrewdness, craftiness, prudence, cunning
- Knowledge (*da'at*) – knowledge ranging from factual to intimate
- Discretion (*mezimmah*) – discretion, planning, purpose, scheming
- Learning (*leqah*) – learning, persuasiveness, teaching
- Guidance (*tahbulah*) – guidance, counsel, direction, steering, advice

Many of these terms present the wisdom endeavor as dividing between two ways (discern, discretion), or being able to see through a murky situation (insight, prudence, shrewdness), one that requires specific direction (knowledge, learning, guidance), and a choice that leads to successful living (righteous, justice, equity). Studying this passage illustrates the multiple facets that make one wise. Wisdom includes everything encompassed in its word-field: knowledge, discernment, prudence, justice, etc.

The recurring image of a choice between two paths—wisdom and folly, life and death—forms a fundamental framework for understanding the pursuit of wisdom. As Genesis makes clear, the Lord understands that the intent of the heart of humanity is evil from their youth up (Gen 6:5, 8:21). Proverbs refers to this human intent as folly, the will of humans to go their own way in their own understanding. Consequently, foolish humanity requires instruction, correction, and even rebuke to find the path of wisdom and step back upon it. The proper response to such instruction and rebuke is to fear the Lord, the beginning of all wisdom (Prov 9:10). This imagery of the two paths paints wisdom as a journey full of choices across time. The wise person stays on the path of wisdom by choosing wisdom time and time again.

Another passage defining wisdom comes from the building of the tabernacle in Exodus 35. In this chapter, the Lord gives special wisdom to Bezalel of Judah to design the tabernacle:

> 35:30 Then Moses said to the people of Israel, "See, the Lord has called by name Bezalel the son of Uri, son of Hur, of the tribe of Judah;
>
> 31 and he has filled him with the Spirit of God, with **skill**, with **intelligence**, with **knowledge**, and with all **craftsmanship**,
>
> 32 to **devise** artistic designs, to work in gold and silver and bronze."

Again, considering the wisdom word-field helps the reader better define wisdom. In this passage, the word *hokmah* is translated as "skill" instead of "wisdom," and the word intelligence, *tebunah*, is related to the root verb *bin*, "to understand." *Da'at*, "knowledge," refers to Bezalel's intimate knowledge of his craft (*mela'kah*). The Lord gave Bezalel these wisdom gifts so that he could creatively devise (*hashab*) designs for the tabernacle. This description of Bezalel echoes the Proverbs 1 passage above, drawing from the same word-field. Experts in their craft know exactly how to use their tools in just the right way, in just the right place, toward a successful end. Their insight and discernment produce a creative and high-quality outcome. Wisdom, then, is likened to skillful craftsmanship: doing the right, just, and equitable deed to the right person, in the right context, in the right way, at the right time, for the good of the other.

In any study, looking closely at specific passages proves useful, yet zooming back out for a view of the larger context also helps define ideas well. Proverbs 3:19 reads, "by wisdom (*hokmah*) the Lord founded the earth; by understanding (*tebunah*) he established the heavens." This passage implies that the biblical context for wisdom begins with the Lord's work of creation in Genesis 1-2. Human beings made in the image of God were created in wisdom, fashioned to live their lives conforming to God's creational wisdom. Humanity should make their lives fit into—work in harmony with—the rest of creation created by God's wisdom. Wisdom is not just an aspect of correct human living; wisdom is woven throughout the fabric of creation. As a creature, living rightly in creation is living wisely.

This creation starting point begins a creation/wisdom theme that runs throughout the Writings. As will be discussed below, the Writings begin with the book of Chronicles; Chronicles begins with a 9-chapter genealogy of the people of Israel, starting with Adam. Even with no narrative surrounding Adam's name, every Bible reader—ancient or contemporary—knows to fill in Adam's story from Genesis 1-4[5]: God created Adam in His image and placed him in the garden to

---

[5] See Toews, Brian G. "Genesis 1-4: The Genesis of Old Testament Instruction," in *Biblical Theology: Retrospect and Prospect.* Ed. Scott J. Hafemann. Downers Grove, IL: InterVarsity, 2002: 38-52.

keep God's commands, but Adam played the fool, bringing death and judgment on himself and all creation. Consequently, Adam is exiled from the garden but given hope for redemption through his offspring. By beginning with "Adam," the book of Chronicles establishes a creational context for itself as well as for the Writings as a whole: wisdom is found by reading these texts against the backdrop and through the filter of creation.

After Chronicles, each book in the Writings continues to treat wisdom within this creational context. For instance, the book of Job reveals that only the Lord as Creator knows where wisdom is found (Job 28:23-28). Humans cannot find wisdom (Job 28:12-13); it is not in the land of the living, but must be given to humanity by the One who stands outside of creation and so understands it all: the Creator Himself. Ecclesiastes echoes the God/man, *'elohim/'adam*, relationship of Genesis and considers the vanity (*hebel*) seen in creation's apparently profit-less repetitive cycles. In Ecclesiastes, as in Genesis 3, humanity is ultimately just dust. The Song of Songs presents a garden-like picture of a man and a woman searching for and finding each other, anticipating a joyful union. The Song extends Adam's poetry in Genesis 2:23: "This [woman] is now bone of my bones, / And flesh of my flesh." The following diagram illustrates how firmly Genesis 1-4 roots the books in the Writings:

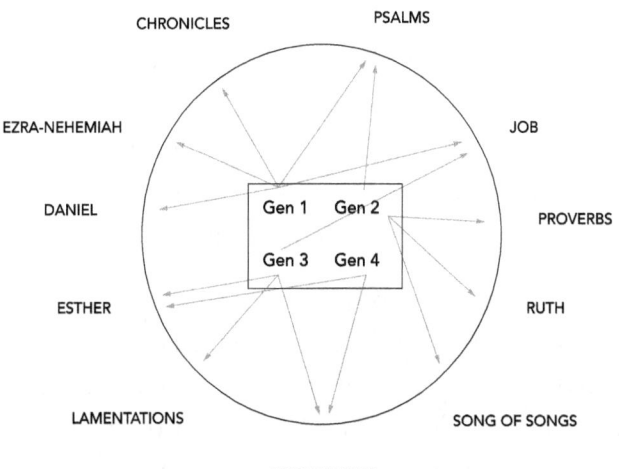

Given the relevance of the wisdom books' relationship with Genesis 1-4, each chapter of *Voices of the Sages* will include a short discussion of the creation themes threaded throughout that specific text. Each book's direct link to the creation account functions to contextualize the Writings so their content can be applied more generally and universally. The Writings typically do not make explicit references to their own OT context: Mosaic Law, sacrifices, feast days, or specific places in the land, except for Jerusalem. Instead, the Writings portray wisdom as unbound by historical time periods and events. Since Genesis 1-4 forms the backdrop for all humanity, the Writings offer themselves as a repository of wisdom for all humans across time and place.

The Books in the Writings: Dates, Authors, Order

The above notwithstanding, the Writings still exhibit marks of the history of Israel. For instance, the book of Psalms illustrates the compilation of the Writings across the OT timeframe. The variety of psalms from different biblical periods—Moses (Ps 90), David (half the Psalter), Solomon (Ps 72), exilic (Ps 74, 79), and post-exilic (Ps 126)—indicates that the final collection of the 150 psalms must have taken place in Israel's post-exilic period. Similarly, the Writings contain texts from pre-exilic, exilic, and post-exilic times; the collecting and curating of the Writings collection must have taken place during or after the Persian or Greek phases of the post-exile but before the Christian era. Thus formed, the Writings address God-fearers in the post-exile and beyond. Even in these years after the exile, Israel's older books or texts, like David's psalms, remain relevant and meaningful; the NT's numerous quotations from and allusions to the Writings demonstrate how valuable these texts were and are to the NT and the Church.

The question of authorship of the individual books of the Writings naturally surfaces in this discussion. Like so much of the OT, most books in the Writings derive from an anonymous author; the texts themselves do not provide a clear window into their authorship. We simply do not know who compiled the Psalter or Chronicles, for example.

The books of Ruth, Esther, and Job are anonymous as well. Parts of the book of Proverbs are Solomon's, but in light of the additional proverbs added by the wise men of Hezekiah (Prov 25:1), we do not know who compiled the final edition of Proverbs. However, since these books have been received as the Word of God (2 Tim 3:15-16), this anonymity does not create a problem. *Voices of the Sages* will point out each book's history and historical context when such information is clear from the texts and relevant to the conversations between the books. Though the Writings were written over hundreds of years by different authors in different historical contexts, *Voices of the Sages* will read the Writings as a single unified collection curated to communicate a consistent wisdom message with related theological themes.

The next question is that of book order. The Protestant Bible divides the OT into four sections: Pentateuch, History, Wisdom, and Prophets. The Hebrew Scriptures or "**TaNaK**" groups the same books into only three categories:

- The Law or *Torah*: Genesis, Exodus, Leviticus, Numbers, Deuteronomy

- The Prophets or *Nebi'im*, further subdivided into:

    - Former Prophets: Joshua, Judges, 1-2 Samuel, 1-2 Kings

    - Latter Prophets: Isaiah, Jeremiah, Ezekiel, the Twelve Minor Prophets

- Writings or *Ketuvim*: Chronicles, Psalms, Job, Proverbs, Ruth, Song of Songs, Ecclesiastes, Lamentations, Esther, Daniel, Ezra-Nehemiah

Comparing these two ways of ordering the OT reveals different "canonical neighborhoods" of books. For example, in the Hebrew Scriptures, the book of Daniel resides not with the Prophets but between two post-exilic narratives, and the book of Ruth is bracketed by two wisdom books. *Voices of the Sages* explores the Writings in their Hebrew grouping; this context fosters interpretive insights within the grouping far more difficult to see in the traditional Protestant OT book order.

To complicate matters a bit further, the order of the books in the grouping of the Writings varies slightly between two major Jewish traditions.[6] However, the basic structure of the Writings remains similar. Since one must choose an order to proceed in any kind of orderly fashion, *Voices of the Sages* will use the order of the Writings in the Masoretic Text (MT), the authoritative version of the Hebrew Scriptures, for two reasons. First, pre-Christian evidence references the three divisions of the Hebrew Bible[7], meaning that the Hebrew TaNaK is the Bible that Jesus, the apostles, and the early Church read and studied. Jesus' reference in Luke 24:44 to the OT as "the Law of Moses, the Prophets, and the Psalms" illustrates this three-part scheme. Although Jesus selects only one book from the third division for his presentation to the disciples, He may have chosen the Psalms because they contain so many important passages relating to His coming as the Messiah. In this case, the Psalms could function as a representative book for the collection of the Writings.

Second, the MT is the authoritative Hebrew text for the Jewish community, the scholarly community, and any work of translation from the Reformers to the present. When one studies the Old Testament, one uses the MT; the MT's order of books is therefore worth consideration. In fact, the latest print edition of the scholarly Hebrew Bible, *Biblia Hebraica Quinta*, adopts the order of the books in the MT: the Writings/*Ketuvim* collection begins with Chronicles and ends with Ezra-

---

6 Regarding the Writings, Timothy J. Stone states, "The evidence is late and scant, but from what survived, the Talmudic and Masoretic orders for the Writings in the Jewish tradition are the only two attested prior to the twelfth century C.E." Timothy J. Stone. *The Compilational History of the Megilloth: Canon, Contoured Intertextuality, and Meaning in the Writings.* Tübingen: Mohr Siebeck, 2013: 111. The Talmudic order for the Writings is Ruth, Psalms, Job, Proverbs, Ecclesiastes, Song of Songs, Lamentations, Daniel, Esther, Ezra-Nehemiah, and Chronicles.

7 The best evidence comes from the Prologue to the book of Sirach, dated at 132 BCE. In the Prologue, the text refers three times to the Law, the Prophets, and the other books. There are three different names for the third division: "the others that followed them" ("them" being the Law and the Prophets), "the other books of our fathers," and "the rest of the books." Though the name of this third division is not set, the third division itself is clearly established.

Nehemiah.⁸ For these reasons, *Voices of the Sages* will proceed using the order of the Writings found in the MT even as it seeks to broadly study the books in the Writings in conversation with one another, highlighting each book's different angle on wisdom themes.

Themes in the Writings

The books in the Writings, at first glance, seem like a haphazard collection of disparate texts—narrative, poetry, genealogy, long texts, short texts, songs, etc. Two major themes flow through this eclectic collection, providing thematic unity: creational wisdom and the Davidic kingdom.⁹ Like a montage that juxtaposes two distinct pictures to form one whole idea, so the first section of the Writings foregrounds creational wisdom and is juxtaposed with the second section highlighting the Davidic kingdom. Together, these two parts contribute to this overview: the Writings serve to instruct the exiled people of God to seek Wisdom, as they wait for the coming David and his kingdom. Alternatively, this statement can be simplified to "the Writings are the *torah* of David." Chronicles and Psalms treat both wisdom and the kingdom as central themes, one as a narrative and the other as a collection of poetry. As synoptic versions of each other, they serve as a double introduction to the collection.¹⁰

As illustrated below, Chronicles begins the Writings and introduces the main themes by narrating the lives of wise David and wise Solomon, who rule over the Lord's kingdom and build His

---

8 Previously, the *Biblia Hebraica Stuttgartensia*—the fourth edition of the Hebrew text (1968-1976)—ordered the Writings in a mediatorial fashion between the Talmudic order and the MT order, situating Chronicles last in the collection. The *Biblia Hebraica Quinta*—the fifth edition—will follow the order of books in the Leningrad Codex, the oldest known complete copy of the MT.

9 Steinberg and Stone present similar themes of two sub-divisions in the Writings, charting that the wisdom series describes the way of the individual together with God as a development from sorrow to joy, and the national-historical series describes the way of the people, again as a development from sorrow to joy. See Julius Steinberg and Timothy J. Stone. *The Shape of the Writings*. Winona Lake: Eisenbrauns, 2015: 153.

10 For more on Chronicles and Psalter as a double introduction, see Gunnar Begerau, "Strukturelle und Inhaltlich–theologische Verbindungen der Ketuvim in der Anordnung der BHS." *Das Heilige Herz der Tora: Festschrift für Hendrik Koorevaar zu seinem 65 Geburtstag*. Aachen: Shaker, 2011: 135-151. See also Stone, *Megilloth* 175-77, for a discussion of the chiasm of the *Megilloth* with Ecclesiastes at the center, also discussed in Chapter 9 on the book of Lamentations.

temple. These David and Solomon narratives contrast the foolishness of the house of David after Solomon's death. Chronicles continues, urging Israel to walk in the ways of David and Solomon within the context of kingdom living (2 Chron 11:17). The temple, the house of God, provides the reference point for the book as a whole. After the death of Solomon, Chronicles consistently presents the Davidic kings as either wisely seeking the Lord or foolishly forsaking Him—the house of David's repeated folly ultimately leads to exile in Babylon. Readers end Chronicles introduced to the twin themes of creational wisdom and the Davidic Kingdom.

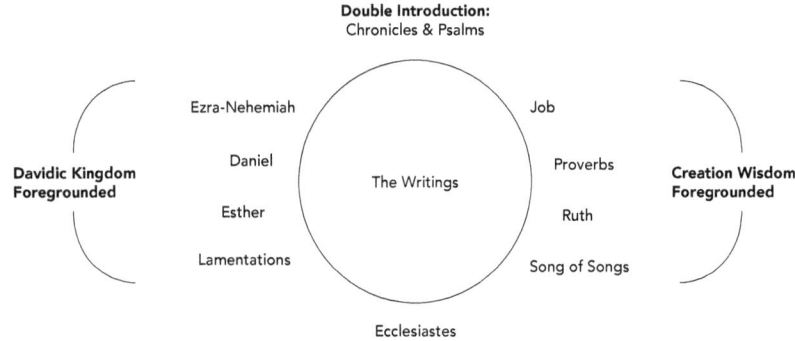

The Writings then focus on the consequences of Israel's folly: the loss and restoration of the Davidic kingdom in exile and post-exile. As the diagram demonstrates, the first and second halves of the Writings foreground one theme over the other; however, the wisdom section does not lack elements of the Davidic kingdom (see Proverbs and Ruth) and vice-versa (see Esther and Daniel). Though the groupings' emphasis changes, key words, sub-themes, and motifs connect the two sections and shape a unified perspective in the collection of books.

After Chronicles, the book of Psalms continues the introduction of the Writings' central themes. Psalm 1, a wisdom psalm, introduces the Psalter by presenting the two paths of wisdom and folly along with the key wisdom ideas of paths, ways, meditation, life, and death. Psalm 1 establishes the Psalter as a wisdom book, buttressed by the wisdom psalms introducing Books III, IV, and V of the Psalter (Pss 73, 90, and

107 respectively). Psalm 2, closely bound up with Psalm 1[11], introduces the certainty of the rule of the Lord's anointed king over fools who do not submit to him. Thus, Psalms 1 and 2 serve to introduce the overall message of the Psalter – only the wise can ascend to Zion to dwell with the Lord and His messianic king. After the Psalter, Job and Proverbs, traditionally recognized as wisdom books, focus on the fear of the Lord, one of the central wisdom concepts in the OT.

The next five books, traditionally called the *Megilloth*, showcase women and connect to wisdom themes presented in Chronicles, Psalms, and Proverbs particularly. The book of Ruth appears immediately after Proverbs 31. Ruth, an excellent woman (Ruth 3:11), serves as a narrative example of the concluding proverb about the excellent woman in Proverbs 31:10-31. The Song of Songs' association with Solomon (Song 1:1) and his wisdom puts the Song in the wisdom category (1 Kings 4:30-34), but prompts a substantive conversation on the book's subject matter, as will be discussed in Chapter 7. In contrast, Ecclesiastes overtly treats wisdom and folly in its content, themes, and conclusion regarding the fear of the Lord. The alphabetic acrostics[12] in Lamentations parallel the acrostic in the woman of virtue proverb (Prov 31:10-31) and those in the Psalms (Pss 34, 37, 119). The very form of the acrostic seems to carry wisdom overtones. From a content perspective, Lamentations mourns Lady Jerusalem's playing the fool and dying, living out the consequences of embracing folly as predicted by Lady Wisdom in Proverbs (Prov 7:24-27, 9:18). Finally, echoing the book of Ruth and Lady Wisdom in Proverbs, the book of Esther offers a woman as the central agent of deliverance of the people. Just as the excellent woman works for the good of her family and town, and Ruth works for the good of Naomi, Esther's role as queen forms the conduit for the deliverance of the Jews. Thus, the wisdom thread in these books emerges in a serial reading, but, as *Voices of the Sages* will explain, takes

---

[11] The word "blessed" (*ashrey*) brackets the beginning of Psalm 1 and the end of Psalm 2, linking the two psalms into a unified whole.

[12] An alphabet acrostic is a series of 22 verses, each beginning with a successive letter of the Hebrew alphabet starting with the first (*Aleph*) and ending with the last (*Tav*).

on more depth when considered in dialogue with the other texts of the Writings.

The final two books in the Writings continue to focus on wisdom in a post-exilic context. Daniel 1 depicts Daniel as the consummate wise man, seeking to honor the Lord in exile. As he waits for Israel to be restored, Daniel walks in wisdom; through him, the God of Israel reveals mysteries that will take place after the Babylonian phase of the exile. Lastly, Ezra-Nehemiah narrates Israel's return to the land, the rebuilding of the temple, the reestablishment of the Israelites' lives according to the word of God, and the rebuilding of Jerusalem. Although Ezra-Nehemiah does at times employ wisdom language (Neh 8), its content centers on examining whether the people who returned from exile are walking in wisdom or folly. Are they people living according to "the wisdom in Ezra's hand," the Law of God (Ezra 7:25)? The prayers of confession in Ezra 9 and Nehemiah 9 answer clearly: Israel continues to commit folly by intermarrying with unbelievers, among other sins. The concluding disaster at the temple in Nehemiah 13 repeats Solomon's folly with the foreign women who turned his heart away from the Lord (Neh 13:26). Neither wise Solomon nor those who returned to the land heed Lady Wisdom's instruction about resisting the woman of Folly.

As mentioned above, the Writings are the *torah* of David. The Hebrew Bible uses the word *torah* to refer to the Law of Moses but also to refer to any type of teaching or instruction, such as the *torah* of one's mother (Prov 1:8). The *torah* of David allows for the Writings to be instruction by David and David's son as well as instruction about David and David's house, tying together the twin themes of wisdom and kingdom. Echoing the *torah* of Moses, the *torah* of David provides a synoptic version of the Lord's instruction for the people of God in exile. This is true of the whole of the Writings, but also of particular books in the Writings. For instance, as Chapter 5 will discuss, Proverbs seems to present a synoptic version of the laws in Deuteronomy without the framework of life in the land. In the post-exile, the Writings serve as a *torah* for those people who cannot live under the Law in the promised land.

Thinking of the Writings as *torah* in the post-exile welcomes even contemporary readers to listen to the Writings in pursuit of a life of wisdom. The Writings describe Israel's life in the post exile:

- The Temple is rebuilt but the divine presence is gone (Ezra-Nehemiah).

- The City of David stands, but no Davidic King/Messiah sits on the throne (Ezra-Nehemiah; 2 Chron 36).

- The people return to the land but still live in exilic conditions (Neh 9:36 - slaves on their own land).

- The people suffer crises and grief (Dan 6, visions in Dan 7 and 11; Esther; Ezra-Nehemiah; Lam 5).

- Israel continues their folly and covenant infidelity (Ez 9; Neh 9, 13 - foreign women) because there is no New Covenant written on their heart (Jer 31).

- The source of *torah*/wisdom is Scripture, the written word of God (Ez 6-7; Neh 8).

- The Lord works providentially behind the scenes (Ezra-Nehemiah; Esther; Daniel 1; Ruth).

The relevance of the Writings to the Church should emerge clearly from this list. The book of Acts and Church history recount suffering and persecution, and yet Christians continue to hope for the promised return of King Jesus, the Son of David. The life of the Church is sustained by the written word of God, the Old and New Testaments. Christians trust in the Lord as a good Shepherd who works sovereignly and providentially for His purposes and the good of His children. Thus, the life-context of those who read and collected the Writings parallels that of the Church today; the Writings offer Christians wisdom and strength as we seek to walk in the way of the Lord Jesus Christ.

A Primer on Hebrew Poetry

Several books in the Writings are or contain poetry. Most Bible readers have not studied OT Hebrew and find themselves at a disadvantage when studying Hebrew texts, poetry in particular. However, all is not lost. Hebrew poetry weathers translation well—with a little instruction, the careful reader can draw out a number of valuable observations from the English versions of these poems.

First, as is true in poetry the world over, formatting matters. Breaking up lines of poetry to fit into multiple columns on a page does not help readers see the relationships between the lines. Consider reading a Bible paginated in a single column to see the poetic formatting of the text in contrast to prose passages.

Second, when studying, using a Bible in the King James Bible tradition (RSV, ESV, NASB) is helpful because the translators sought to translate more literally and consistently. For instance, they attempt to translate a specific Hebrew word, wherever it appears, with the same English word.

Third, Hebrew poetry revolves around the repetition of thoughts or meaning.[13] Typically, two lines of poetry comprise a single verse—an A line and a B line, such as here in Proverbs 5:1:

A Line: My son, be attentive to my wisdom;

B Line: Incline your ear to my understanding,

These two lines are called "parallel" lines, and this pattern is "parallelism." However, the relationship between the two lines goes beyond repetition and parallelism. These two lines are bound together by a kind of poetic glue; they form two parts of a whole and should be read off of each other. The reader should read the A line, then the B line, and then go back to the A line. The B line typically develops the A line or advances and adds to it. The lines read, "A, and what's more,

---

[13] See Adele Berlin, *The Dynamics of Biblical Parallelism*. Bloomington: Indiana University Press, 1985.

B."[14] Discovering what the B lines adds requires analyzing the meaning of both A and B lines together. The more comfortable a reader is with grammatical categories[15], the more the reader can see a variety of observations and explanations. Feel free to mark up your study Bible to pair the related terms in the A line and the B line. Here is Proverbs 5:1 again:

A Line: My son, be attentive to my wisdom;

B Line: Incline your ear to my understanding,

The relationship between the parallel lines brings out the repeated concepts. The A line begins with "My son," addressing the target audience of the proverb. "Be attentive" is repeated in "incline your ear," but the repetition is not an exact one—the B line builds on the A line. "Incline your ear" draws attention to the specific organ for listening and involves body movement. "My wisdom" is repeated by "my understanding," but the pairing moves the meaning from a general word for wisdom to a more specific word: "understanding" or *tebunah*. The two lines of Proverbs 5:1 therefore ask the son/reader not just to pay attention, but to specifically turn himself to the proverbs for both general wisdom and specific understanding.[16]

Exact repetition is rare in Hebrew poetry, so when it happens, the focus highlights the word in question. Consider Psalm 1:2:

A Line: But his delight is **in the law of the Lord,**

B Line: And **on His law** he meditates day and night.

Here the word "law" (*torah*) is repeated exactly in the B line, but with the pronoun "His" replacing its antecedent, "the Lord," from the A line. Somewhat surprisingly, the noun "delight" is related to the verb

---

14 See James Kugel, *The Idea of Biblical Poetry*. Baltimore: Johns Hopkins University Press, 1998.

15 Consult an introduction to English grammar. Even readers with a limited grammar vocabulary can learn to analyze paired words that fulfill the same function.

16 Wisdom/understanding is a common word pair, a set of terms that typically appear together in parallel lines. Wicked/sinners is another common one (Ps 1, for example).

"meditate." Because of the poetic glue binding the lines together, the reader is forced to combine "delight" and "meditate" to draw out the implications of the pairing of these two words. This relationship points to the reality that the things we delight in are where we spend a lot of mental, emotional, and psychological energy. We think on them often and for long periods of time—we meditate on them. The repetition and pairing in the two lines of Psalm 1:2 highlight how naturally and delightfully the blessed man ponders and meditates on the Lord's instruction, His *torah*.

A fourth guideline of Hebrew poetry is fixed line length; this limitation forces authors to choose what to include very carefully. The Psalm 1:2 couplet works well again as an example here. When you look at words on the page, you notice that line pairs in Hebrew poetry are roughly the same length; maintaining that proverb's shape is crucial. [17]The B line contains a phrase with no corresponding expression in the A line; by using "His" instead of "of the LORD," the psalmist made room in the line for the words "day and night." We can label this new information a "plus." Since only so many words can fit into each line, the lines form a kind of poetic straitjacket. Hebrew poets use any extra space to fit in another word or two to further expand the idea of the A line. In this case, "day and night" weaves in the notion of the blessed man continually meditating on the law of the Lord. The extra space in the line is used to add notions of time and consistency to the two lines' focus on joyful meditation.

Another technique called ellipsis allows writers to create space for additional words in the B line. Ellipsis happens when the B line borrows a word from the A line but does not include it in the actual wording of the B line. Psalm 1:5 provides a good example:

A line: Therefore, the <u>wicked</u> **will** <u>not</u> **stand** <u>in the judgment</u>,

B line: <u>Nor</u>----<u>sinners</u>----<u>in the congregation of the righteous</u>.

---

[17] While scholars agree that Hebrew poetry intentionally limits line length, there is no consensus on what those limitations are.

"Wicked"/"sinners" are parallel and form a word pair. "Not"/"nor" make each line negative. The verb "will ... stand" is omitted from the B line but also assumed as a building block in the meaning of the B line. The reader borrows the verb from the A line and fills it in while reading. This ellipsis creates space for the poet to repeat and expand the idea of judgment with the phrase "the congregation of the righteous." The couplet now communicates that the wicked/sinners will not stand or join with the righteous before the Lord. They are driven away like chaff (Ps 1:4) in the judgment, leaving only the assembly of the righteous standing before Him, firmly rooted as living trees (Ps 1:3). When reading Hebrew poetry, watch for ellipses and the spaces they create for extra helpful information.

You now know the basics of how to read Hebrew poetry. A slow, careful reader of biblical poetry can make insightful observations from the text and form an in-depth understanding of the lines and verses. Marking the relationships between words and phrases between the A and B lines brings out the ideas that the poet left for readers to reflect and meditate on. Though the following chapters will analyze the poetry in a bit more depth, you are now equipped to see its basic meaning for yourself, in your English Bible.

We are now prepared to listen to the conversation of the books in the Writings. Picture a welcoming room with a round table, and the books themselves sitting in a conversational circle. The books are talking about their contents, seeking wisdom together. What might they be saying to one another?

Further Reading

On Poetry:

Alter, Robert. *The Art of Biblical Poetry*. Vol. Rev. and Updated. New York: Basic Books, 2011.

Berlin, Adele. *The Dynamics of Biblical Parallelism.* Bloomington: Indiana University Press, 1985.

Kugel, James. *The Idea of Biblical Poetry.* Baltimore: John Hopkins University Press, 1998.

On the Writings:

Morgan, Donn F., ed. *The Oxford Handbook of the Writings of the Hebrew Bible.* Oxford Handbooks. 2018. Online edition. Oxford: Oxford Academic, November 7, 2018.

Steinberg, Julius and Timothy J. Stone. *The Shape of the Writings.* Winona Lake: Eisenbrauns, 2015.

Stone, Timothy J. *The Compilational History of the Megilloth: Canon, Contoured Intertextuality, and Meaning in the Writings.* Tübingen: Mohr Siebeck, 2013.

Chronicles: The House that Wisdom Built

Old Testament Background to Chronicles

- Creation: Gen 1-4
- Genealogies: Gen 5, 10, 11
- Building of the tabernacle: Ex 25-40
- Disobedience, exile, sabbaths, and forgiveness: Lev 26:27-46
- Duties of Levites: Num 3-4
- Saul and David: 1-2 Samuel
- Solomon and the kings of Judah and Israel: 1-2 Kings
- The fall of the house of David: Book III of the Psalter, Pss 73-89
- The Lord reigns: Book IV of the Psalter, Pss 90-106
- Going up to the house of the Lord: the Songs of Ascents, Pss 120-134
- 70-year exile to Babylon: Jer 25:12, 29:10

Chronicles' Creation Framework: The Son of David as a Second Adam

In the Hebrew scriptures, Chronicles is a single book. As discussed in the introduction, the genealogies of 1 Chronicles 1-9 set the creational context for the narrative by starting the reader in Genesis 1-4. Humanity (*'adam*) was created in the image of God to rule and subdue creation in the garden, filling the whole creation with other image bearers to God's glory (Gen 1:26-28). After Adam's sin, the Lord promises redemption through the seed of the woman, a future second Adam. Chronicles' genealogies link Adam to David, setting the stage for the narrative's focal flow: David, Solomon, and the house of David. The Davidic promise of 1 Chronicles 17:7-14 frames the promised son of David as a second Adam; the son of David will live out the kingly responsibilities the first Adam failed to fulfill. As will be discussed in this chapter, David's son Solomon builds a "garden" house for the

Lord—the temple—pre-figuring the coming Messiah's eternal reign in the new Jerusalem for the good of Israel and all humanity (*'adam*) (2 Chron 6:33; Rev 21:1-22:5).

1-2 Chronicles: An Outline

1 Chronicles 1-9 - Genealogies

> Beginning with Adam in 1:1, the genealogies of 1 Chronicles 1-9 focus on the bloodlines of Judah, David, Levi, and Benjamin, ending with those who returned from exile in 1 Chronicles 9:2-34.

1 Chronicles 10-29 - The Davidic covenant and preparations for the house of the Lord

> Chronicles begins the wisdom theme by contrasting Saul, who did not seek the Lord (1 Chron 10), with David, who sought the Lord by bringing the ark to Jerusalem (1 Chron 13-16). David makes preparations for Solomon's construction of the "garden" temple and charges Solomon to be wise and seek the Lord (1 Chron 21-29).

2 Chronicles 1-9 - Wise Solomon builds the house of the Lord

> Solomon's construction of the temple is bracketed by his prayer for wisdom in 2 Chronicles 1 and the Queen of Sheba's visit to Jerusalem to seek Solomon's wisdom (2 Chron 9).

2 Chronicles 10-36 - The Davidic House from Rehoboam to the Cyrus decree

> These episodes about David's sons serve as object lessons, examples, or parable-like narratives of the wisdom theme in Chronicles.[18] The kings who seek the wisdom of God are blessed, and those who do not are judged. Like Adam, David's house falls and is exiled east to Babylon. Chronicles then concludes by

---

18 See Begg, Christopher. "'Seeking Yahweh' and the Purpose of Chronicles." *Louvain Studies* 9 (2): 128-141. Begg likens this section in Chronicles to an extended parable, like Jesus' parables, clearly assigning a wisdom focus to the book (Begg, "Seeking," 139).

jumping forward 70 years to Cyrus king of Persia allowing the exiles to "go up" to Jerusalem to rebuild the house of the Lord (2 Chron 36:23).

Chronicles and Ezra-Nehemiah: Bracketing the Writings

As mentioned above, Chronicles concludes with the decree of Cyrus (2 Chron 36:22-23), and Ezra-Nehemiah begins with that same decree (Ezra 1:1-4). This narrative connection links the two books chronologically, giving the reader a beginning-to-end narrative canvas for the entirety of the history of Israel from "Adam" through the exiles' return to Jerusalem to rebuild. This Chronicles/Ezra-Nehemiah juxtaposition also situates the reader of the Writings between the two books: in the post-exile, eager for restoration (see 1 Chron 9:2). The Jews in exile awaiting the Messiah with no temple or holy city and contemporary readers ask the Writings the same question: while we wait for the coming King, how do we live wisely in a world shaped by the consequences of our sin? Ezra-Nehemiah ends the Writings by recounting how those who return to Jerusalem to rebuild the temple again commit folly, the folly of Solomon (Neh 13:26). The Writings thus end with a clear message: the return from exile is a disaster—the redemption of Israel is yet to come.

Major Themes: the House of the Lord, the House of David, and the Two Ways

1. The House of the Lord

The construction of the house of the Lord dominates the Chronicles narrative (1 Chron 22-2 Chron 7). When the Lord appears to Solomon in 2 Chronicles 1, Solomon asks Him for wisdom and knowledge to rule Israel. After the Lord grants this request, Solomon applies this God-given wisdom to the task before him: building the house of the Lord (2 Chron 2-8). Wisdom language infuses Solomon's choices and planning. The designer of the temple, Huram-abi, is described as a skilled (*hakam*) man with knowledge and understanding (*binah*) (2 Chron 2:7; also Ex 31:1-6). Likewise, the musicians and composers understood their craft (*bin*) (1 Chron 25:7). Wise choices guide the entire enterprise of building the house of the Lord. The temple is a house of wisdom: constructed by a wise king and wise designer, indwelt by the Lord who created everything by His wisdom, sheltering the tablets of wise *torah* in the ark of the covenant, and fostering worship from wise musicians. Only the wise should approach such a house and God.

2. The House of David

In 1 Chronicles 17, the Lord denies David the privilege of building the temple. Instead, the Lord outlines his intent to build David a "house," a dynasty. The Lord promises that, after David's death, He will:

- Raise up and establish the kingdom of one of David's sons (his seed), who will build the Lord a house (17:11-12a).

- Establish David's throne forever (17:12b).

- Be a Father to David's son/seed (17:13).

- Settle David's son/seed in the Lord's house and kingdom forever (17:14).

These four promises constitute the Davidic covenant. By beginning with "Adam," Chronicles links the kingdom language in the Lord's charge to Adam with His promise to David. Readers should read David and his son/seed as a second Adam–a king to rule as God's representative on earth from a sacred place. In multiple places, Chronicles presents Solomon as the fulfillment of the Lord's promise to David (2 Chron 1:9, 6:4-9, 10-11, 15). In 2 Chronicles 6:16, Solomon himself refers again to the Davidic promise and looks to the future, asking the Lord to keep His promises to David if the house of David walks in the wise paths (*torah*) of David and Solomon (2 Chron 6:16).

3. The Two Ways: Seek and Forsake

Chronicles also contains a seek/forsake theme (*darash/'azab*), categorizing kings by whether they seek the Lord or forsake Him. For instance, Saul dies because he consulted a medium instead of seeking (*darash*) the Lord (1 Chron 10:13-14). After David establishes his kingdom and secures Jerusalem as the capital, his first task is to seek (*darash*) the ark of the covenant—the presence of the Lord—because "they did not do so in the days of Saul" (1 Chron 13:3). When David charges Solomon with building the temple, he asks the Lord to supply Solomon with insight (*sekel*) and understanding (*binah*) so that he can keep God's law/instruction (*torah*). At the end of his preparations, David addresses Solomon again, charging him to keep and seek (*darash*) all God's commands, warning him against forsaking (*'azab*) the Lord (1 Chron 28:7-9). In turn, Solomon's first task as king echoes his father's in 1 Chronicles 13: he seeks out (*darash*) the bronze altar to offer sacrifices (2 Chron 1:5). That very night, the Lord appears to Solomon and asks what He can give him. Solomon's request for wisdom aligns him with his father David, in opposition to their predecessor Saul.

The remaining and also the majority of the seek/forsake passages then follow in Chronicles' accounts of the kings of Judah after Solomon (2 Chron 10-34). Most narratives tell how the king started well by seeking (*darash*) the Lord but then forsook (*'azab*) Him and suffered the consequences of such folly. Rehoboam's story in 2 Chronicles 11-12 epitomizes this pattern. The consistency of this seek/forsake language throughout the Chronicles narratives reinforces the role of wisdom and folly in the life of Israel and her kings. Though the sons of David occasionally seek the Lord, in the end, they play the fool and bring about His judgment on themselves and the kingdom entrusted to them: exile.

The Sages in Conversation

1. The House of the Lord

As discussed above, Chronicles provides the narrative background for the Writings. However, similarly to the way the three synoptic gospels recount the life of Christ, several texts in the Writings provide synoptic perspectives of key OT events narrated in Chronicles, adding layers of complexity and insight for the reader. This conversation reveals areas of overlap between Chronicles and Psalms, Lamentations, Ezra-Nehemiah, and Daniel.

A natural first part of this conversation centers on the intersection of Chronicles and the Psalms in two areas: temple worship and the resolution of the exile. David's preparations for Solomon's construction of the temple include work with Levitical singers (Asaph, the sons of Korah, Heman) and the temple psalmody (1 Chron 25), directly connecting Chronicles to the book of Psalms. David himself is the named author of 73 of the 150 psalms; he is the primary composer and curator of the Psalter, accompanied by the Levitical singers mentioned above. Many psalms' superscriptions, for instance "For the choir director" (Ps 18), imply that David collected his poetry, his psalms, to give to the choir director for temple worship.[19] Furthermore, Psalm 18 concludes with language from the Davidic covenant conversation of 1 Chronicles 17, indicating that the psalm has been redacted, shaped—by David or others—between the time he became king and the exile. The implication, therefore, is that many Psalms were curated for temple worship, collected on purpose for worshipping the Lord in His house in Jerusalem.

Such worship comes to an abrupt end in 586 BCE: Nebuchadnezzar destroys the temple and exiles the people of Israel to Babylon. What did the exiles take with them into captivity? Their Psalter. Even with no house of the Lord, no city of David, and the nation scattered, the Psalter allows the people of Israel to remember the temple worship of the era of Solomon, to revisit the spiritual life of their nation. The Psalter functions as a kind of "traveling temple"; wherever the dispersed Israelites find themselves, they can seek the Lord by worshipping Him through the Psalter, their repository of instruction and hope. The fact that those returning from exile restored

---

19 Some Psalms include a superscription: text appearing before the first verse of a psalm and giving information about the author, historical context, psalm genre, music, and/or choir director. For instance, Psalm 18's superscription is "For the choir director. Of David the servant of the LORD, who spoke to the LORD the words of this song in the day that the LORD delivered him from the hand of all his enemies and from the hand of Saul. And he said," (Ps 18).

Davidic psalmody (Ezra 3:10-11) illustrates the centrality of the Psalms to Israel's temple worship. The written Psalms allow the temple worship of Chronicles to travel through time and space, guiding worshippers into wisdom even into the present.

Within this discussion of exile, Lamentations offers a synoptic portrayal of the destruction of the temple. The Chronicler describes the tragedy and horror of the Babylonian invasion: the slaughter of young men, women, and the sick; the removal of the temple vessels; the burning of the house of God and fortified buildings; the breach of the walls; and the exile of survivors to Babylon (2 Chron 36:14-21). The author of Lamentations echoes these events, adding the loss of the temple, the priests, and Israel's temple activities to the list (Lam 1:3-4, 2:6-8, 4:11-15). As poetry does, Lamentations presents an insider's perspective of these tragic events in graphic and emotional terms, communicating not only the events themselves but their impact on the people of Israel as they suffer the consequences of forsaking the Lord.

However, unlike Chronicles, Lamentations presents Jerusalem personified as a woman and contains her confession of sin and folly, the cause of the Lord's judgment (Lam 1:8, 14, 18). Chronicles ends with no such confession. The Chronicler's hope is found earlier in the book: in his prayer of dedication, Solomon prays for the Lord to forgive His people when they confess their sin and turn (*shub*) to Him with all their heart (2 Chron 6:36-39), even in exile. The hope in Lamentations 5:19-21 echoes this "turning" language, but instead of the people themselves turning to their God, the people pray that the Lord might turn (*shub*) them back to Him and renew the days of old: a Davidic king and temple. Chronicles narrates Israel's sin, judgment, and exile while Lamentations outlines Israel's future restoration: only the Lord can bring about a renewal of heart and kingdom.

Chronicles and Psalms also intersect over each book's resolution of Israel's exile, with additional contributions from the sages of Ezra-Nehemiah and Daniel. The Chronicler clearly outlines how David's house played the fool by being unfaithful and rejecting God's law/instruction (*torah*), resulting in exile (2 Chron 36:14-16). However, Chronicles ends with the Lord commanding Cyrus to build the temple. This proclamation certainly provides hope for Israel: "build [the LORD] a house in Jerusalem [...] Whoever there is among you of all His people, may the LORD his God be with him, and let him go up!" (2 Chron 36:23). Yet this resolution to the exile also proves unsatisfying—according to 1 Chronicles 17, a son of David is supposed to build the house and sit on the Lord's throne forever. While Cyrus may fear the Lord, he is no son of David.

Ezra-Nehemiah provides an update on the reconstruction of Jerusalem. Although the Lord required the building of the Second Temple (2 Chron 36:22-23; Haggai 1; Ezra 5:1-5), this temple differs from the first in several ways. Crucially, there is no Davidic king on the throne and no divine glory in the house of the Lord (Ezra 3:12-13). Instead of building a house of wisdom with wise expert designers like Huram-abi, this second temple is tarnished by the people's folly with unbelieving Gentiles, men and women (Ezra 9; Neh 9 and 13). Though the people restore the liturgy of David (Ezra 3:10, 12:45-47) and Ezra teaches the people the Lord's wisdom (Ezra 7:25; Neh 8), this temple remains a pale version of the original. Like Chronicles, the end of Ezra-Nehemiah also leaves the reader puzzled about this return from exile, looking to the future for a more satisfying fulfillment of the Lord's promises through His prophets.

Here the book of Daniel chimes into this conversation with Daniel's prayer in chapter 9. When reading Jeremiah, Daniel realizes that the 70-year exile is over and so prays that the Lord would fulfill His promise concerning His people, His city, and His temple. The Lord responds by giving Daniel another vision of the future and the wisdom to understand that vision. Though the temple must be rebuilt to accomplish the word of the Lord and the direction of His prophets (Ezra 5:1-2), in the end, the house of the Lord will be built by David's greatest son, the Messiah. The Lord tells Daniel that the full resolution of the exile is pushed off into the future, the so-called 70 "weeks" of

Dan 9:24-27 (see Chapter 11).

The sages' conversation then returns to the Psalms. Book III of the Psalter (Pss 73-89) emphasizes the fall of the kingdom of David, including the destruction of the temple (Ps 74) and the removal of David's sons from the throne (Ps 89). In Book V, the Songs of Ascents (Pss 120-134) depict the people ascending to Jerusalem under the son of David. Psalms 110 and 132 specifically serve as songs looking ahead to the time when the people will "go up" to Jerusalem under a Davidic King and the house he builds for the Lord. While the Lord did fulfill His promise to bring His people back to the land under Cyrus (Jer 25:11; Isaiah 44:28-45:7), the editors of the Psalter point readers to the ultimate realization of the Davidic promise not in Cyrus, but in a future son of David.

This conversation between the books of Chronicles, Psalms, Lamentations, and Daniel allows readers of the Writings to place Cyrus and his decree within a larger vision of Israel's future. Cyrus is not the final word on king, temple, and kingdom. As Israel looks forward to the future fulfillment of the Davidic Covenant, they cling to the promise that ultimately, they will be part of the wise ones who will go up to join the Son in Zion.

2. The House of David

Both Chronicles and Psalms prominently feature King David. As mentioned above, at least 73 of the 150 Psalms are specifically attributed to David, and Chronicles spends 19 chapters recounting David's rule as king over Israel. While these texts certainly differ in their form and content, the editors of each of these books cast this main character in a dual light: David is both the model saint and the model sinner.

Chronicles narrates how David sought the Lord, passionately made preparations for the temple, and instructed Solomon to seek the Lord and build His house (1 Chron 13-29). While recounting these events, the Chronicler also highlights David as the model God-fearer and standard for all the sons of David (2 Chron 6:16, 7:17, 11:17, 34:2).

In turn, the Psalms give an inside view of David's wise walk with the Lord, for instance in Psalm 19. After opening with a stanza about how creation reveals God's glory, David describes the *torah* of the Lord as wisdom in proverbial terms: making wise the simple, enlightening the eyes, cultivating the fear of the Lord, being more desirable than gold, keeping him from sin (Ps 19:7, 8, 9, 10, 13). He concludes the psalm by praying that the meditation (*higgayon*) of his heart be acceptable in God's sight. This focus on the *torah* in Psalm 19 illustrates the fundamental wisdom skill of meditation (Ps 1:2). What is the wise saint to do? Meditate on the *torah* of the Lord.

Furthermore, Psalm 19 is bracketed by two "entrance into Zion" psalms: Psalms 15 and 24. In each, David asks who may ascend the hill of the Lord and dwell in His holy tent (Ps 15:1, 24:3).

> 15:1 O Lord, who shall sojourn in your tent?
>
> Who shall dwell on your holy hill?
>
> 2 He who walks blamelessly and does what is right
>
> And speaks truth in his heart ...
>
>
> 24:3 Who shall ascend the hill of the Lord?
>
> And who shall stand in his holy place?
>
> 4 He who has clean hands and a pure heart,
>
> Who does not lift up his soul to what is false
>
> And does not swear deceitfully ...

The answers again sound like a collection of proverbs: those who walk in integrity, who speak truth, who do not lend money out with interest, who do not swear deceitfully (Ps 15:2-5, 24:4-5). In these three psalms, David sings of the path of wisdom leading to the house of wisdom, the house of the Lord. Like David, those who seek the Lord in His house must walk the path of wisdom. The Chronicler reinforces this idea in 1 Chronicles 13, David's first attempt to bring the ark into Jerusalem. Initially, because David and Israel were not wise and did not follow Moses' instructions, the Lord killed Uzzah and the ark remained en route, in the house of Obed-edom. In fear of the Lord, David turns from his initial folly to wisdom in 1 Chronicles 15. This time, David followed the *torah* regarding the role of the Levites, appoints Asaph to sing a psalm of thanksgiving and praise (1 Chron 16), and successfully moves the ark into its new place in Jerusalem. In quite a literal sense, this episode illustrates the Psalms: only the wise can ascend the hill—"go up" to Jerusalem—and dwell in the presence of the Lord. Solomon echoes these principles during his dedication of the temple when he confesses Israel's sin and calls on the Lord to "arise to your resting place, you and the ark of Your might" (2 Chron 6:40-42; Ps 132:8). Through their King David passages, Chronicles and Psalms both agree: the all-wise God of Israel will only dwell with wise people in His house of wisdom.

And yet the Chronicler and the Psalter also present David as the model sinner. Though David was foolish in his first attempt to bring the ark into Jerusalem, David's great sin in Chronicles is his numbering of the people for war (1 Chron 21).[20] Pressed by a military adversary, David resorted to trusting in the number of his soldiers instead of in the Lord. The Lord punished this evil with pestilence: 70,000 men of Israel died (1 Chron 21:7, 14). David emphasizes his lack of wisdom in his confession: "I have sinned greatly in that I have done this thing [...] I have acted very foolishly" (1 Chron 21:8). Right before the angel of the Lord is about to destroy Jerusalem, David again confesses his wickedness, purchases the threshing floor of Ornan the Jebusite, builds an altar, presents offerings, and calls on the God of Israel. The

---

20 The Psalter might ask the Chronicler why David's sin with Bathsheba is not included in Chronicles. 1 Chronicles 3:5 names Solomon as the son of David without specifically referencing Solomon's mother Bathsheba. Chronicles appears to focus on the house of David and the house of the Lord; David's two recorded acts of folly relate to the temple: the ark of the covenant and the site of the temple (1 Chron 13 and 21). David's sin with Bathsheba falls outside the Chronicler's focus. That being said, 2 Samuel 11 narrates the Bathsheba episode as King David's most significant sin, a condemnation the Psalter echoes repeatedly.

Lord answers with fire and commands the destroying angel to restore his sword to its sheath. This threshing floor, the exact location of David crying out in repentance, becomes the site of Solomon's temple (2 Chron 3:1). Thus, any sinner going to pray to the Lord in the temple is physically and spiritually mimicking David's turn away from folly, cry for forgiveness, and sacrifice to the Lord (2 Chron 6; 1 Chron 21:28-22:1). King David, the model sinner, guides Israel into repentance.

Many psalms reference David's sinfulness, though Psalms 51 and 32 offer the most detail. In Psalm 32, David sings of his uncovering of his sin and confession to the Lord (Ps 32:3-7), followed by the wisdom he learned after his repentance (Ps 32:8-10). Specifically within the context of David's sin with Bathsheba, Psalm 51:1-17 provides the most detailed portrait of sin and forgiveness, David's model "sinner's prayer":

> 51:4 Against you, you only, have I sinned
>
> And done what is evil in your sight,
>
> So that you may be justified in your words
>
> And blameless in your judgment.
>
> 51:6 Behold, you delight in truth in the inward being,
>
> And you teach me wisdom (*hokmah*) in the secret heart.

Again, David emphasizes that confession and truth result in wisdom. It seems the Psalms editors appended verses 18-19 to the end of David's prayer to remind Israel that the future of Zion/Jerusalem depends on the people of God confessing their sin. These closing verses look forward to a rebuilt Jerusalem and renewed temple worship:

> 51:18 Do good to Zion in your good pleasure;
>
> Build up the walls of Jerusalem;

19 Then will you delight in right sacrifices,

In burnt offerings and whole burnt offerings;

Then bulls will be offered on your altar.

For Psalms readers in the post-exile, the parallel is stark. David sinned, suffered consequences, repented, and was restored. Likewise, the city of Jerusalem and the temple were destroyed because of the people's folly. Thus, the Lord's restoration depends on Israel's contrite heart and repentance. David's confessional psalms welcome the post-exilic Israelites back onto the path of wisdom, ultimately leading to Jerusalem/Zion.

3. The Two Ways: Seek and Forsake

As mentioned earlier, the verbs "seek" (*darash* and *baqash*) and "forsake" (*'azab*) occur repeatedly in the Chronicler's narrative, establishing a wisdom perspective of the lives of Saul, David, and Solomon. This pattern grows in strength and continues in 2 Chronicles 10-36, the narrative of the house of David from after Solomon to the exile. In turn, Proverbs also uses seek/forsake language to characterize the wise man and the fool. This next conversation unpacks the layers seek/forsake language reveals in these wisdom texts.

In Chronicles, people can seek the Lord or forsake Him at various points in their lives. Seeking the Lord often results in building projects (2 Chron 14:4-7), rest (2 Chron 15:12-15, 20:3-30), wealth and honor (2 Chron 17:4-6), or proper temple worship (2 Chron 34:3-7). These elements constitute the height of temple worship and divine blessing under King Solomon. Thus, when Israel continues to seek the Lord after the death of Solomon, they enjoy the blessings of wise Solomon's reign. Forsaking the Lord results in the opposite: military defeat (2 Chron 12:5, 21:10, 24:4), exile (2 Chron 29:9), and the destruction of Jerusalem and the temple (2 Chron 34:25)—exactly what God warned Israel would happen. In 1 Chronicles 28:9, David tells Solomon, "If you seek Him, He will let you find Him; but if you forsake Him, He will reject you forever." Azariah the prophet repeats this paradigm in 2 Chronicles 15:2: "The Lord is with you while you are with Him. If you seek Him, He will be found by you, but if you forsake Him, He will forsake you." The blessed man of Psalm 1 seeks the Lord by meditating on His instruction and so prospers (*salah*); the same is true for the kings of Israel: King Uzziah "continued to seek the Lord in the days of Zechariah [...] and as long as he sought the Lord, God prospered (*salah*) him" (2 Chron 26:5).

After Solomon, most kings of Israel start out seeking the Lord but, in time, forsake Him. The opposite is true of only one king: Manasseh. Seduced early in his reign by the idolatry of the nations, Manasseh led Israel astray and was exiled to Babylon. In exile, he sought the Lord and humbled himself before Him (2 Chron 33:12). Because of Manasseh's repentance, the Lord eventually restores him to Jerusalem, where, in turn, Manasseh restores proper temple worship. As the only king who begins a fool but turns to wisdom, Manasseh's story illustrates Solomon's prayer that those taken into captivity who turn to the Lord will be forgiven (2 Chron 6:36-39, 7:14). These kings' narratives serve as a series of parables[21] or case studies for Israel to learn from. The lesson is clear: seeking folly will ultimately remove you from the Lord and His house/Jerusalem, but seeking wisdom will bring you near to Him and His blessings. Chronicles' seek/forsake language shows how a person can be both wise and a fool in turn, living in the consequences of wisdom and folly.

The book of Proverbs also repeatedly uses seek/forsake language with respect to the wise and the fool. However, in contrast to Chronicles, Proverbs presents the wise and the foolish as two separate characters. According to the opening message of Lady Wisdom, fools have no interest in forsaking their folly (Prov 1:22-26):

---

21 Christopher Begg writes, "And if so, Chronicles might be viewed as an extended parable. But as a parable, like those of Jesus, all that it relates leads up to a challenge to decision, a challenge which, however, again as with many of Jesus' parables, remains unspoken, being left to the hearers/readers to grasp and articulate for themselves" (Begg, "Seeking," 139).

1:22	How long, O simple ones, will you love being simple?
	How long will scoffers delight in their scoffing
	And fools hate knowledge?
23	If you turn at my reproof,
	Behold, I will pour out my spirit to you;
	I will make my words known to you.
24	Because I have called and you refused to listen,
	Have stretched out my hand and no one has heeded,
25	Because you have ignored all my counsel
	And would have none of my reproof,
26	I also will laugh at your calamity.

According to this passage, fools love their folly, and when called to turn in repentance (*shub*), they refuse. By asking a rhetorical question, Lady Wisdom does not allow the possibility that these fools respond to her call in verses 22-23. Verses 24-26 form a verdict, predicting the coming calamity of these fools. Several other passages in Proverbs reinforce this perspective on fools: for instance, Proverbs 13:19 calls it "an abomination" for fools to turn from evil; such a practice is "against their religion." Proverbs 27:22 describes the fool as so settled in his folly that even being disciplined cannot help him:

27:22	Crush a fool in a mortar with a pestle
	Along with crushed grain,
	Yet his folly will not depart from him.

Proverbs 14:24 insists on how deeply fools are consumed with folly; the parallelism indicates folly is the crown of fools.

> 14:24 The crown of the wise is their wealth,
>
> But the folly of fools brings folly.

Fools consistently seek out folly and forsake wisdom. On the other hand, the wise seek Lady Wisdom and find her (Prov 8:17):

> 8:17 I love those who love me,
>
> And those who seek (*shahar*) me diligently find me.

Seek (*shahar*) is related to the Hebrew word for dawn, suggesting the nuance of the seeker being anxious to get started in their search, be it for wisdom or folly. Although Lady Wisdom calls the fool to forsake his folly and live (Prov 9:6), Proverbs holds out little hope for fools. Simply put, the book of Proverbs does not seem to indicate that fools repent from their sin and turn to wisdom. Such is only the practice of the wise.

At this point, one must consider the issue of forgiveness. Chronicles teaches that when Israel repents and seeks the Lord, the Lord forgives their sin (2 Chron 7:14, 30:18-20). The turn from forsaking to seeking is crucial to repentance and consequently, to forgiveness. The only verses in Proverbs addressing any possible teaching about forgiveness are Proverbs 16:6 and 28:13.[22] The NIV translates Proverbs 16:6 in keeping with Lady Wisdom's message:

> 16:6 Through love and faithfulness sin is atoned for;
>
> Through the fear of the Lord a man avoids evil.

A close analysis of the parallelism between the A line and the B line suggests that, in this case, atonement means avoiding evil, not the

---

[22] R. N. Whybray sees this possibility in Proverbs 16:6, stating, "[T]his is the only verse in Proverbs which refers to God's forgiveness of the penitent sinner." R. N. Whybray. "Proverbs." *New Century Bible Commentary*. Grand Rapid, MI: Eerdmans, 1994: 393.

forgiveness of evil.[23] Sin is kept at bay by love, faithfulness, and the fear of the Lord. The wise avoid evil by seeking love and faithfulness; fools embrace sin by seeking the path of folly. On the other hand, Proverbs 28:13 clearly addresses confession and forgiveness:

> 28:13   Whoever conceals his transgressions will not prosper,
>
> But he who confesses and forsakes them will obtain mercy.

Although the Lord does show mercy to those who confess and forsake their transgression, this verse appears to be addressing forgiveness in interpersonal relationships, not divine forgiveness. The text does not specifically refer to the Lord, and the book of Proverbs consistently focuses on humans acting in righteousness, justice, and equity with one another (Prov 1:3). Other proverbs also touch on transgressions being covered through human actions[24]; for instance, Proverbs 10:12 reads:

> 10:12   Hatred stirs up strife,
>
> But love covers all offenses.

Even if these two verses do teach something about divine forgiveness, the overall purpose of Proverbs is for the wise to increase in wisdom (Prov 1:5) by diligently seeking Lady Wisdom and not committing folly to begin with. At its very center, Proverbs 16:17 says:

> 16:17   The highway of the upright turns aside from evil;
>
> Whoever guards his way preserves his life.

In sum, Proverbs teaches the wise to guard their way by avoiding the disastrous consequences of evil and folly. The emphasis appears to be on the wise acting rightly, not forgiveness.

---

[23] The passive verb in the A line makes "sin" a subject acted upon by an agent not included in the line. "Sin" is therefore parallel to "evil." The one who does the atoning is not included in the proverb line at all.

[24] See also Proverbs 17:9 and 19:11.

Chronicles and Proverbs differ in their perspective of the wise and fools. Why does Proverbs not present teachings about fools turning from their folly and seeking the Lord? The answer lies in each text's purpose and audience. Chronicles is a narrative of the house of David, written in the post-exile. The Chronicler reviews the story of Israel from Adam to the return to Jerusalem, picking and choosing events and data to include. The Chronicler focuses on the people's relationship with the Lord; at times, the king and Israel seek the Lord, forsake evil, and enjoy His blessing. At other times, they play the fool and forsake Him. Chronicles functions as an exhortation for Israel to repent, be forgiven, and seek the Lord, all within the context of the promised land, the City of David, and the temple. In contrast to Chronicles, Proverbs is a collection of instructions for wise kingdom living even when the kingdom is off the scene. Proverbs describes fools in a book meant for the wise to increase their learning (Prov 1:1-6). Since the fool is not Proverbs' target audience, human repentance and divine forgiveness are not the topic of the book.

Toward the New Testament

1. Jesus, the Fulfillment of the Davidic Promise

The NT picks up the Chronicler's message that the seed of David will build a house for the Lord. Solomon states that the Lord fulfilled this promise in Solomon's construction of the first temple, but he also asks the Lord to keep His promise in the future (2 Chron 6:16). Even David understands that the Lord spoke promises to him about the distant future (1 Chron 17:17). The NT presents Jesus as this distant future fulfillment of the Davidic promise. For instance, Hebrews 1:5 describes Jesus as the Son of God, quoting 1 Chronicles 17:13: "I will be a father to him and he will be a son to me." By referencing Chronicles, Hebrews clearly frames Christ as the fulfillment of the Lord's promise to David. Immediately after this verse, Hebrews continues, stating that Jesus is the firstborn over all creation and will return to "the world" again (Heb 1:6). This word for "world" (*oikoumene*) comes from a compound Greek word meaning "a house which is inhabited" (*oikou + mene*). This "house" wordplay may allude to the specifics of the Davidic covenant: son, house, and kingdom. Jesus will found a future new creation "house" where angels will worship and serve Him as he sits on his eternal throne (Heb 1:8-13), echoing Chronicles' temple worship under Solomon.

In keeping with this house language, Jesus declares that he will build his church upon the foundation of his messiahship (Matt 16:16-18). Whereas the house that Solomon built was a physical dwelling place for the Lord, the NT borrows language from Chronicles, teaching that the church is a spiritual house consisting of those in Christ. The church is the house of God (1 Pet 2:3) and a holy temple (Eph 2:21) with Jesus Christ as the foundation (1 Cor 3:11), cornerstone (1 Pet 2:6), and Son over it (Heb 3:6). Jesus is the faithful and obedient Son of David and Son of God who builds God's church upon his person, words, and works. Jesus, Son of David and Son of God, will fulfill all God's promises to David.[25]

2. Jesus, Son of David, Son of Adam, Son of God

Though the house of David played the fool in Chronicles, Jesus, wise Son of David, will inherit David's throne. The Gospel of Luke introduces the child of Mary as the son of the Most High who will reign on the throne of David forever (Luke 1:32-33). Luke also presents Jesus as one who grows in wisdom and stature (Luke 2:40, 52). After being separated from his parents, Jesus is found in the temple dialoguing with the teachers of Israel, amazing everyone with his wisdom and understanding.

As always in biblical texts, genealogy matters; the NT includes two genealogies of Jesus. Luke 3:23-38 takes Jesus' line back to Adam, the first son of God, and presents the same Adam-David theology as the Chronicler. As such, Jesus Christ is the king of the earth: Son of David, Son of Adam, and Son of God. Complementing this perspective, the Gospel of Matthew presents Jesus as the Messiah, Son of David, Son of Abraham (Matt 1:1). This reference recalls the

---

25 In John 2:19, Jesus says, "Destroy this temple, and in three days I will raise it up" in reference to the "temple" of His body and His resurrection.

Lord's promises to Abraham: land, seed, and blessing to all nations (Gen 12:1-3, 22:16-18). Matthew's genealogy of Jesus also focuses on the Davidic line and includes significant women (Tamar, Rahab, Ruth, and Bathsheba) as well as the Babylonian exile. Through these choices, the Gospel of Matthew frames the coming of Jesus, the Messiah, as the resolution to the ending of Chronicles. Jesus will save Israel from their sins, end their exile, bring them to their land, and permanently fulfill God's promises to David and Abraham, blessing Israel and ultimately all nations.

3. Jesus, the Path of Wisdom

If Jesus is indeed the promised son of David and son of God, then He must walk on the path of wisdom and avoid folly. As mentioned above, Jesus was wise even as a youth (Luke 2). The temptation accounts in the Gospels indicate that Jesus avoided evil and sought the Lord and His word (Matt 4:1-11; Luke 4:1-13). Jesus answers each of the three temptations of the devil by quoting Deuteronomy: when presented with the two paths, Jesus chooses the path laid down by the *torah* of God. Jesus heeds the admonitions in Chronicles to seek the Lord and keep His commandments. During His temptations, Jesus the wise king of Israel also demonstrates that He is greater than the temple and greater than Solomon (Matt 12:6, 42).

The Sermon on the Mount presents Jesus as the sage-king (Matt 5-7). In this passage, Jesus teaches the people with royal authority; His sermon sounds like a lecture on wisdom containing blessings, parables, figurative language, and picturesque descriptions of wise living. In Matthew 7, He concludes with a presentation of the two gates, the two trees, and the two foundations. These illustrations each echo the OT wisdom texts: the wise path leads to life and the foolish one leads to death. Jesus concludes by teaching that the wise will listen to His words and act upon them, but the foolish will not listen and so suffer devastating consequences. On the mount, like Solomon before Him but better, Jesus is the sage-king, the source of wisdom. He Himself is the path that the wise walk upon (John 14:6). Unlike all the sons of David and Solomon, Jesus begins wisely and ends wisely: He thoroughly keeps the wisdom of God and embodies wisdom itself.

Further Reading

Begg, Christopher T. "Seeking Yahweh and the Purpose of Chronicles." *Louvain Studies* 9 (2): 128–41.

Blenkinsopp, J. "Wisdom in the Chronicler's Work." *In Search of Wisdom*. Edited by Leo G. Perdue and J. W. William. Westminster: John Knox Press, 1993.

Endres, John C. "Chronicles and the Writings." in *The Oxford Handbook of the Writings of the Hebrew Bible,* Oxford Handbooks. Edited by Donn F. Morgan. Online edition. Oxford Academic, 2018.

Japhet, Sara. *The Ideology of the Book of Chronicles and Its Place in Biblical Thought.* English edition. Winona Lake: Eisenbrauns, 2009.

Oeming, Mafred. "Wisdom as a Central Category in the Book of the Chronicler: The Significance of the Talio Principle in a Sapiential Construction of History." *Studies in the Bible, its Exegesis and its Language*. Edited by Moshe Bar-Asher et al. Jerusalem: Bialik Institute, 2007: 125-141.

Wallace, Howard N. "What Chronicles Has to Say about Psalms." *The Chronicler as Author: Studies in Text and Texture*. Sheffield, England, 1999: 267-91.

Witherington, Ben, III. *Jesus the Sage: The Pilgrimage of Wisdom*. Minneapolis: Fortress Press, 2000.

The Book of Psalms: The Wise Ascend to Zion

Old Testament Background for the Psalter

- Creation: Gen 1-4
- Egypt, Red Sea, Sinai, wilderness journey: Ex 1 to Num 32
- David-Saul-Absalom sequence: 1 Sam 16 to 2 Sam 18
- David and the temple: 1 Chron 11-29
- Solomon's reign: 1 Kings 2-10; 2 Chron 1-9
- Temple worship: 1 Chron 25
- The fall of Jerusalem and exile: 2 Kings 25; 2 Chron 36
- The return to the land after the exile: Ezra-Neh
- The Law as wisdom: Deut 4:6
- The Davidic covenant: 2 Sam 7; 1 Chron 17

Creation and the Psalms: Flourishing and the King in Zion

Psalms 1 and 2 introduce the reader to the book of Psalms. Psalm 1 presents two paths: the way of the righteous and the way of the wicked. The blessed man of Psalm 1:1 meditates on the *torah* of the Lord, resulting in his thriving like a living tree (also Pss 19 and 119). Both these ideas hearken back to Genesis 2, when the Lord places Adam and Eve in a garden of flourishing trees and establishes two paths for the man and the woman: freely eat of all the trees in the garden, and do not eat from the tree of the knowledge of good and evil (Gen 2:16-17). If the man and the woman obey His commandments, they will live; if they disobey Him, they will die. Through this garden imagery and language, Psalm 1 establishes that when the righteous walk according to the Lord's instruction (*torah*), they can live a kind of garden-life even outside Eden, enjoying the blessings of wisdom and creation as God intended at the beginning.

Psalm 2 introduces another theme for the book of Psalms: God's messianic king. Although opposed by His enemies, in the end he will subdue the nations, inherit the earth, and reign from Zion. This king's dominion echoes Genesis 1:26, God's creation of humanity (*'adam*) in His image to rule over the whole of creation; the son of God of Psalm 2 fulfills the creational design of Genesis 1 (see Pss 8, 72, 110). The persecution of and opposition to the Lord's king stem from Genesis 3: the enmity between the "seed" of the serpent and the seed of the woman (Gen 3:15). Psalm 2 continues, emphasizing the wise flourishing as they follow *torah* and take refuge in the Messiah, eagerly anticipating the Lord's deliverance and their procession up to Zion to "kiss the son" (Ps 2:12). In a fitting conclusion, the Psalter as a whole ends with a crescendo of praise to the Lord from all creation (Ps 148 especially). God's Genesis creation design will be complete when the King reigns in Zion with those who love Him to the praise of His glory.

The Psalter: An Outline

The five books of the Psalter present a loose chronology of David and his kingdom. The individual psalms serve as pieces of a mosaic picturing the story of David and his house. Though poetic in form, the Psalms form a synoptic version of the events in Chronicles.

Book I: Psalms 1-41 are attributed to David and focus on his sufferings, his refuge in the Lord, and his love of God's wisdom.

Book II: Psalms 42-72 begin with a collection of psalms of Korah about the promised King who will save the people from exile and establish Zion. This book also includes Davidic laments and songs of trust and praise. Solomon's psalm about the glorious kingdom ends Book II by affirming that the Lord has been faithful to His promise to David (Ps 72).

Book III: Psalms 73-89 shift their focus to the people of Israel, discussing the apparent blessings of the wicked, their own unfaithfulness, exile, and hope for the future. Psalm 89 concludes the book with the fall of the Davidic kingdom and the exile of the people.

Book IV: Psalms 90-106 feature the exile experience of God's people as they look to the Lord's heavenly reign.

Book V: Psalms 107-150 record the songs of the redeemed from exile. Those who love God's *torah*-wisdom (Ps 119)—the redeemed—will ascend to Zion and her king with shouts of praise.

Major Themes: *Torah*-Wisdom, Suffering to Glory, the Lord and His Son Reign in Zion with the Wise

1. Torah-Wisdom

The book of Psalms emphasizes the relationship between God's *torah*-wisdom and going up to Zion to be with Him and His king. The three great *torah* psalms—Psalms 1, 19, and 119—each emphasize wisdom, teaching that loving the *torah* leads to abiding in the Lord's presence. The wise of Psalm 1 find refuge in the Messiah installed in Zion (Ps 2:6). Psalm 19 sits between two psalms about dwelling on God's holy hill (Pss 15 and 24). Following Psalm 119, the Songs of Ascents (Pss 120-134) sing of deliverance as the redeemed ascend Zion. This collection reaches its climax in Psalm 132, in the union of the seed of David and the house of the Lord. Throughout all 150 chapters, the Psalter's message remains consistent: those who receive the Lord's wisdom and instruction will abide with Him and His king in Zion.[26]

2. Suffering to Glory

Over 60 psalms fall into the lament category, making suffering a central theme of the Psalter. In a typical lament, the psalmist addresses the Lord, describes his trouble, petitions the Lord for deliverance, and concludes with praise, trust, or hope yet without any resolution to his trouble. Psalm 13 illustrates this pattern well:

13:1   How long, O Lord?

---

[26] The Psalter's wisdom emphasis also appears at the beginning of Books III, IV, and V. The center of the Psalter, Psalm 73, treats the wisdom question of the wicked prospering and the righteous suffering (see discussion in the Job chapter). It is no wonder both the Christian and Jewish traditions place the Psalms with the other wisdom books.

2	How long will my enemy be exalted over me?
3-4	Answer me, O Lord, my God
5-6	I will trust and sing praise to You

Laments ring loud and clear in the psalms. The first half of the Psalter focuses on David's lamentable situations but concludes with the glorious reign of the king (Ps 72, the end of Book II). The Psalter's second half begins with the fall of the kingdom in Book III, culminating in a crescendo of praise (Ps 146-150). This same pattern emerges from the psalms of David: while David's first psalm, Psalm 3, offers a lament within the context of the Absalom rebellion, his last psalm, Psalm 145, leads readers into the final chorus of praise. David's psalms and the Psalter as a whole follow the same arc: they move from suffering to glory.

3. *The Lord and His Son Reign in Zion with the Wise*

The Psalms also highlight the reign or rule of the Lord. Consistently in the Psalter, the Lord's reign and the human king's reign are united. As mentioned above, those who receive the Lord's wisdom and instruction abide with Him and His king in Zion (Ps 2, 132). However, during the time of the Psalms editors, there is no Davidic king on the throne. Book IV addresses this issue by focusing on the divine King, the LORD[27] of heaven, as the people wait for His salvation and their return from exile (Ps 106:47). Psalm 93:1-2 epitomizes the Psalter's teaching about the Lord's reign:

93:1	The Lord reigns; he is robed in majesty;
	The Lord is robed; he has put on strength as his belt.
	Yes, the world is established; it shall never be moved
2	Your throne is established from of old;
	You are from everlasting.

---

[27] The "the LORD reigns" psalms in Book IV use the covenant name of God, YHWH, translated as LORD in the English Bible tradition.

This theme of the Lord's reign begins in Psalm 2:4-6 with the heavenly King installing His messianic King in Zion and continues throughout the Psalter. In particular, Book IV contains a collection of psalms repeating the expression "the Lord reigns" (Ps 93:1, 95:3, 96:10, 97:1, 99:1). This truth is significant within Book IV: with no Davidic king on the throne, the Lord appears absent and His promises forgotten. During such times, the psalmists' wisdom is to appeal to the Lord's eternal and heavenly rule. Book V resolves this absence of the messianic king by focusing on the Lord's promise to David: his son will indeed sit upon His throne (Pss 110 and 132).

The Sages in Conversation

1. Torah-Wisdom

As discussed above, Psalm 1 establishes meditation on *torah* as a wisdom pursuit, providing a hermeneutical lens for understanding the rest of the Psalter. Following *torah* and seeking wisdom yield the same result: going up to Zion to dwell with the King. In this conversation, the Psalter discusses this link between *torah* and wisdom with Ezra-Nehemiah, Proverbs, and Deuteronomy.

Ezra-Nehemiah specifies the close relationship between wisdom and *torah*. Ezra 7:10 reads, "For Ezra had set his heart to study the law of the Lord and to practice it, and to teach His statutes and ordinances in Israel." Later in the same chapter, the Persian king Artaxerxes gives Ezra authority to execute justice according to "the wisdom of your God which is in your hand" (Ezra 7:25).[28] This statement implies that because of Ezra's character and teaching, Artaxerxes rightly equates the wisdom of Ezra's God with the *torah* of the Lord. Wisdom and *torah* are bound up with one another in the Hebrew Scriptures, the book in Ezra's hand.

The book of Proverbs offers a far more developed relationship

---

28 In Deuteronomy 4:6, Moses makes the same point: "Keep them and do them, for that will be your wisdom and your understanding in the sight of the peoples, who, when they hear all these statutes, will say, 'Surely this great nation is a wise and understanding people.'" Following the statutes of the Lord makes one wise.

between *torah* and wisdom. Proverbs 1-9 repeatedly clusters *torah* terms and wisdom terms; for example, Proverbs 2:1-3 reads:

> 2:1 My son, if you receive my **words**
>
> And treasure up my **commandments** with you,
>
> 2 Making your ear attentive to **wisdom**
>
> And inclining your heart to **understanding**;
>
> 3 Yes, if you call out for **insight**
>
> And raise your voice for **understanding** ...

This passage pulls several terms from the wisdom word-field (see Introduction): "wisdom," "understanding," and "insight." However, Proverbs 2 also includes "commandments" (*mitswah*), bringing the Law into the frame of reference. *Torah* and *mitswah* again appear together in Proverbs 3:1 and 7:1-2:

> 3:1 My son, do not forget my **teaching** (*torah*),
>
> but let your heart keep my **commandments** (*mitswah*).
>
> 7:1 My son, keep my words
>
> and treasure up my **commandments** (*mitswah*) with you;
>
> 2 keep my **commandments** (*mitswah*) and live;
>
> keep my **teaching** (*torah*) as the apple of your eye;

Both texts liken the father's teaching (*torah*) to the Lord's commandments (*mitswah*) for His son Israel, recorded in Deuteronomy. In fact, after the prologue of Proverbs 1:1-7, the very next verse exhorts the son to listen to his parents' *torah* instruction (Prov 1:8):

> 1:8 Hear, my son, your father's **instruction** (*musar*),
>
> and forsake not your mother's **teaching** (*torah*).

This verse begins with the call "Hear, my son" (*shama'*), paralleling the famous Shema in Deuteronomy 6:4: "Hear, O Israel ..." With this exhortation to hear, Proverbs signals that it is beginning with a Shema of its own.[29] The expression "hear, my son" (*shama'*), also serves as a division marker for several sections within Proverbs 1-9 (4:1 and 10, 5:7, 7:24). This refrain positions Proverbs 1-9 as a wisdom Shema, the foundation of the wisdom of Solomon (see Prov 10:1, 25:1).[30]

The relationship between Proverbs and the Shema of Deuteronomy 6 emerges even more clearly if one compares the wording in both texts. The chart below uses Proverbs 3:1-3, but could also be worked out with Proverbs 6:20-23 or 7:1-3:

Deuteronomy 6:4-9	Proverbs 3:1-4
6:4 Hear, O Israel: The Lord our God, the Lord is one.	3:1 My son, do not forget my teaching, but let your heart keep my commandments,
5 You shall love the Lord your God with all your heart and with all your soul and with all your might.	2 for length of days and years of life and peace they will add to you.
6 And these words that I command you today shall be on your heart.	3 Let not steadfast love and faithfulness forsake you; bind them around your neck; write them on the tablet of your heart.
7 You shall teach them diligently to your children, and shall talk of them when you sit in your house, and when you walk by the way, and when you lie down, and when you rise.	4 So you will find favor and good success in the sight of God and man.
8 You shall bind them as a sign on your hand, and they shall be as frontlets between your eyes. 9 You shall write them on the doorposts of your house and on your gates.	

---

29 See Bernard Schipper and D. Andrew Teeter. "Wisdom and Torah: The Reception of 'Torah' in the Wisdom Literature of the Second Temple Period." Supplement to the *Journal for the Study of Judaism*. Leiden: Brill, 2013.

30 For further discussion on the Shema and other proverbs echoing Deuteronomy, see Gary E. Schnittjer. *Old Testament Use of Old Testament*. Grand Rapids: Zondervan, 2022: 568-573.

By drawing from the same word field as the Shema, the book of Proverbs positions itself as a Shema for those in exile. Just as Deuteronomy is the *torah* of Moses, so, in a way, is the book of Proverbs the *torah* of Solomon. For Israel to live and flourish in the promised land, they need to observe the *torah* of Moses, outlined in Deuteronomy. However, exiled Israel is unable to exactly obey these Deuteronomic commandments while under Gentile authority in a foreign land. The book of Proverbs, then, provides a Deuteronomy-like *torah* for those God-fearers seeking to live a kingdom life amidst the nations. Proverbs brackets out the promised land-specific elements of Deuteronomy—laws of the temple/sanctuary, clean and unclean animals, the sabbatical year, landmarks, warfare, feasts, etc—and instead presents parallel instruction: wisdom applicable by humans anywhere. In so doing, the book of Proverbs becomes a synoptic version of Deuteronomy for life in exile. Ultimately, Proverbs functions not only as wisdom for Israel under Solomon but also as *torah* for those in exile and beyond.

The Psalter itself echoes this idea that *torah* and wisdom are closely related. In addition to the three *torah* Psalms mentioned above, a number of other psalms also treat *torah* and wisdom together. Psalm 78, for instance, combines wisdom terms with *torah* language, creating a "proverbial psalm":

78:1		**Give ear**, O my people, to my **teaching** (*torah*);
		Incline your ears to the **words** of my mouth!
2		I will open my mouth in a parable (*mashal*)
		I will utter **dark sayings** (*hidah*) from of old,
3		Things that we have heard and known,
		That our **fathers** have told us.
4		We will not hide them from their **children** (*ben*),
		But tell to the coming generation

> The glorious deeds of the Lord, and his might,
>
> And the wonders that he has done.

In these opening verses, the psalmist sets his agenda: to recount Israel's history with the Lord, highlighting the teaching the next generation is to glean from Israel's past. The terms "dark sayings" (*hidah*) and its parallel "parable" (*mashal*) bring wisdom language into this introduction.[31] By using these terms, the psalmist frames the purpose of the psalm as the pursuit of wisdom, calling on the people to reveal this wisdom to their children.

In the next few verses, the psalmist presents the general moral of his parable: the Lord established a *torah* for Israel so that fathers could teach their children (*ben*, or sons) to keep God's commandments, thereby avoiding the sins of their own stubborn and unfaithful forefathers. Psalm 78:5-8 continues with more *torah* language:

> 5   He established a testimony in Jacob
>
>   And appointed a **law** (*torah*) in Israel,
>
>   Which he **commanded** (*tsawah*) our fathers
>
>   To **teach** (*yarah*) to their **children** (*ben*),
>
> 6   That the next generation might know them,
>
>   The **children** (*ben*) yet unborn,
>
>   And arise and tell them to their **children** (*ben*),
>
> 7   So that they should set their hope in God
>
>   And not forget the works of God,
>
>   But keep his **commandments** (*mitswah*);
>
> 8   And that they should not be like their fathers,

---

31 For a discussion of wisdom and "dark sayings" (*hidah*), see the chapter on the book of Daniel.

> A stubborn and rebellious generation,
>
> A generation whose heart was not steadfast,
>
> Whose spirit was not faithful to God.

The verbal parallels between these two segments—teaching, law, fathers, children—knit the psalm together. Within his introduction, Asaph links his *torah* in verse 1 with the Lord's *torah* in verse 5: both lead to wisdom. The remainder of this lengthy psalm (verses 9-72) provides Asaph's *torah*-parable about Israel's failure to faithfully keep God's *torah* and the Lord's repeated compassion and forgiveness, two of the main thematic threads in the OT.

In sum, Ezra-Nehemiah, Proverbs, and Psalms all present wisdom and the keeping of *torah* as the same pursuit. Reflecting this focus, pocket New Testaments today often include the books of Psalms and Proverbs; these two *torah*-wisdom books contain God's universal and creational wisdom for those living between the promise of the kingdom and its fulfillment.

2. Lament in the Psalms and the Writings

The 60+ laments in the Psalter make lament a major theme of the book as well as a worthy conversation topic with other sages in the Writings. Wisdom books often include laments for the obvious reason that humans going through trial and tragedy frequently petition God in their time of need, seeking solace and comfort. During trials, the temptation is to resolve our troubles through our own understanding when in fact, the God-fearer should seek the Lord and respond according to His wisdom. However, as this conversation will demonstrate, Job, Psalms, and Lamentations provide quite a wide variety of laments for the God-fearer to consider.

Both David and Job pour out their souls in lament to God. As demonstrated earlier in this chapter with Psalm 13, David's laments follow a consistent pattern: each lament psalm speaks directly to God, narrates David's suffering at the hands of his enemies, asks for deliverance, and ends with trust or praise. Job's laments do not follow this pattern. Job's trials begin in Job 1 and find no resolution until the end of the last chapter, Job 42. Initially in Job 1-2, Job seems to take the high road, blessing the Lord while willingly receiving evil (*ra'*) from His hand. Job's words turn to lament in chapter 3 when he curses his life, decrying his entire existence from the moment of his conception through to his present sufferings. His profound despair continues in his other laments: chapters 6-7, 9-10, 13-14, 16-17, 19, and 23-24.

The chart below summarizes similarities and differences between David's and Job's laments:

David's Laments	Job's Laments
1. Directly <u>address the Lord</u>	1. Mostly <u>address Job's friends</u>

2. Describe trials:
  - Sufferings, sickness
  - <u>Wicked enemies</u>
	2. Describe trials:
	  - Sufferings, sickness
	  - <u>Friends as enemies</u>
	  - **God as an enemy**

3. <u>Petition</u> the Lord for deliverance	3. <u>Complain about/to the Lord</u>
4. Conclude with praise, trust, or hope	4. **Nothing**

The underlined and bold points indicate subtle and significant differences between these two men's laments; suffering and sickness constitute the only clear common ground. In contrast to David's consistent laments addressed to his Lord, Job turns his complaint to God directly only on occasion, using "you" in three of his laments: chapters 6-7, 9-10, and 13-14. Even within his addresses to God, usually near the end of each chapter, Job's stark language stands out:

- Remember me (7:8, 10:9)

- You terrify, try, gaze, oppress, hunt me (7:14, 18, 20, 10:3 and 16)

- Why do you target, contend, consider me Your enemy? (7:20,

10:2, 13:24)

- Make me know my sins (13:23)

- You seek my guilt, but You know I am not guilty (10:5-7)

- Remove Your hand so that we can speak (13:21-22)

- Hide me, conceal me until Your wrath is spent (14:13)

In keeping with this questioning and aggressive attitude, Job's last words to God summarize Job's charges against Him (Job 30:20-23):

30:20 I cry to you for help and you do not answer me;

I stand, and you only look at me.

21 You have turned cruel to me;

With the might of your hand you persecute me.

22 You lift me up on the wind; you make me ride on it,

And you toss me about in the roar of the storm.

23 For I know that you will bring me to death

And to the house appointed for all living.

As these words indicate, Job not only adds God to his list of adversaries, but he also ends his laments mired in complaint, never demonstrating a turn to the trust or hope so comforting to David, at least up to this point in the story.

Given these dramatic differences in perspective, a natural conversation between psalmists like David[32] and Job focuses on attempting to resolve this disparity within their laments. Though David at times affirms his innocence the way Job does (for instance in Ps 7:3-9), David would probably ask Job why he resists declaring

---

[32] In terms of tone and language, Psalm 88 of Heman the Ezrahite shares aspects of both Job's and David's laments, and does not end with a declaration of trust or praise.

God to be his refuge in the midst of his troubles.³³ In turn, Job might ask why God would be his refuge when he believes God is the one attacking him. Job remains confident that if he could present his case to God, he would surely be vindicated (Job 13:15-19). So why is God, whom David sees as a "righteous judge" against his enemies (Ps 7:6, 11, 17), oppressing His servant Job? In a sense, Job's continued entreaties to God are themselves evidence of his faith in God's justice and righteousness. David might then highlight the difficulty of Job's situation vis-à-vis God: Job "knows that his vindicator (*goel*) lives" (Job 19:25). That vindicator is God Himself (also in 16:19), but at the same time, God seems to be Job's adversary, the source of his suffering. From David's perspective, Job's position seems untenable—how can the Lord be Job's enemy and vindicator at the same time? David's laments consistently reiterate that God is his only hope while Job maintains that God is the problem and needs to become the solution. At this point, David may just be appalled into silence, ending the conversation in a stalemate, just like Job's conversation with his three friends. How can Job and the Lord both be vindicated?

While Job's laments offer no resolution, the book of Job as a whole does. Job ends chapter 31 still asserting his innocence and crying out for the Lord's response: "Let the Almighty answer me!" (Job 31:35). In Job 38-41, the Lord breaks His silence and in turn questions Job. As a result, Job ceases his ignorant speaking:

> 40:4 Behold, I am of small account; what shall I answer you?
>
> I lay my hand on my mouth.
>
> 5 I have spoken once, and I will not answer;
>
> Twice, but I will proceed no further.

---

33 The difficult Hebrew of Job 13:15 allows for opposite meanings in translation. The majority of the English versions follow the ESV: "Though he slay me, yet I will hope in him." However, the NRSV reads: "See, he will kill me; I have no hope." The majority of Job's statements about hope (*tiqwah* and *yahal*) indicate that he has none (Job 6:11, 7:6, 14:11, 17:15, 19:10) other than occasional hope for death (Job 6:8, 14:14, 17:13).

When confronted with the might, power, and knowledge of the Almighty Creator, Job understands his place as a creature. Instead of cursing his life as he did earlier, in the end he retracts his ignorant words while still sitting in dust and ashes (Job 42:6).[34] Still in the misery and suffering he has undergone since chapter 1, he proclaims his trust in the Lord and petitions for continued instruction from Him (Job 42:4). Were David still listening to Job at this point, he would probably shout for joy, embrace Job, and join him in petitioning God for mercy to the tune of one of his favorite psalms.

Ultimately, David and Job both assert their trust and confidence in the Lord. Both declare their faith in Him and their hope for future deliverance while still in the midst of their trouble. The length of the book of Job appears to allow for an extended treatment of suffering and lament lacking in a comparatively short psalm. In turn, David's songs, while poignant, seem to offer a summary of lament, not a play-by-play of the psalmist's lengthy time of suffering and struggle with God. Though the end point is the same, these two books offer paths to that end varying in depth and scope.

Enter the book of Lamentations. True to its title, this series of laments brings a third sage into the conversation. The various characters in the book—personified Jerusalem, a prophetic observer, a suffering man, and the people of Israel—weep and mourn over the destruction of the temple and the city of David by the hand of the Lord. Unsurprisingly, Lamentations offers additional nuance when compared to the laments of Job and David.

Perhaps the most glaring particularity in Lamentations is that three of the five laments end with a petition for vengeance on Israel's enemies instead of praise or trust in the Lord (Lam 1:21-22, 3:64-66,

---

[34] One of the most important verses in the book, Job 42:6, has been understood by translators and commentators in different ways. See Sandra L. Gravett. *An Introduction to the Hebrew Bible: A Thematic Approach*. 1st ed. Louisville: Westminster John Knox Press, 2008: 454-55.

4:21-22).³⁵ Maybe these prayers for destruction make sense given that the Lord executed His judgment through Gentile nations. Like Job, the very fact that the people seek the Lord in prayer may itself be evidence of their trust and faith in His justice. However, paralleling Job's lament pattern, Lamentations does not arrive at the point of explicit statements of praise or trust in God. Instead, Israel continues to seek the Lord's vengeance.

Unlike Job but similarly to some of David's penitential laments (Pss 32, 38, 51), Lamentations includes confession: in Lamentations 1, personified Jerusalem confesses her sins (Lam 1:14, 18, 20). Normally, confession is followed by an indication of forgiveness, yet no such statement exists for Israel in Lamentations. The only statement about forgiveness in the entire book specifies that the Lord has not pardoned or forgiven Israel's transgressions (Lam 3:42) but instead was the One who brought devastation upon them (3:43-51). The text of Lamentations consistently describes the Lord's wrath against His people in the destruction of Jerusalem, giving no hint that He has turned to His people to forgive. Lamentations implies that after His judgment, the Lord is still angry, and He is silent. The man of Lamentations 3 briefly returns to the hope that the Lord will demonstrate His compassion and lovingkindness (*hesed*):

> 3:31 For the Lord will not
>
> Cast off forever,
>
> 32 But, though he cause grief, he will have compassion
>
> According to the abundance of his steadfast love (*hesed*);

This brief hope aside, Lamentations consistently bemoans the suffering of the people, admitting transgression against the Lord but

---

35 David does petition the Lord to judge his enemies (Ps 69:20-28, 109:6-20), but these requests are found in the midst of his psalms, not at their endings. So placed, they seem to form part of the process of lament and not its conclusion.

then returning yet again to complaint about His harsh treatment. Lamentations 2:20 even echoes the Job-like sentiment that the Lord has gone too far in His anger:

> 2:20 Look, O Lord, and see!
>
> With whom have you dealt thus?
>
> Should women eat the fruit of their womb,
>
> The children of their tender care?
>
> Should priest and prophet be killed
>
> In the sanctuary of the Lord?

These rhetorical questions assume the answer "No. God dealt with us, His people, too harshly." Israel seems to charge the Lord with committing an injustice against them by judging the people beyond what their sins deserved. Prior to the Lord's instruction in Job 38-41, Job would agree with Israel that God brings calamity without just cause (Job 10:2-8). David might then remind Job and Lamentations that the Lord is blameless when He judges sin (Ps 51:3), whatever that judgment might be. Also, the people should perhaps have anticipated cannibalism as a consequence of breaking the covenant (Deut 28:57; Jer 19:9, 23:11-12). Regardless, these chapters expand a fundamental part of the lament process: crying out to God from the depths of one's suffering, anguish, and anger.

Lamentations offers yet another theme to this lament conversation: turning or returning (*shub*) to the Lord. In chapter 3, the man who represents suffering Jerusalem urges the people to return (*shub*) to the Lord (Lam 3:40-41). Then, the people's prayer in chapter 5 calls for the Lord to return or restore (*shub*) them to Himself (Lam 5:21). The final verses of the book end with pointed and dramatic ambiguity:

> 5:21 Restore us to yourself, O Lord, that we may be restored!

>   Renew our days as of old—
>
> 22   Unless you have utterly rejected us,
>
>   And you remain exceedingly angry with us.[36]

According to OT patterns, turning or returning to the Lord (*shub*) should result in the reversal of Israel's fortunes, an easing of her suffering, a turn from death to life, from calamity to blessing. For instance, in the laments of Psalms 80 and 85, returning to the Lord leads to salvation and the end of God's anger because of His lovingkindness (Ps 80:3, 7, 19, 85:4, 10-13). Although the center of Lamentations mentions hope in the Lord's lovingkindness (Lam 3:21-26), Lamentations ends with no further reference to this hope. Both David's laments and the book of Job end with clear trust, confidence, and praise to God, even in the midst of suffering, but Lamentations has not yet taken that turn. The people have confessed their sin, asked to be returned to the Lord, but the text contains no hint of a response from the Lord. Instead, the book ends with questions: has the Lord completely rejected us? Has the covenant been annulled?

As these sages have discussed, laments provide wisdom on how to walk on the Lord's path in times of suffering. The wisdom books do not expect all laments to follow the typical structure of David's lament psalms. This conversation between David, Job, and Lamentations reveals a less restrictive approach to the handling of suffering, allowing each lament to take a shape reflecting the sufferer's time-bound journey through pain, mourning, and seeking the Lord to understand and respond wisely.

3. The Lord and His Son Reign in Zion with the Wise

As briefly discussed above, the Psalter foregrounds a wisdom/king/Zion cluster of themes. Many so-called royal psalms speak of a human to reign as king; in Psalm 2:4-6, for instance, the Lord states that He

---

36 For various translation options, see H. J. Flowers. "The Book of Lamentations." *Review & Expositor* 31 (4): 452–60.

has installed His king upon Zion, His holy mountain. The Psalms also allude to God's promise to David to place one of his sons on Israel's throne in Jerusalem forever. For example, Psalm 132 pinpoints Zion as the Lord's resting place, where He will sit along with His king (132:11-12, 13-14). What is this interplay between Israel's king in Jerusalem, the Messiah's earthly reign from Zion, and the reign of God from heaven over all the earth? The sages of Psalms, Chronicles, Lamentations, and Daniel take up this conversation.

Chronicles offers an initial picture of the relationship between these kings. The Chronicler presents the Lord's reign through David and Solomon's relationship with the ark of the covenant, the symbol of God's presence. By bringing the ark into Jerusalem the way he finally does, with reverence and praise, David publicly demonstrates his submission to the kingship of the Great King, the Lord. In turn, at the dedication of the temple, Solomon welcomes the ark as the symbol of the Lord's sovereignty and reign over him and all creation. Chronicles' David-Solomon-temple-ark narratives highlight how both these kings recognized their role as a delegate, an intermediary between the heavenly king and the people.[37] The Davidic line derives its authority from the supreme authority and the promise the Great King of heaven made to David.

Lamentations, written after the destruction of Jerusalem, connects to the Chronicles narrative by describing Israel's waiting for salvation in exile. Lamentations 5 depicts life after the destruction of the city and temple; the people in the land labor to eke out a daily existence. There is no king in Jerusalem, the people think the Lord has forsaken them, and yet just a few verses before the conclusion of the book, Lamentations 5:19-20 reads:

> 5:19   But you, O Lord, reign forever;
>
> Your throne endures to all generations.

---

[37] The David and Solomon ark narratives are bracketed by Asaph's psalm in 1 Chronicles 16 (itself a reworking of Psalms 105:1-15, 96:1-13, and 106:1, 47-48) and Solomon's quotation of Psalm 132:8-9 in 2 Chronicles 6:41.

> 20   Why do you forget us forever,
>
> Why do you forsake us for so many days?

Even in the midst of Israel's petitions for restoration of the former glory days (city, people, temple, and king), the people acknowledge the reign of the Great King of heaven. In fact, Lamentations as a whole is a wail of grief to a God Israel believes to be sovereign over all people, Israel and Gentile alike. Israel knows their judgment stems from the authority and covenant of the Great King of heaven, against whom they have sinned. Even while questioning whether He has completely rejected His people, Lamentations affirms the Lord's reign.

The Psalter now interjects, certifying the hope Lamentations merely grasps for. The psalms also ask if the Lord has rejected His people, but these same psalms end with hope (Ps 60:12, 79:12-13, 80:18-19). Book V looks forward to the promised Davidic king; in Psalm 110:2, *YHWH*[38] declares to the promised Messiah, "The Lord sends forth from Zion your mighty scepter. Rule in the midst of your enemies!" In Psalm 132:12-13, the psalmist again states that David's son shall rule on his throne forever, immediately specifying that *YHWH* has chosen Zion as His dwelling place. Affirming *YHWH* as the King of creation, the Psalter foresees the future renewal of Israel: *YHWH* will execute His reign through the coming Messiah, the king in Zion.

At this point, the book of Daniel enters the conversation with new revelations about the timing of this ultimate restoration and the Lord's reign over Israel and the nations.[39] Daniel's interpretation of Nebuchadnezzar's dream (Dan 2) and Daniel's own vision (Dan 7) present similar timelines:

- Daniel 2: four phases of Gentile dominion, ending in the eternal kingdom of God

---

[38] The tetragrammaton, *YHWH*, is used here because Psalm 110:1 references both to the LORD (*YHWH*) and the Lord (*'adon*) in the statement "The LORD says to my lord."

[39] For a discussion of the content of Daniel's visions, see Chapter 11.

- Daniel 7: four phases of Gentile dominion, ending in a human/Messianic reign with the people

Through these visions and their explanations, the book of Daniel reiterates that God reigns over the world and that He has temporarily handed over the dominion of the earth to the Gentile kings. Furthermore, this text places the restoration of the earthly reign of the Great King through the Messiah far in the distant future, after Babylon, Greece, Medo-Persia, and an undesignated end-time fourth phase of Gentile dominion are judged (Dan 9). In the end, the eternal heavenly kingdom of God will break into the world; Daniel 7:13-14 reads:

> 7:13　I saw in the night visions,
>
> And behold, with the clouds of heaven
>
> There came one like a son of man (*'enosh*)[40]
>
> And he came to the Ancient of Days
>
> And was presented before him.
>
> 14　And to him was given dominion
>
> And glory and a kingdom,
>
> That all peoples, nations, and languages
>
> Should serve him;
>
> His dominion is an everlasting dominion,
>
> Which shall not pass away,
>
> And his kingdom one
>
> That shall not be destroyed.

This passage in Daniel 7 puts a human face on the reign of God, the heavenly king. According to the royal psalms (Pss 2, 8, 72, 89, 110, 132,

---

40 Daniel 7 was originally written in Aramaic. *'enosh* is the Aramaic word for the Hebrew "man" (*'adam*).

for example), this son of *'adam* receiving the kingdom is none other than the promised son of David, the Messiah. Once again, the Ancient of Days delegates His rule (Daniel 7:9-10). Interestingly enough, Daniel's angelic interpreter indicates that the coming kingdom will be given to the people of God (Dan 7:27), linking the son of *'adam* with the saints, the redeemed of Israel. This turn of events echoes the covenant-like bond between king and people.

Thus all earthly kings—of Israel, a gentile nation, or the Messiah Himself—derive their authority from the Great King over all. David prefigures the Messiah, serving as a narrative type of His coming kingship. The Messiah—the son of Adam, Son of David, the Son of God—will follow the pattern of David, His father: he will defeat the Lord's enemies, submit his rule to the Great King, and establish a place for the Lord to dwell and reign. By doing so, the Messiah will fulfill the Davidic covenant, finally allowing the wise to ascend to Zion to dwell with the Lord and His king.

Toward the New Testament

1. Law and Wisdom: The Gospel of Jesus Christ

As discussed above, the Psalter offers a wisdom perspective on the law. The wise meditate on *torah* and flourish, prospering in all they do (Ps 1:2-3). In turn, the *torah* restores or regenerates the life of the wise (Ps 19:7). Throughout Psalm 119, the psalmist speaks of the life-giving power of the *torah* (Ps 119:25, 37, 40, 88, 93, 107, 149, 154, 156, 159). It is no surprise, then, that the psalms also combine the wisdom of creation and the wisdom of *torah*, such as in Psalm 19. *Torah* creates life.

In like fashion, the Gospel of Jesus Christ brings the believer from death to life, as dramatized by baptism. The Gospel makes a new creation of the children of Adam (2 Cor 5:17; Col 3:10-11). Just as the *torah* in the Psalter forms the way, truth, and life of the God-fearer, so also Jesus proclaims that He Himself is the way, truth, and life (John 14:6). According to Jesus' words in Luke 24:44, the Psalms find their culmination in the death, burial, and resurrection of Jesus. Not only is the *torah* the royal law and the law of liberty (James 2:5, 2:12), but the *torah* is also the Gospel of life, life in Jesus Christ.

2. Suffering to Praise

The overall arc of the Psalter and its laments moves from suffering to praise. This arc parallels the arc of the life of Christ. According to 1 Peter 1:10-11, the OT prophets sought to know about the sufferings of the Messiah and the glories to follow: the incarnation and humiliation of Jesus followed by His resurrection. While suffering on the cross, Jesus quotes David's lament in Psalm 22:1: "My God, My God, why have you forsaken me?" (see also Ps 69). The crucifixion of Jesus marks the most lamentable moment in human history. The Son of God, nailed to the cross for sins He did not commit, cries out in anguish to His Father, asking why He has been abandoned to suffering. Today, the church refers to this day as Good Friday, "good" because of the resurrection of Jesus to come on the first day of the week. Easter morning marks the most glorious moment of the incarnation: the Father has remembered His Son and through Him, vanquished sin and death. Following the same arc as the Psalter, the death, burial, and resurrection of Jesus move from suffering to praise.

The life of a Christian, one who is in Christ, follows the same suffering-to-glory trajectory. In Romans 8:18, Paul declares that the sufferings of the present time do not compare to the glories that follow (see also 1 Pet 4:13); those in Christ, as well as the creation, will participate in Christ's resurrection (Rom 8:19-25). The arc of Jesus' life is repeated in the life of the church, again paralleling the laments in the Psalter.

3. God Reigns and the Son Reigns

The Writings make clear that God the Father, the Great King of heaven, has delegated His authority to the Son to rule over all creation (Pss 8, 110, 132). The NT also describes the close association between the rule of God and the messianic king, the son of David and Adam. Before Jesus ascends to the Father, He states that all authority has been given to Him in heaven and earth (Matt 28:18). The NT repeatedly reiterates this authority structure (Eph 1:20-22; Phil 2:9-10; 1 Peter 3:22). 1 Corinthians 15:20-28 details how Jesus fulfills the rule of the son of Adam predicted in Psalm 8: Christ must reign and put all things under His feet in victory, including death. Once all things are under His rule, Christ then hands the kingdom back to God the Father, who gave Christ this authority in the first place.

Lastly, in Jesus' beatitudes, He describes who is "blessed": the poor in spirit, those who mourn, the gentle, those who hunger and search for righteousness, the merciful, the pure in heart, the peacemakers, those who have been persecuted for the sake of righteousness, those who have been insulted, persecuted, and lied about for the sake of Christ (Matt 5:3-12). This list comes straight out of the Writings: these are the characteristics of the wise. Echoing the Psalter while on the Mount, Jesus Himself affirms that the wise will inherit the kingdom.

Further Reading

Brown, William P. "Reading Psalms Sapientially in the Writings." *The Oxford Handbook of the Writings of the Hebrew Bible*, Oxford Handbooks. Edited by Donn F. Morgan. Online edition. Oxford Academic, 2018.

deClaissé-Walford, Nancy L. et al. *The Book of Psalms*. Grand Rapids: Eerdmans, 2014.

Estes, Daniel J. *Psalms 73-150: An Exegetical and Theological Exposition of Holy Scripture*. Nashville: Holman Bible Publishers, 2019.

Mays, James Luther. *The Lord Reigns: A Theological Handbook to the Psalms*. 1st edition. Louisville: Westminster John Knox Press. 1994.

McCann, J. Clinton. *A Theological Introduction to the Book of Psalms: The Psalms as Torah*. New York: Abingdon Press, 1993.

Job: Human versus Divine Wisdom

Old Testament Background for the Book of Job

Creation and the Book of Job: Job as an Adam Figure

- Creation, Adam, Eve, the serpent, the fall, Cain/Abel: Gen 1-4
- YHWH, the covenant name of Israel's God: Ex 3
- "God Almighty" (*shadday*), a pre-covenant name of the Lord: Gen 17:1; Ex 6:3
- Shuah and Teman, ancestors of Job's friends: Gen 25:2, 36:11
- Edom/the land of Uz, Job's home: Lam 4:21

One of the OT's greatest passages on wisdom and creation, Job 38-41 offers a detailed, poetic version of Genesis 1. In His response to Job, the Lord reveals His wisdom and power, displayed in His creation and management of that creation. Again, treating creation, Job 28 explains that only the Creator knows where wisdom is found; humans cannot find wisdom on their own (Job 28:23-28, 12-13). Wisdom does not exist in the land of the living; wisdom must be given to humans by the Creator Himself, the One who stands outside of the created world and thoroughly understands His own work.

The opening narrative of the book of Job also subtly parallels Genesis 1-4. Both narratives revolve around God the Creator, a character in opposition to God, a man, and his wife. This parallel casts Job as an Adam figure, this time one who obeys the Lord and does not rebel against Him. Like the serpent, Job's mysterious adversary (*satan*) plots to encourage the man and his wife to choose sin and folly. In contrast to Adam, Job does not listen to his wife's foolish advice to "curse God and die" (Job 2:9-10). Job's wife clarifies the easy way out of Job's affliction, increasing the tension in the story: readers read on to see if Job will give in and curse God. If he does, will the consequences be further ruin or deliverance from suffering? These parallels between

Genesis 1-4 and Job 1-2 increase the stakes in Job's dilemma; Job and the readers wait for God to speak into the situation.

Job: An Outline

Job 1-2: The Debate about Job's Motivation for Fearing God

> Since the Lord blesses and protects Job, the adversary (*satan*)[41] asks the Lord whether Job fears God "for nothing" (Job 1:9). The Lord allows Job's calamities to reveal the answer to this question.

Job 3-31: Dialogues between Job and his Three Friends

> Job and his friends discuss Job's righteousness or wickedness and the Lord's justice. In the end, Job seeks vindication from the Lord. Within these dialogues, Job 28 declares that only the Lord knows wisdom: only He can answer these questions.

Job 32-37: Monologue of Elihu

> Elihu presents his human "wisdom," bridging Job's petition for the Lord to answer him (Job 31:35) and the awaited response from the Almighty.

Job 38:1-42:6: The Lord's Instruction to Job

> The climax of the book: the Lord answers Job and teaches him wisdom.

Job 42:7-9: Job's Friends Chastened by the Lord

> Job, the Lord's servant, is vindicated before his friends and intercedes for them.

Job 42: 10-17: Job Restored and Blessed by the Lord

> In the end, the Lord "increased all that Job had two-fold" (Job 42:10).

---

[41] English versions translate the Hebrew *satan* as *Satan* (see the marginal notes in your Bible); however, the Hebrew text includes a definite article with *satan*: "the *satan*." Since Hebrew does not use articles with personal names, the best way to translate the Hebrew is "the adversary," a title for an angelic creature in opposition to both the Lord and His servant Job.

Major Themes: The Fear of the Lord, Wisdom Manifest in Creation, Actions and their Consequences

1. The Fear of the Lord

The book of Job begins with a description of a man from Uz: both the book's narrator and the Lord Himself call Job "blameless, upright, one who feared God and turned away from evil" (1:1, 8, 2:3). The whole town recognizes Job's blameless life: he defends the poor and needy and stands up to evil (Job 29:7-17). The text repeatedly describes Job as a man without reproach, one on the wisdom path.

In Job 1:9, the Lord brings up His servant Job, and the adversary (*satan*) challenges His view of this man, asking if perhaps Job fears God "for no reason" (*hinnam*). The adversary argues that of course Job fears God: the Lord has put a hedge of blessing around His servant, his family, and his possessions. Job experiences nothing bad, only blessings and prosperity from God (Job 1:10). The adversary (*satan*) predicts that if the Lord stretches out His hand against Job, Job will cease being blameless and curse God to His face (Job 1:11). This dialogue establishes the focus of the entire book: will Job curse God or will he remain the servant of the Lord when he suffers the total loss of family, possessions, and health? Is Job really the man described in Job 1:1, or is his reverence for God simply a divine-human transaction? The Lord allows the adversary (*satan*) to afflict Job, His blameless servant, to answer these questions.

2. Wisdom Manifest in Creation

The conversation between Job, his three friends, and another friend, Elihu, make up the bulk of the book of Job (Job 3-37). These chapters, the words of humans trying to puzzle out what happened to Job and why, build up to the Lord's dramatic entrance into the conversation. Ever since chapter 28 revealed that humans cannot find wisdom, readers have been waiting for the Lord to enter the conversation, speak wisdom, and set the record straight. And the Lord does not disappoint. Speaking out of a whirlwind, He accuses Job of obscuring wisdom with ignorant speeches and calls the words of his three friends' "folly" (Job 38:2, 42:7-9). The Lord's instruction in Job 38-41 then teaches Job and the readers that the Creator governs His creation in wisdom, even when that wisdom is not readily accessible to humans. No created being in heaven or earth can understand the Lord's wise governance, even as we are and live in its clearest manifestation: creation.

3. Actions and their Consequences

Both the narrator and the Lord make it clear that Job's calamities are not the result of his sin. From Job 1-2, readers know the Lord destroyed Job (2:3) through the adversary (*satan*) to demonstrate that Job's fear of the Lord was genuine, untethered to His blessings. However, only the Lord, the adversary, and the readers know this; Job and his three friends remain uninformed of the heavenly context of Job's experiences. Naturally, then, their dialogues go back and forth unresolved: Job claims his innocence while charging God with injustice, and his three friends insist Job sinned, bringing on himself the righteous judgments of God. The three friends hold to traditional OT act-consequence wisdom thinking: if you obey Him, God blesses you, and if you sin, He punishes you. This act-consequence discussion forms the focus of the human dialogue in the book. Knowing he is blameless, Job finds himself unable to agree with this position; why do the righteous suffer what looks like judgment from the Lord?

The Sages in Conversation

1. The Fear of the Lord

As discussed above, the entire book of Job focuses on the answer to the adversary's question: Does Job fear God for no reason? Other OT wisdom texts also treat the fear of the Lord: Proverbs, Ecclesiastes, and Psalms in particular. Although the expression "the fear of the Lord" (*yirat YHWH*) is the same in each book, the meaning of this phrase varies according to its contexts. For example, according to Proverbs 1:7, the fear of the Lord "is the beginning of wisdom" whereas in Job 28:28, the fear of the Lord "is wisdom." Those are not the same statements.

Intrigued, the sages sit down to examine this phrase, its meaning, and the way they each use it differently.

In Job 1-2, Job's fear of the Lord serves as his defining characteristic. The Lord describes Job as "blameless, upright, fearing God, and turning away from evil" (Job 1:1, 8); the adversary condenses this description to a simpler shorthand in his question "Does Job fear God for no reason?" (Job 1:9). When urging Job to repent of his sin, Job's friend Eliphaz asks (Job 4:6):

4:6   Is not your <u>fear of God</u> your confidence,

And the <u>integrity of your ways</u> your hope?

Using language similar to Job 1:1[42], this verse parallels the fear of God and the integrity of one's ways. In turn, Job later equates fearing the Lord with departing from evil and embracing or embodying wisdom and understanding (Job 28:28). Thus throughout the book of Job, fearing the Lord describes a life of integrity, a servant of the Lord on the path to wisdom.

The sage of Proverbs now speaks. The phrase "the fear of the Lord" provides structure for the book of Proverbs, bookending the text at the beginning and the end (Prov 1:7, 31:30) and resurfacing in the book's internal seams (Prov 9:10, for instance). Proverbs 1:7, "The fear of the Lord is the beginning of wisdom," serves as the thematic statement for the whole book. The Hebrew word for "beginning" (*reshit*) can also mean "first" or "best," allowing for the fear of the Lord to be the first step, a gateway into a life of wisdom, but also the best part of wisdom. As discussed in the Proverbs chapter, the book's wisdom content does not technically begin until the superscription of Proverbs 10:1, "the proverbs of Solomon." Proverbs 1-9 serves as the introductory call, urging readers to step onto the path of wisdom, eager for the coming wisdom in Proverbs 10-31. Thus, Proverbs 1:7 and Proverbs 1-9 describe the foundational attitude one must possess to

---

42 The Hebrew word "integrity" is *tam*; in Job 1:1 and 8 and 2:3 and 9, the Hebrew word for blameless is *tom*. Both terms derive from the verb *tamam*, whose core idea is completeness.

acquire wisdom: one must fear the Lord.

The sage continues: Proverbs 1:7 offers yet more insight. The A line assumes the text is referring to the wise who seek wisdom, described in Proverbs 1:1-6:

> 1:7 **The fear of the Lord is** the beginning of <u>knowledge</u>;
>
> **fools despise** <u>wisdom and instruction</u>.

The B line expands "knowledge" with the words "wisdom and instruction." "The beginning of" is entirely left out of the B line, leaving "the fear of the Lord" parallel with "fools who despise" (*buz*) wisdom. Parallel lines always play off of each other; while the B line frequently expands the A line, the pairs can also contrast one another. In this pair, the two lines are antithetic. Those who fear the Lord are the opposite of the fools who despise wisdom. In other words, the fear of the Lord is love for the Lord's wisdom, and by extension, the Lord Himself. In keeping with this perspective, love (*'ahab*) appears repeatedly in Proverbs 1-9. For instance, Proverbs 4:6 calls for the "son" to love wisdom, and Lady Wisdom loves those who love her (Prov 8:17, 21). On the other hand, fools love their folly (Prov 1:22); Lady Wisdom mentions that those who hate her love death (Prov 8:36). Proverbs 1-9 defines the fundamental relationship between the wise and the Lord as a love relationship, also called the fear of the Lord.[43] The fear of the Lord causes people to run toward God, not away from Him but away from evil.

The sages pause, processing the contrast between the texts of Job and Proverbs. The sage of Ecclesiastes speaks next, offering yet another voice in the group's study. As discussed in depth in Chapter 8, Ecclesiastes uses an editor's frame to bookend the words of the Preacher (*qohelet*), its major middle section. In the frame itself (Eccl 1:1-11, 12:8-14), the editor refers to the Preacher in the third person:

---

[43] Deuteronomy 10:12-13 uses similar language: "Now, Israel, what does the LORD your God require from you, but to fear the LORD your God, to walk in all His ways and love Him, and to serve the LORD your God with all your heart and with all your soul, and to keep the LORD's commandments…"

"he." Inside the editor's frame (Eccl 1:12-12:7), the Preacher refers to himself in the first person: "I." 8 of the 9 references to the fear (*yare'*) of God occur in the Preacher's sermon, revealing several aspects of his understanding of the concept:

- God has dealt with humanity in such a way that they should fear Him (Eccl 3:14). Instead of being frustrated with the way God has ordered human life, people should trust or have faith in God—"fear Him."

- In Ecclesiastes 5:7, the Preacher contrasts the vanity (*hebel*) of foolish, hasty words and dreams that lead to nothing with their opposite: fearing God. This passage suggests respect and guardedness as the proper attitudes toward an eternal God: since God is in heaven and humans are on the earth, people need to be careful of their words before Him (also Eccl 5:2).

- Ecclesiastes 8:12 adds a modifier, speaking of fearing God "before His face." The Preacher distinguishes the consequences of the two paths: "it will be well" for those who fear God before his face, but "it will not be well for the evil man ... because he does not fear God" (Eccl 8:12-13).

Once the Preacher is finished, the frame narrator uses fear (*yare'*) at the very end of the book.[44] After restating the Preacher's theme of vanity (*hebel*, Eccl 12:8), the frame editor ends the book with his response to the central human issue that all is *hebel*. In this summary verse, the frame editor adds an important modifier; though most of Ecclesiastes is written in prose, formatting Ecclesiastes 12:13 in poetic verse brings out its textual relationships:

> 12:13   The conclusion of the matter when **all** has been heard:

---

[44] Scholars debate whether *Qohelet* and the frame editor use "fear" (*yare'*) the same way: does the expression refer to being afraid of God or is it comparable to trusting/obeying God? Ecclesiastes 9:2 and 12:5 do seem to use fear in the sense of being afraid. For example, see Tremper Longman III. "'The Fear of God' in the Book of Ecclesiastes." *Bulletin for Biblical Research* 25 (2): 13-21.

God <u>you must fear</u> and *his commandments* <u>you must keep</u>,

For this is for **all** humanity. (translation mine)

The interpretation of the B line rests on the meaning of the Hebrew conjunction "and." The "and" could simply add a second idea or it could introduce an explanation of the original idea. In the first case, this line from Ecclesiastes sounds like the wisdom sequence in Proverbs: begin the wisdom journey by fearing God and then proceed, keeping His commandments. In the second case, this line echoes the book of Job: fearing God means keeping His commandments. The sages' eyes twinkle with delight at Ecclesiastes' explanation, teetering together on the brink of insight.

Ecclesiastes continues. Echoing the Preacher's use of "the fear of God" to describe humans' proper response to the *hebel* of all things, the frame editor uses fear (*yare'*) to describe the way humans connect to the eternal God—by fearing Him with faith, trust, love. In this sense, the book appears to reflect the use of fear in Proverbs 1:7. Agreeing that all is *hebel*, the frame editor pushes the reader to adopt an attitude of fear of God and consequently, to keep His commandments. Within the context of the discussion of *hebel*, Ecclesiastes 12:13 manages to synthesize Proverbs and Job: since in the end God will bring all human deeds to judgment (Eccl 12:14), one's posture toward God and the totality of the life of a God-fearer matters eternally, beyond this *hebel* world.

After a long, reflective pause, the Psalter takes his turn to speak. The Psalms use fear (*yare'*) of the Lord as a general phrase to describe those who belong to the Lord, those who revere the Lord, or those who might be afraid in their troubles. Related to the conversation above, these verses offer a sample of the parallelism featuring "fear" (*yare'*) within the Psalter:

- Psalm 31:19 - fear//take refuge
- Psalm 33:18 - fear//hope for lovingkindness
- Psalm 40:3 - fear//trust
- Psalm 86:11 - fear Your name//walk in truth
- Psalm 112:1 - fear//delight in His commandments
- Psalm 119:63 - fear//keep Your precepts
- Psalm 119:79 - fear//know Your testimonies
- Psalm 128:1 - fear//walk in His ways
- Psalm 147:11 - fear//wait for His lovingkindness

These passages describe those who fear the Lord as taking refuge, finding hope, and trusting in Him; these persons also demonstrate their fear by walking in His ways and keeping His commandments, precepts, testimonies. The Psalter thus uses fear (*yare'*) similarly to the book of Job, as a general descriptor of a servant of the Lord. Job is a God-fearer like the psalmists are God-fearers. Yet Psalm 111:10 also repeats the central thematic statement of Proverbs: "The beginning of wisdom (*hokmah*) is the fear of the Lord."

The Psalter continues, offering a unique contribution to this discussion: the Psalms teach that in time, not only the Lord's servants, but everyone will fear the Lord. Psalm 33:8 reads:

> 33:8 Let all the earth fear the Lord;
>
> Let all the inhabitants of the world stand in awe of Him!

Although the Psalter certainly contains passages suggesting Israel and the nations should be afraid of the Lord, other passages such as this one also foretell that the nations will fear the Lord in humble submission. Psalm 2:10-11 introduces this idea early in the Psalter by instructing the kings of the earth to wise up and worship the Lord with fear and reverence. The Psalter then continues this theme throughout its pages, urging readers to look to the future time when all the earth will fear the Lord (Ps 47:1-2, 64:9, 65:8, 67:7, 102:15).

The sages' discussion of the fear (*yare'*) of the Lord certainly deepens readers' understanding of what it means to be a God-fearer. Each book uses the same term, but with a variation in meaning: fearing God is not a monolithic idea within the Writings. This conversation serves as a good reminder that fully understanding the texts' nuances requires their words to be carefully considered within their distinct contexts.

2. Wisdom Manifest in Creation

As mentioned above, Job 28 ties together the central themes of the book—God, the creation, and wisdom—affirming that only the Lord knows where wisdom is found; humans cannot find it on their own. The Lord's two lessons for Job in Job 38-41 further develop chapter 28, contrasting the misguided words of Job, his three friends, and Elihu. After listening to the sage of the book of Job, the Psalter and Ecclesiastes offer their own perspectives on wisdom and creation.

Specifically, Job 28 uses humans' search for precious ores to illustrate how elusive wisdom is. Humans dig mines, seeking and finding the earth's treasures (Job 28:1-11), but wisdom cannot be found by searching the earth or the deep waters (*tehom*, also in Gen 1). Job 28:20 asks, "Where is the place of understanding?" Even death does not know; wisdom is hidden from both the living and the dead (Job 28:21-22). Yet God knows wisdom. At creation, "He established [wisdom], and also searched it out" (Job 28:27).[45] The picture here is a creator full of knowledge and skill shaping everything just right, designing each aspect of creation perfectly. The intricacy and complexity of the created world are themselves the manifestation of God's wisdom.

---

45 Anthropomorphically, the Lord models the wisdom path by "searching out" (*haqar*) wisdom. Unlike humans, He succeeds since creation comes from Him to begin with.

Since a created being cannot stand outside creation to assess it and fully see how it reveals wisdom, the Creator offers His human creation a wisdom directive to follow: "the fear of the Lord is wisdom, and to turn from evil is understanding" (Job 28:28). Though Job does not realize it yet, these words of his lead to the resolution of his crisis.

The climactic discussion of wisdom and creation comes from the Lord's responses to Job in Job 38-41, as He speaks out of a whirlwind. In His first response, the Lord asks Job questions about inanimate and then animate creation (Job 38:4-38, 38:39-39:30), showing Job that he has muddied his perspective of wisdom by uttering words without knowledge (Job 38:2). Within this first lesson from inanimate creation, the Lord lists several elements that seem to oppose Him and humans:

- Proud waves (Job 38:11)

- The wicked (Job 38:13, 15)

- The deep (Job 38:16)

- The gates of death (Job 38:17)

- Snow and hail (Job 38:22)

- Flood and thunderbolt (Job 38:25)

- Times of distress, war, and battle (Job 38:23)

This list does not present the same idyllic picture of creation as Genesis 1, when God saw that everything He made was good. Instead, the Lord calls Job's attention to the uncontrollable forces Job can see and experience in his own life. God points out that He restrains and orders these terrifying elements. The power and forces of the natural world submit to God's control and wisdom over them. Through these examples, the Lord teaches Job He knows how to wisely govern and guide both the good and the apparently wild or problematic aspects of the created order (also Ps 148:7-8).

The Lord then transitions to another object lesson: the "ostrich" (Job 39:13-18). In this passage, the Lord describes a bird who lays her eggs and then abandons them, forgetting that a wild animal might trample them. The ostrich treats her young cruelly when she leaves them alone, yet the bird laughs, unconcerned that her labor might have been in vain[46] (Job 39:13-16). The ostrich acts this way "because God has made her forget wisdom and given her no share in understanding" (Job 39:17). In this statement, God adopts Job's limited perspective: when one sees the world through human eyes, many aspects of the created order seem out of joint, as if the Creator has bungled his dealings with humans and animals. But God's perspective reveals that even the ostrich lives as part of His wisdom; if Job cannot understand a bird, how can he understand what the Lord does in the complexity of creation and his own life?

God pauses for a moment, allowing Job to respond and acknowledge his own insignificance in the face of the Lord's wisdom (Job 40:4). Unsurprisingly, Job reconsiders his claim that God has forgotten wisdom and justice in Job's case. But God is not finished. He continues, this time instructing Job through the Behemoth and the Leviathan, the most powerful land and sea creatures He made (Job 40:15). Still speaking from the whirlwind, the Lord explains these creatures' power and might, reiterating that He made them magnificent and terrifying. Offering these wondrous and terrifying beasts as examples of divine wisdom in creation and management of that creation, the Creator again reminds Job of his place as a creature and corrects Job's perspective.

Chastened to his core, Job voices his adjusted perspective by declaring that the Lord has the power to do all things and His wisdom cannot be thwarted (Job 42:2). Through God's instruction, Job has finally come to understand the full meaning of his own words in Job 28: only the Lord knows where wisdom is found. Still in the

---

[46] The Hebrew word used for this bird is *renanim* and comes from the verb *ranan*, "to shout for joy." This name appears to be a play on words: this bird utters loud "cries for joy" even at the possible destruction of her eggs.

midst of his suffering, Job does not curse God to His face, nor does he again charge Him with injustice. Instead, with a proper perspective of his situation vis-à-vis his Creator, Job chooses to learn wisdom over speaking ignorantly (Job 42:3, 6). He retracts his words and God vindicates him (42:6-9). The case of Job, servant of the Lord, is "settled out of court," as it were. God has used creation as a canvas to give Job wisdom insight even as he suffers calamities.

Similarly to the book of Job, the Psalter contains several poetic presentations and commentary on God's creation in Genesis 1 (Pss 8, 19, 24, 33, 102, and 104). In a unique contribution to this conversation, several times within the Psalter the psalmists juxtapose creation language with salvation language. The passages in question describe the Exodus/Red Sea event. Psalm 136 recounts the Lord's creation of the heavens and earth (Ps 136:1-9) and His deliverance of Israel from Egypt and other mighty kings (Ps 136:10-22). Psalms 74:12-17 and 77:11-20 use creation language to describe these specific events. These two psalms interpret Genesis 1 as God delivering creation from the darkness and the deep (Gen 1:2); once God completes His work of creating light and dividing the waters, He brings forth the dry land. The Lord's salvation of Israel at the Red Sea follows this same pattern: God brings Israel through the waters on dry land. For the psalmists, God's great deeds of creation and salvation of His people parallel one another.

Unsurprisingly, creation wisdom in Ecclesiastes takes a completely different turn. The opening verses of the book form a creation poem and present its most prominent theme: all is vanity, *hebel*.[47] This assessment clashes with the creation account in Genesis 1, where all is "good." The language and themes in Ecclesiastes sound similar to God's judgment on the man in Genesis 3:17-19: human life consists of cycles of hard labor outside the garden, ending in the dust of death—all is vanity (*hebel*). *Hebel* is also the same word as "Abel" in Genesis 4. Abel, too, was but a vapor, present and then gone.

---

47 *Hebel* literally means "vapor" or "breath." English versions have translated *hebel* as "vanity, meaninglessness, uselessness, emptiness, or futility." Given this breadth of meaning, it seems best to allow each verse's context to guide the interpretation and translation of the word.

Ecclesiastes' language of vanity, hard labor, and death describes the created order outside the Garden of Eden.

Ecclesiastes next discusses the question naturally following this theme: if all is vanity (*hebel*), do human laborers gain any profit from all the work they do under the sun? (Eccl 1:3) In other words, do humans gain any advantage from their lifelong toil? At first, Ecclesiastes 1:3-11 seems to answer "no." The whole creation—the sun, the wind, the rivers, human eyes and ears—works hard only for the creation cycles to wipe out profit, disallowing any gain. And yet a closer look reveals small transitory or temporary advantages, like a vapor (*hebel*). The sun does provide sunshine while it is out. The eye does see even though it is not satisfied. Even though people will not be remembered, they do accomplish some things during their lifetimes. Is all vanity? Yes. Sooner or later, everything vanishes like a vapor (*hebel*).

The Preacher uses this argument to lead to his next point—why this fleeting gain or profit does not satisfy humans. Because God has put eternity in the human heart (Eccl 3:11), a life of hard labor cycles ending in death fails to fulfill men and women. Human beings are created to seek meaning beyond this life. The Preacher's solution points humans back to the Creator: only the fear of the Lord can satisfy and bring lasting advantage beyond death. Though *hebel* is the context of human life, humans crave eternity, seeking relationship with the Creator through the fear of the Lord (Eccl 3:14).

The sages of Job, the Psalter, and Ecclesiastes each urge readers to look to creation to know God. The wonders, powerful beasts, and cycles of the created world all ultimately testify to the wisdom and care of the Creator.

3. Actions and their Consequences

The Writings often discuss the lives of the righteous and wicked. The third dialogue in this chapter focuses on one's actions and what consequences, if any, humans should expect from God because of those actions. The sages of the books of Job, Psalms, Proverbs, and

Ecclesiastes sit down to talk through the connections between actions and their consequences.

As mentioned above, the conversation between the men in Job 3-37 debates the cause of Job's suffering. Job and his three friends fail to reach a resolution: Job maintains that he suffers while still being righteous, but according to his friends, Job is being judged by the Lord—he should submit to God's reproof and repent of his sin. Job's friends each present the same understanding of human actions and their consequences: God blesses the righteous, and He judges the wicked. In the words of Eliphaz, the leader of the three friends (Job 4:7-8, 5:17):

> 4:7 Remember: who that was innocent ever perished?
>
> Or where were the upright cut off?
>
> 4:8 As I have seen, those who plow iniquity
>
> And sow trouble reap the same.
>
> 5:17 Behold, blessed is the one whom God reproves;
>
> Therefore despise not the discipline of the Almighty.

Throughout their conversation, the three friends do not deviate from their message; they only intensify their words. In chapters 21 and 24, Job responds with his own questions:

> 21:17 How often is it that the lamp of the wicked is put out?
>
> That their calamity comes upon them?
>
> That God distributes pains in his anger?
>
> 24:1 Why doesn't the Almighty bring the wicked to judgment?
>
> Why must the godly wait for him in vain? (NLT)

Job asks his friends to open their eyes; their simplistic doctrine of divine judgment on the wicked does not fully describe reality. Looking about them, Job sees plenty of wicked seemingly at liberty to enjoy the good life instead of God's judgment. At odds with his friends, Job waits in suffering for God to answer him.

The Preacher in Ecclesiastes concurs with Job. The Hebrew word *hebel* can also imply absurdity. Sometimes in life, situations seem unreasonable, meaningless, or ridiculous. The Preacher observes (Eccl 2:11, 3:16, 19):

> 2:11   Then I considered all that my hands had done and the toil I had expended in doing it, and behold, all was vanity and a striving after wind, and there was nothing to be gained under the sun.
>
> 3:16   Moreover, I saw under the sun that in the place of justice, even there was wickedness, and in the place of righteousness, even there was wickedness.
>
> 3:19   For what happens to the children of man and what happens to the beasts is the same; as one dies, so dies the other. They all have the same breath, and man has no advantage over the beasts, for all is vanity.

In these statements, the Preacher repeatedly draws attention to the absurd realities of life, those times when a situation is illogical or one's actions are met with an illogical consequence. Hard work yields nothing. A courthouse hands down an injustice. These examples resonate with the reader as honest assessments of the absurdity of life under the sun. Ecclesiastes 8:14 specifically echoes Job:

> 8:14   There is a vanity that takes place on earth, that there are righteous people to whom it happens according to the deeds of the wicked, and there are wicked people

to whom it happens according to the deeds of the righteous. I said that this also is vanity.

Job and the Preacher agree: plenty often, the wicked prosper and the righteous are afflicted. At the center of the Psalter, Asaph struggles with a similar issue: His experience so troubled him that he almost gave up his faith in the Lord (Ps 73:2-3):

> 73:2 But as for me, my feet had almost stumbled,
>
> My steps had nearly slipped.
>
> 3 For I was envious of the arrogant
>
> When I saw the prosperity of the wicked.

Psalm 73 continues, describing the good life of the wicked. Then, in verses 13-14, Asaph lays out his dilemma:

> 73:13 All in vain have I kept my heart clean
>
> And washed my hands in innocence.
>
> 14 For all the day long I have been stricken
>
> And rebuked every morning.

These verses describe Asaph's crisis of faith even as he remains blameless from sin; like Job, Asaph clings to the way of the righteous and still experiences great suffering. Asaph continues:

> 73:16 But when I thought how to understand this,
>
> It seemed to me a wearisome task,
>
> 17 Until I went into the sanctuary of God;
>
> Then I discerned their end.

Again like Job, Asaph finds a resolution to his dilemma in the presence of the Lord. There, Asaph sees the end of the wicked; they "are destroyed in a moment" (Ps 73:19). Psalm 73 adds to Job's perspective on the Lord's dealings with the righteous and the wicked: during their lifetime, the wicked may experience blessing, and the righteous may not. However, in the end, the righteous will be blessed and the wicked judged. Asaph closes his psalm by teaching his readers how to navigate this interim period (Ps 73:28):

> 73:28   As for me it is good to be near God;
>
> I have set the Lord YHWH as my refuge,
>
> That I may tell of all your works. (translation mine)

Asaph's psalm and Job's narrative present similar processes. At the beginning, one fears the Lord and enjoys His blessing. Then the God-fearer, still righteous, goes through a period of suffering, striving to stay faithful to the Lord (Job 42:1-9). During their affliction, the Lord's servant wrestles with the Lord's apparent injustice as He blesses the undeserving and withholds blessing from the faithful. While under duress, both Asaph and Job learn anew to take refuge in the Lord, to listen to His wisdom and trust His wise governance of creation. In the end, the righteous will be blessed and the wicked judged.

At first glance, the book of Proverbs seems to align with Job's three friends and their theological framework: the righteous are blessed and the wicked are judged.[48] Many proverbs confirm this prescription, as illustrated here by Proverbs 10:16:

> 10:16   The wage of the righteous leads to life,
>
> The gain of the wicked to sin.

---

[48] Bruce Waltke explains, "A more precise formulation is a character > conduct > consequence connection—that is, what you are determines what you will become" in "Chapters 1-15." *The Book of Proverbs*, Grand Rapids, MI: Eerdmans, 2004: 73.

However, Proverbs also reveals exceptions.[49] The "better is ..." proverbs[50] teach that all is not well for the righteous all the time:

> 15:16 Better is a little with the fear of the Lord
>
> Than great treasure and trouble with it.

Proverbs like this one allow for the righteous to experience less than bountiful blessings, even scarcity. At this point in the conversation, Job and Asaph would nod in agreement, looking to Proverbs for further explanation.

Proverbs' varied emphases on divine retribution seem to fall in line with the purpose of the book: to provide instruction so the wise increase in wisdom, beginning with the fear of the Lord (Prov 1:1-7). God-fearers should obey this wisdom instruction as *torah*—not suggestions but commandments from God. Since living in wisdom is akin to living in harmony with the wisdom built into creation (Prov 8:22ff), the retribution principle reflects the natural order of creation. Most of the time, the wicked suffer and the righteous prosper. Having said that, the wise should not be surprised if in God's wise sovereignty, the righteous suffer and the wicked prosper. Proverbs 16 repeatedly emphasizes the Lord's sovereignty over human affairs (Prov 16:1, 33, also Prov 16:2-4, 9, 11):

> 16:1 The plans of the heart belong to man,
>
> But the answer of the tongue is from the Lord.
>
> 16:33 The lot is cast into the lap,
>
> But its every decision is from the Lord.

Echoing the book of Job, the middle of Proverbs describes the Lord as the sovereign wise Creator who oversees the actions of humans. However,

---

[49] Lindsay Wilson writes, "The book as a whole endorses the principle of retribution, but it does not describe all the ways in which God is at work in his world" in *Proverbs: An Introduction and Commentary*. Downers Grove, IL: InterVarsity Press, 2018: 21.

[50] See also Proverbs 16:8 and 19, 19:1, and 28:6. These proverbs are also discussed in Chapter 5.

that management allows for exceptions within the general prevailing pattern. Summer will be hot, and winter will be cold, but this reality still allows for occasional warm winter days. Passages like "better is a little with the fear of the Lord" acknowledge these exceptions, guiding the sufferer to stay the course on the wisdom path. Proverbs teaches the wise to expect both regular patterns and those exceptions; at all times, the wise trust the Lord and follow His wisdom *torah*.

As this conversation between sages illustrates, the Writings contain a variety of instruction about actions and their consequences. Although the books uphold traditional divine blessing and retribution, the Writings also repeatedly attend to the central issue of why the righteous suffer and for how long. During such times, the sages all encourage the righteous to take refuge in the Lord and trust Him, suffering in confidence that the Lord will bless them in the end.

Toward the New Testament

1. *The Fear of the Lord*

As explained above, the OT wisdom texts use fearing the Lord as a general description of the life of a wise person and as the beginning or foundation of wisdom. The NT uses the fear (*phobos*) of the Lord/God as a life descriptor as well, but rarely, instead calling such a person a "saint" (*hagios*) or a "believer" (*pisteuo*). Fear of God language in the NT describes:

- A Gentile worshipper of the God of Israel, like Cornelius (Acts 10:2, 22, 13:4, 17:4)

- People who humbly respect or are in awe of God, such as the men of Israel Paul speaks to in Jerusalem on his first missionary journey (Acts 13:16, 26; 1 Pet 2:17; Phil 2:12; 2 Cor 5:11)

- The life of a Christian, particularly in the church (Acts 9:31; Col 3:22; Eph 5:21; 2 Cor 7:1)

- A righteous person, like those Peter finds among the Gentiles (Acts 10:35; John 9:31; Luke 1:50 quoting Ps 103:17)

Though not directly involving the Writings, the NT depicts Abraham as the quintessential believer and God-fearer. After the sacrifice of Isaac (Gen 22:12), Abraham is called a God-fearer: he believed God's promise from Genesis 15:6 to the point of sacrificing his son. James 2:22-23 uses Abraham to illustrate the proper relationship between faith, works, and righteousness. In this regard, God-fearing in the OT is roughly equivalent to "believing" in the NT. Believing God signals entrance into a relationship with Him; the believer's life is then described as a walk of faith. Thus, like the fear of the Lord, belief functions as the beginning of wisdom and a life of wisdom.

2. Wisdom Manifest in Creation

Colossians provides perhaps the best Christological treatment of creation and wisdom in the NT. Although 1 Corinthians 1-2 presents a concentrated discussion of wisdom and the gospel, Paul treats wisdom all throughout Colossians. Following his usual pattern, the prayers at the beginning of Colossians provide themes to follow in the rest of the letter. The thanksgiving and prayer of Colossians 1 echo several OT wisdom texts:

- Offering thanksgiving and prayer (1:3, 9) – the Psalter

- Bearing fruit (1:6, 10) – Psalm 1

- Understanding the grace of God in truth (1:6) – Proverbs

- Being a faithful servant (1:7) – Job

- Knowledge of God's will in all spiritual wisdom and understanding (1:9, 10) – Proverbs

- Walking in a manner worthy of the Lord (1:10) – Proverbs

- Cultivating steadfastness and patience (1:11) – Job

Paul continues chapter 1 with the topic of Jesus and creation before moving to the relationship between Christ and wisdom (Col 1:25-29, 2:1-3). Thus, Paul intertwines Jesus/creation teaching with wisdom language and a wisdom perspective on the gospel.[51] These wisdom overtones continue with Colossians 1:15-20, widely considered a Christ hymn or psalm. This Colossians passage can be read as an expansion of Proverbs 3:19:

> 3:19   The Lord by wisdom founded the earth;
>
> By understanding he established the heavens;

As a psalm, Colossians 1:15-20 can be helpfully formatted as poetry:[52]

> He who is the image of the invisible God,
>
> The firstborn of all creation,
>
> For in Him all things were created
>
> In the heavens and upon the earth,
>
> The visible things and the invisible things,
>
> Whether thrones or dominions
>
> Whether rulers or authorities;
>
> All things through Him and for Him were created.
>
> And He Himself is before all things
>
> And all things in Him hold together,

---

51 NT Wright observes, "The poem clearly transfers to Christ language and predicates which had, in some form or other, belonged in Judaism to Wisdom and Torah ... All that Judaism had hoped to gain by belief in the one God, whose Wisdom was given to them in the form of Torah, was now to be gained through Christ. For Him, and not for Israel, all things were created. Having Christ, God's true wisdom, the Colossian church possesses all that it needs (cf. 1 Cor 3. 22 f.)." in "Poetry and Theology in Colossians 1:15-20." *New Testament Studies* 36 (3): 464.

52 The translation is mine, but the formatting follows the Nestle-Aland Greek New Testament, 27th ed.

> And He Himself is the head of the body, of the church;
>
> He who is the beginning,
>
> The firstborn of the dead,
>
> In order that in all things He Himself might come to be first,
>
> For in Him [God] was pleased to have all the fullness to dwell
>
> And through Him to reconcile all things to Himself,
>
> Having made peace through the blood of His cross,
>
> Through Him whether the things on earth
>
> Or the things in the heavens.

This Christ hymn uses language and concepts echoing Word-wisdom-creation passages such as the word at creation (Gen 1), creation through the word of the LORD (Ps 33:6-9), and wisdom at creation (Prov 8:22-30). These passages dovetail to trace OT creation wisdom to its ultimate realization in Jesus, the Messiah. Jesus Christ is the Word and Wisdom of God through whom He created and sustains all things.

3. Actions and their Consequences

The action-consequences framework in the NT echoes that of the OT, acknowledging consequences in this life while emphasizing an eternal perspective. Echoing Proverbs, the NT offers several examples of one's actions carrying consequences in this life. For example, after healing the paralytic at the pool of Bethsaida, Jesus tells the man to sin no more, lest something worse happen to him (John 5:14); Ananias and Sapphira are struck down in real time because of their lies to God

(Acts 5:1-5).[53]

Nonetheless, the NT emphasizes eternal consequences over present ones. At the judgment seat of Christ, believers will be recompensed according to what we have done through our bodies, whether good or bad (2 Cor 5:10). God will also judge unbelievers according to their deeds at the great white throne judgment (Rev 20:11-15). As articulated in Ecclesiastes 12:13-14, even though in the present the righteous may suffer and the wicked may prosper, everything humans do in this life matters eternally (1 Cor 10:31). The parable of the tares even acknowledges that humans cannot accurately distinguish between the righteous and the wicked in this life; the Lord allows the wheat from the good seed to exist right alongside tares from the bad seed (Matt 13:24-30).[54] As summarized in Galatians, though God allows both to live side by side in the present life, in the end He will correctly distinguish between the righteous and the wicked (Gal 6:7-8):

> 6:7   Do not be deceived: God is not mocked, for whatever one sows, that will he also reap.
>
> 8   For the one who sows to his own flesh will from the flesh reap corruption, but the one who sows to the Spirit will from the Spirit reap eternal life.

Like Asaph reminds readers in Psalm 73, Christians should seek counsel and guidance from the Lord, taking refuge in Him and staying on the path of wisdom (Ps 73: 24, 28).

---

53 For more passages on divine retribution, see Romans 1:18, Romans 12:19, 1 Corinthians 11:30, 2 Timothy 4:14, and James 5:14-16.

54 David DeSilva comments that Paul's Galatians 6:7 maxim that you reap what you sow "is notably (and appropriately) common in wisdom literature, which is based to a great extent on the observation of the created order and the application of the principles observed therein to the lives and practices of human beings. The maxim captures an undeniable truth of agriculture, proven year after year, crop after crop. The truth of the natural order supports, by analogy, Paul's claim about the moral order of God's economy. The consequences of one's choices (whether to live for the impulses of the flesh or to live for the cultivation of the Spirit's fruit) will prove that mortals cannot outwit God." From *The Letter to the Galatians*. Grand Rapids, MI: Eerdmans, 2018: 492.

The NT also weaves in another dynamic for the Church. Not only should Christians expect to reap the consequences of their actions in the present and in eternity, but NT saints should also expect suffering because of their allegiance to Christ. As Jesus was persecuted, so will His saints be persecuted (John 15:20-25). This teaching adds a uniquely NT layer into the actions-consequences framework: in the life of the Church, for the sake of Christ, good will be accompanied by hardship. Living a Christ-like life, a righteous life, promises to incur suffering.

Further Reading

Dell, Katharine J., "The Book of Job in the Context of the Writings." Donn F. Morgan, Ed. *The Oxford Handbook of the Writings of the Hebrew Bible*, Oxford Handbooks, 2018; online edition, Oxford Academic, 7 Nov. 2018.

Hartley, John E. *The Book of Job*. Grand Rapids, MI: Eerdmans, 1988.

Wilson, Lindsay. "Job 38-39 and Biblical Theology." *The Reformed Theological Review* 62 (3): 121-138.

Zuck, Roy B. *Sitting with Job: Selected Studies on the Book of Job*. Grand Rapids, MI: Baker Book House, 1992.

Proverbs: Wisdom Loves Those Who Love Her

Old Testament Background for Proverbs

- Creation, Adam, Eve, God in the garden: Gen 1-4
- Solomon's wisdom and reign: 1 Kings 1-11; 2 Chron 1-9
- The Davidic covenant: 2 Sam 7; 1 Chron 17
- Other proverbs/riddles/parables:
  - Samson: Judges 14:12-20
  - Nathan: 2 Sam 12:1-7
  - Wise woman of Tekoa: 2 Sam 14:1-20
  - Narrative parable: Ps 78
  - The writing on the wall: Dan 5
  - Prophetic parables: Ez 17:2-4, 24:3-14

Creation and Proverbs: Lady Wisdom at Creation and in the Son's Life

Proverbs 1-9 introduces the Lord's wisdom personified as a woman: Lady Wisdom. Her speech in Proverbs 8 explicitly refers back to the creation account in Genesis 1 (see also Prov 3:19), when she declares that the Lord possessed her before He began to create the heavens and the earth (Prov 8:22). Lady Wisdom worked alongside the Creator as His architect ('amon), His expert or skilled worker. Her fingerprints cover every aspect of creation: the created world is a wisdom-shaped world. By extension, then, all the wisdom in the book of Proverbs is creational wisdom.

Lady Wisdom and "the son" in Proverbs 1-9 form a second creational backdrop for this text. The language of Genesis 3 casts the Fall as a wisdom event: the woman saw the forbidden fruit as able to make one wise (Gen 3:6). The man listened to the woman; they both played the fool and died, exiled from the Garden of Eden, destined to return to the dust. Paralleling man, God, and woman in the garden,

Lady Wisdom represents God's wisdom, calling the son to listen to her life-giving voice and turn away from the Woman of Folly, who leads to death (Prov 7:24-27, 9:18). Proverbs casts the wisdom decision as a Genesis 3, creation-like moment: its life and death implications will define the son's entire existence.

Proverbs: An Outline

Proverbs 1-9: To Begin, Choose Wisdom

The fear of the Lord is the beginning of wisdom, leading to understanding and just living. King Solomon, the son of David, instructs his son and his people to seek out and become one with Lady Wisdom, that they may live.

Proverbs 10-31: The Words of the Wise

These proverbs constitute the "commandments" or *torah* of the kingdom. They naturally divide into two parallel sections, each containing a collection of Solomon's proverbs followed by other wise persons' contributions:

    I. The First Collection: Proverbs 10-24

- Solomon - 10:1-22:16
- "The words of the wise"- 22:17-24:22
- "The sayings of the wise"- 24:23-34

    II. The Second Collection: Proverbs 25-31

- Solomon - 25:1-29:27
- "The words of Agur"- 30:1-33
- "The words of King Lemuel"- 31:1-31

Before continuing in this chapter, it may be helpful to reread the Introduction's primer on Hebrew poetry. Here are a few additional notes:

- Proverbs is attributed to Solomon, son of David. The introductory superscription sets Solomon as the source for Proverbs' wisdom.[55] However, internally, Solomon's collection references other wise men and introduces their wisdom with superscriptions of their own: the words of the wise men (Prov 22:17, 24:23), Agur (Prov 30) and Lemuel (Prov 31). The parallelism in Proverbs 22:17 equates "the words of the wise" with "my [Solomon's] knowledge"; the words of the wise become part of Solomon's wisdom and, as a good scholar, he cites his sources in his book.

- Solomon's proverbs usually follow the pattern of two paired lines; proverbs from "the wise" vary this form, often containing 3 or more lines and a variety of structures.

- Although frequently translated "proverb," the Hebrew word *mashal* can also refer to a longer wisdom saying, a "parable" such as in Ezekiel 17:2-4 and 24:3-14. In a stunning intersection of form and content, Proverbs' concluding passage on the wife of virtue embodies excellence; the parable is written as an alphabetic acrostic of 22 verses matching the 22 letters of the Hebrew alphabet. For more on Proverbs 31, see the chapter on the book of Ruth.

Major Themes: the Fundamentals of Wisdom, Lady Wisdom or Lady Folly, and Wisdom with Wisdom

1. The Fundamentals of Wisdom (Prov 1:1-7)

As many books do, Proverbs 1:1-7 begins by offering a hermeneutical lens for reading the text well. This passage clearly articulates four purposes for the book of Proverbs:

1. To know and discern wisdom

---

[55] The superscription in 1:1 connects Proverbs with the Song of Songs and Ecclesiastes, naturally generating conversation between these books.

2. To instruct in wise behavior: righteousness, justice, and equity

3. To give wisdom to the naïve and young, simultaneously allowing the wise to increase their wisdom

4. To understand proverbs, enigmatic sayings, and riddles

From within these purpose statements, Proverbs 1:7 reveals the thematic foundation for the entire book of Proverbs: the fear of the Lord is the beginning of wisdom. This idea of the fear of the Lord is discussed in detail in the chapter on the book of Job. Proverbs 1-9 develops this verse, preparing the son and the readers to receive the proverbial wisdom of Proverbs 10-31.

2. Lady Wisdom or Lady Folly (Prov 1-9)

The characters of Lady Wisdom and the Woman of Folly dominate Proverbs 1-9, as they compete for the attention of "the son." The text uses these women's voices to present the son's two options: the way of wisdom and the way of folly. In doing so, these chapters parallel other OT wisdom texts by emphasizing the high stakes of the son's decision—the way of wisdom leads to life while the way of folly leads to death.

The superscription of the book, "the proverbs of Solomon, the son of David, king of Israel," presents Solomon as the wise father, teaching his son wisdom. Thus, Proverbs' primary recipient is the heir to the throne; he needs wisdom to rule and reign righteously. However, within these introductory chapters, the call to wisdom also goes out to "sons," plural (Prov 4:1, 5:7, 7:24), indicating a wider audience beyond the crown prince. The book as a whole continues this widening from the specific household of Solomon to the wise more generally. Proverbs 1 describes the wise person as one who increases in learning (1:6), who heeds the instruction of his mother and father (1:8). In Proverbs 8:32, Lady Wisdom also addresses her "sons," beseeching them to listen to her voice. By the end of the book, wisdom is extended from the royal house to every house; the excellent wife of chapter 31 is clearly not the wife of a king but of a commoner. Given these criteria for being wise, by implication, any reader of the book of Proverbs can be a child of wisdom.

3. Wisdom with Wisdom

Proverbs also provides wisdom to understand wisdom (1:6). Though the book contains some longer parables, for instance in chapters 8 and 31, most of Proverbs is written as a series of seemingly unrelated short statements. These sayings each provide a summary or a conclusion of what is true, a snippet of how life works within the created order; the wise are thus prompted to ponder the truth of each individual proverb within the context of their own life. Since wisdom is multi-faceted and applied situationally, the best tool for pondering wisdom is more wisdom, a fuller picture of the nuances of a topic. Proverbs draws these pictures by addressing the same topics in a variety of places and from several perspectives throughout the book. Perhaps the best example of wisdom in dialogue with wisdom is Proverbs 26:4-5:

> 26:4 Answer not a fool according to his folly,
>
> Lest you be like him yourself.
>
> 5 Answer a fool according to his folly,
>
> Lest he be wise in his own eyes.

Taken separately, these verses offer plenty for the wise to ponder. However, taken together, they highlight the discernment needed to find wisdom in a given situation. Should the wise answer the fool or not answer the fool? Either could be the wise choice. As its etymology divulges, discernment relates to separating two things (di-scernment). "Understanding" (*bin*) has a similar connotation because of its close relationship with the word "between" (*ben*). As this word choice highlights, life often requires deciding between two or more possibly good options and then crafting a wise way to carry out that decision. The wise use wisdom with more wisdom to discern which option is the wisest and most pleasing to the Lord within their particular situations.

The Sages in Conversation

1. The Fundamentals of Wisdom: Righteousness, Justice, and Equity

Like the three NT virtues of faith, hope, and love, the virtues of righteousness, justice, and equity form the three wisdom virtues. After defining these virtues and tracing their development in the book of Proverbs, this section hosts a conversation between the sages of Proverbs, Psalms, and Job about what a life of virtue looks like.

As explained above, Proverbs 1:1-7 lays out the purposes and foundation of proverbial wisdom. OT scholar William Brown reads this passage as discussing three kinds of virtues[56]:

- Intellectual virtues – know, discern (2a), fear of the Lord (7)

- Instrumental virtues – instruction/discipline (2b), give prudence, hearing, acquiring (4-5)

- Moral, communal virtues – righteousness, justice, and equity (3b)

Next, Brown creates a chiasm of these verses,[57] revealing how the passage's structure highlights its center:

> A Comprehensive, intellectual values: 2a
>   B Literary expression of wisdom: 2b
>   C Instrumental virtue: 3a
>   D Moral, communal virtues: 3b
>   C' Instrumental virtue: 4-5
>   B' Literary expression of wisdom: 6
> A' Comprehensive, intellectual values: 7

---

56 William P. Brown. *Character in Crisis*. Grand Rapids: Eerdmans, 1996: 25.

57 A chiasm is a rhetorical device in which ideas, phrases, or themes are arranged in a specific pattern that mirrors or inversely mirrors itself. Its elements or concepts are presented in symmetric or inverted parallelism, often in the form of an "ABBA" or "ABCCBA" structure.

Though admittedly uneven, this chiasm nonetheless underlines the three moral virtues in 1:3b as the heart of knowing and acquiring wisdom. Proverbs casts these virtues as central to wisdom right from the beginning of the book.

These three virtues have different but overlapping meanings, as seen in their use in parallel lines (Prov 8:20) and their various English translations:

- Righteousness (*sedeq*) emphasizes doing what is right according to a standard: God, His Word, or the order of creation.

- Justice (*mishpat*) emphasizes making a correct and fitting decision, such as when a judge formulates a fitting verdict in a legal case.

- Equity (*mesar*) emphasizes doing what is fair, what is right.

Each virtue offers a nuanced focus but cannot be carried out in isolation from the other two. Proverbs and other OT wisdom books call those who do righteousness, justice, and equity persons of virtue (*hayil*). For instance, the woman of virtue in Proverbs 31 is a "*hayil*" woman; as discussed in the chapter on the book of Ruth, Boaz and Ruth are a *hayil* man and a *hayil* woman (Ruth 2:1, 3:11). *Hayil's* root idea is strength, applicable in different directions—wealth, armies, or character—emphasizing a force one cannot dismiss. When used in OT wisdom literature, *hayil* describes a person whose strength of character powerfully transforms their life and by extension, their world.

Proverbs continues its focus on these three virtues in chapters 2 and 8. Proverbs 2 uses these three terms together in the context of the wisdom pursuit. Speaking to the son, the father says:

2:1		If you receive my words ...
3		If you cry for discernment ...
4		If you seek Lady Wisdom as silver ...
5		Then you will discern the fear of the Lord ...

9	**Then you will discern righteousness, justice, and equity, every good path …**
2:12	To deliver you from the evil man …
2:16	To deliver you from the evil woman …

Verse 9 equates the three wisdom virtues with "every good path." When the wise seek wisdom, they walk on the path of righteousness, justice, and equity, safe from evil and folly. In her message in Proverbs 8:4-21, Lady Wisdom also talks about the three wisdom virtues:

- She speaks what is equitable or upright (8:6, 9) and righteous (8:8).

- By her kings and rulers govern with righteousness (8:15-16).

- Riches and righteousness are her gifts (8:18).

- She walks in the ways of justice and righteousness (8:20).

Lady Wisdom lays out her relationship to these three virtues before describing her role in the creation (Prov 8:22-31). The logical flow of the passage emphasizes how Lady Wisdom, a powerhouse of virtue (*hayil*), forms the creation as the Lord's master workman. *Hayil* persons, then, reflect the character of the Creator and His wisdom.

After laying this virtue foundation, Proverbs continues, teaching wisdom through the intellectual, instrumental, and moral virtues. The rest of the book provides a comprehensive portrait of the wise life, the life of righteousness, justice, and equity. Just as Lady Wisdom shaped all of creation, so the wisdom of Proverbs 10-31 shapes every aspect of a human life. Picture a wheel with wisdom at the center. From that center, wisdom impacts and shapes every space inside the wheel. For instance, in Proverbs 31:10-31, wisdom permeates all areas of the *hayil* woman's life, impacting those who surround her for good and blessing. The wise in Proverbs desire a life so completely in sync with the Lord's wisdom that their words and deeds are wisdom's words and deeds.

The sages of Psalms and Job nod their heads in agreement and speak, offering more examples of what the life of virtue looks like. Psalms, for instance, adds several pointed statements about the king's relationship to the wisdom virtues. Psalm 72 begins by defining the wise rule of a Davidic king:

> 72:1 Give the king your justice (*mishpat*), O God,
>
> And your righteousness (*sedaqah*) to the royal son!
>
> 2 May he judge your people with righteousness (*sedeq*),
>
> And your poor with justice (*mishpat*)!

This particular aspect of judging the poor with justice is repeated two verses later:

> 72:4 May he defend (*shapat*) the cause of the poor of the people,
>
> Give deliverance to the children of the needy,
>
> And crush the oppressor!

And later in the same psalm, verses 12-14 again describe the king providing justice for the poor and needy. These repetitions frame the provision of righteousness and justice as the first line of the king's job description: the king is charged with embodying the Lord's righteousness and justice in and for the kingdom.[58] As discussed in the chapter on Chronicles, as the king goes, so go the people. By extension, the whole nation of Israel, from top to bottom, was expected to image the Lord and His wisdom by living a *hayil* life, particularly with respect to the poor and needy.

---

[58] According to 1 Chronicles 18:14, David's reign demonstrated justice and righteousness. 2 Chronicles uses the term "upright" (*yasar*) to summarize the reign of the Davidic sons who feared the Lord: Ahaz (14:2), Jehoshaphat (20:32), Amaziah (25:2), Uzziah (26:4), Jotham (27:2), Hezekiah (29:2, 31:20), and Josiah (34:2).

Though short, Psalm 15 provides another picture of a life of virtue. The psalmist begins by asking who may dwell in the Lord's tent. Verse 2 answers: the one who walks in integrity (*tamim*) and does righteousness (*sedaqah*), speaking truth in his heart. Verses 3-5, the rest of the psalm, continue the description. The one who can dwell with the Lord is the one:

> 15:3 Who does not slander with his tongue
>
> And does no evil to his neighbor,
>
> Nor takes up a reproach against his friend;
>
> 4 In whose eyes a vile person is despised,
>
> But who honors those who fear the Lord;
>
> Who swears to his own hurt and does not change;
>
> 5 Who does not put out his money at interest
>
> And does not take a bribe against the innocent.
>
> He who does these things shall never be moved.

This passage overlaps substantially with Proverbs' descriptions of the wise: a guarded tongue, a person above reproach, one who fears the Lord, etc. The sages of Proverbs and the Psalter cover much the same ground—who can dwell with the Lord? The wise, those on the path of wisdom.

In turn, the book of Job provides yet another picture of a life exuding the wisdom virtues. In Job 1:1, the narrator describes Job as "blameless (*tam*), upright (*yasar*), fearing God and turning away from evil." The Lord Himself confirms this description of Job (1:8). In chapter 29, Job explains why he was so respected in his community:

> 29:11 When the ear heard, it called me blessed,
>
> And when the eye saw, it approved,

12   Because I delivered the poor who cried for help,

And the fatherless who had none to help him.

13   The blessing of him who was about to perish came upon me,

And I caused the widow's heart to sing for joy.

14   I put on righteousness, and it clothed me;

My justice was like a robe and a turban.

15   I was eyes to the blind

And feet to the lame.

16   I was a father to the needy,

And I searched out the cause of him whom I did not know.

17   I broke the fangs of the unrighteous

And made him drop his prey from his teeth.

This passage uses Job's actions vis-à-vis the orphan, the widow, the blind, the lame, and the needy to describe how Job's righteousness manifested itself. Job describes himself putting on righteousness and justice, wearing them as a robe (Job 29:14). When one looked at Job, one saw virtue the way one would see recognizable clothing.

Job continues his case for his innocence in Job 31. This passage describes Job's virtuous life in terms of the sins Job avoided: lusting after women, walking with falsehood, treating people with injustice—especially the poor, trusting in wealth, exulting in the fall of an enemy, lacking hospitality, and hiding his sin like Adam (Job 31:1-34). Each one of these negative statements can be translated into a positive descriptor of Job's righteous life: for example, walking in truth, being hospitable, and being forthright. This list further expands the reader's understanding of Job's blamelessness: his uprightness manifested itself in every area of his life.

As this section has discussed, Psalms 15 and 72 and Job 29 and 31 describe virtue primarily with regard to one's commitments to the poor and needy. While the book of Proverbs does include this teaching in many places, Proverbs' description widens virtue to be much more comprehensive. The Writings as a whole similarly expand the sphere of the application of virtue to loving one's neighbor; however, one's neighbor always specifically includes the poor, the orphan, the widow, and the afflicted. Although Proverbs primarily presents wisdom in terms of an individual's wisdom walk, the individual acts in the context of the broader community, as made explicit in Proverbs 31 being embedded in a town. Persons of *hayil* tie a community together, moving everyone from the king to the neediest of the people toward righteousness, justice, and equity.

2. Lady Wisdom or the Woman of Folly

The wisdom texts shape the discussion of wisdom and folly as the two paths or ways; the path of wisdom leads to life and the path of folly leads to death.[59] Proverbs' unique contribution is the personification of the two paths: Lady Wisdom and the Woman of Folly. Wisdom is consistently written as a woman publicly recruiting those without wisdom to choose her and lead a life fearing the Lord. Proverbs also ends with the parable of the *hayil* woman. Yet in Ecclesiastes 7:23-29, the Preacher states he is unable to find two things: wisdom and a wise woman. How can this be? The following discussion treats this conundrum.

The imagery of the relationship between the son and Lady Wisdom requires examination. As discussed above, Lady Wisdom's words form the bookends of Proverbs 1-9. Between these bookends, these chapters call him to:

---

[59] For the related but distinct discussion of the wicked and retribution, see the Chronicles and Job chapters.

- Seek her, search for her (2:4)[60]
- Find her and hold her fast because of her benefits (3:13-19)
- Do not forsake her; love her, acquire her, prize her, embrace her (4:5-9)
- Take hold of her, guard her (4:13)
- Say to Wisdom, "You are my sister" (7:4)
- Listen, take her instruction (8:1-11)
- Love her (8:12-21)
- Eat my food, drink my wine, as symbols of her wisdom (9:1-6)

This pattern of loving and embracing wisdom casts the relationship between the son and Lady Wisdom as a union; the son is to become one with wisdom. This union carries sexual overtones, especially when considered within a creation framework: in Genesis 2, the man and the woman embrace each other and become one flesh. Proverbs' language also echoes the Song of Songs, a book full of loving and embracing language (Song 2:6, 8:3). All this imagery strengthens Proverbs' picture of the son's decision regarding Lady Wisdom—the commitment to wisdom is full and complete.

Through ambivalence or choice, those who do not follow Lady Wisdom instead embrace the Woman of Folly. Proverbs 1-9 describes the Woman of Folly as a strange or adulterous woman, further deepening the marriage metaphor and illustrating the epitome of folly.[61] Paralleling Genesis 3, the Woman of Folly serves as a voice of "wisdom" to the man, enticing him to follow her guidance; however, since she advocates disobeying the Lord's commands, when the man chooses her instruction, he dies. Unity with the Woman of Folly results in death

---

[60] Some English versions translate the Hebrew feminine pronoun as "it" to refer to wisdom, not Lady Wisdom.

[61] For a discussion of the strange/foreign/adulteress woman, see the Ezra-Nehemiah chapter.

(Prov 2:18, 5:5, 7:27, 9:18). Proverbs' picture of adultery highlights the implications of foolishness: choosing Folly is like violating one's union with one's wife by becoming one with another woman. This decision is a disaster in the making. On the other hand, Proverbs 5 illustrates wisdom as covenant fidelity to one's wife. The wisdom decision is becoming one with wisdom and maintaining that commitment to love her and embrace her. By embracing Lady Wisdom, the wise stay on the path of wisdom and live, increasing in knowledge and understanding (Prov 1:5).

In the MT, the book of Proverbs is followed by a collection of books in the Writings known as the *Megilloth*: Ruth, Song of Songs, Ecclesiastes, Lamentations, and Esther. Four of the five books feature women characters playing a central role:

- Ruth is known as a woman of virtue (*hayil*) (Ruth 3:11).

- The Song of Songs features the woman's voice as the most prominent in the book.

- Lamentations personifies the fallen city of Jerusalem as a woman.

- Esther's wisdom plays a central role in the deliverance of the Jews.

Ecclesiastes is the only book in the *Megilloth* that does not turn on a central female character.[62] However, in Ecclesiastes 7:25-29, the preacher records his observations about wisdom, folly, and women. The words in bold echo Proverbs' language of seeking Lady Wisdom and avoiding the Woman of Folly.

7:23   All this I have tested by **wisdom**. I said, "I will

---

[62] The Hebrew word for teacher or preacher, *qohelet*, is the feminine singular participle of the verb *qahal*, "to assemble." The choice of this feminine form may be a subtle indication that the preacher is speaking for or as Lady Wisdom. However, Ecclesiastes treats *qohelet* as a masculine noun throughout the book—correct grammatical practice based on meaning—except in Ecclesiastes 7:27 where the verb "says" (*'amera*) is feminine third person singular—correct grammar based on form. This grammatical decision seems consistent with the passage's immediate context discussing women.

be **wise**," but it was far from me.

24 That which has been is far off, and **deep, very deep; who can find it out?**

25 I turned my heart to know and **to search out and to seek wisdom** and the scheme of things, and **to know the wickedness of folly** and the **foolishness** that is madness.

26 And I find something more bitter than **death: the woman whose heart is snares and nets, and whose hands are fetters. He who pleases God escapes her, but the sinner is taken by her.**

27 Behold, this is what **I found**, says the Preacher, while adding one thing to another to find the scheme of things—

28 which my soul **has sought** repeatedly, but I have not **found**. One man[63] among a thousand **I found**, but **a woman among all these I have not found.**

29 See, this alone **I found**, that God made man **upright**, but they **have sought** out many schemes.

This difficult passage has produced almost as many interpretations as there are interpreters. Though these verses remain tricky, reading this text against the backdrop of Proverbs produces the following reasonable summary:

- As the underlined words show, *Qohelet* is trying to understand the "scheme"[64] of things, how everything fits together (7:25, 27, 29).

---

[63] The word for man here and in verse 29 is *'adam*, which can refer to humanity as a whole, both male and female. Some translations, such as the Christian Standard Bible, choose to use "person" for *'adam* in verse 28 to emphasize the general meaning of the word.

[64] The Hebrew word for "scheme" is *heshbon* in 7:25 and 27, and *hishshabon* in 7:29. Both words derive from the verb root *hashab*, "to reckon, plan, devise, think, account."

- Wisdom was too far for *Qohelet* to reach. Who can find wisdom? (7:23-24)

- He found the woman who entraps. The wise avoid her; fools are caught (7:25-26).

- He found one person out of a thousand who was wise (7:28).

- He did not find a wise woman among these thousand (7:28).

- He found that God made humanity upright, but they sought many schemes (7:29).

It seems that while seeking to understand the scheme of creation, *Qohelet* tries to play "Lady Wisdom" but fails. He can glimpse some individual truths but not the overall wisdom scheme of the world. Since only God can grasp the wisdom in creation, this failure should not surprise the reader and falls in line with *Qohelet*'s central theme in the second half of Ecclesiastes: humanity's limited wisdom and understanding (Eccl 6:13, 7:14, 8:7, 17, 9:1, 12, 10:14, 11:1-6).

Ecclesiastes 7:24 echoes the question in Proverbs 31:10, "A woman of virtue who can find?" Like *Qohelet*, the voice in Proverbs 31 is looking for this woman of virtue, an embodiment of wisdom, more precious than jewels (Prov 8:11, 31:10). Since he uses the pronoun "I" in 7:25, the Preacher's conclusion appears rooted in his own personal experience: even *Qohelet*, the wise man who has access to everything, cannot find that rarity, a *hayil* woman (see Eccl 1:12-18).[65] Proverbs 19:14 reads:

19:14   House and wealth are inherited from fathers,

But a prudent (*hayil*) wife is from the Lord.

---

[65] Katherine Dell writes, "Could it be Woman Wisdom that Qohelet has not found [...]? [...] I find the argument that she lies implicitly behind this passage both in the language of the quest and in terms of being unreachable quite convincing [...]. This passage then might be a continued reference to the elusiveness of woman wisdom. If we translate אדם [*adam*] as "human being" then he might be making a contrast not between man and woman but between finding a human among a thousand but not that elusive Woman Wisdom." *Interpreting Ecclesiastes: Readers Old and New*. Winona Lake, IN: Eisenbrauns, 2013: 92.

Perhaps the tragic irony is that *Qohelet*, while playing Lady Wisdom, has misunderstood how to find a wise woman. Perhaps, unlike house and wealth, which can be sought after and acquired, a *hayil* woman is a gift from the Lord to a most blessed man.

"A woman of virtue who can find?" The *Megilloth* collection offers itself as an answer. Together, these books both confirm the wise woman's rarity but also highlight examples of such women: the parable of the woman of virtue in Proverbs 31 and Ruth (see Ruth chapter). These texts flesh out the wise life for those in pursuit of wisdom, adding to Proverbs' imagery of the two ways and their two women. Although the book of Proverbs may seem male-centric, the repeated emphases on Lady Wisdom, the woman of virtue, and *torah*-teaching mothers indicate that wisdom is for all who seek it: young and old, rich and poor, men and women, Jew and Gentile.

3. Wisdom with Wisdom

Unsurprisingly, the book of Proverbs contributes the lion's share of wisdom in proverb form to the Writings. As discussed above and in the Psalms chapter, the wisdom in these proverbs functions as *torah* instruction from the king: royal wisdom, the *torah* of Solomon. Furthermore, since the creation has been shaped by Lady Wisdom (Prov 8), living wisely means living in harmony with the Lord's creation. As Lady Wisdom fashioned creation, so the proverbs are designed to shape the totality of a God-fearer's life. Yet as a collection of short, pithy wisdom sayings, the text of Proverbs requires a different reading strategy than other wisdom texts. How should a reader approach this text? The sage of Proverbs offers some advice in this mostly internal dialogue.

Part of the challenge for the reader of Proverbs lies in the reality that people do not usually learn proverbs from a book. People learn and understand proverbs as part of the later stages of language learning: one hears sayings in conversation, eventually coming to acquire and understand them. Using a proverb correctly requires insight into its content and meaning. This book asks the wise to learn proverbs from a text—a new task for any learner. Yet having a text to reference proves helpful for meditating and reflecting on its eclectic contents. Part of the beauty of this text is its depth; Proverbs offers enough fodder for the wise to spend a lifetime revisiting its contents, pondering its insights in refinement of their wisdom.

As far as a concrete reading strategy goes, each proverb begs to be considered in three different contexts. Picture each context as an axis in the diagram below. Separately, picture a book, lying flat and open to a page of the text of Proverbs. Now superimpose the XYZ axis diagram on top of the picture of the open book. The three contexts emerge:

- The X axis is the proverb itself on the page—a few horizontal lines.

- The Y axis is the context provided by the verses surrounding said proverb—the vertical column of scripture.

- The Z axis represents the context of the book of Proverbs as a whole—the thickness of the pages of the 31 chapters.

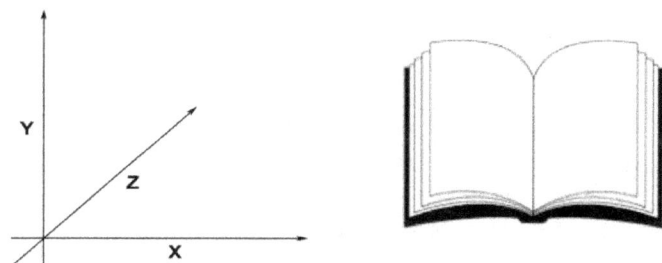

As expected, considering a proverb on the X axis focuses reflection on that single proverb. Each individual proverb functions as a thought unit, prompting both implications and questions. Any proverb can serve as an example here, but 10:1 works nicely:

10:1   A **wise son** makes a <u>glad</u> *father*,

But a **foolish son** is a <u>sorrow</u> to his *mother*.

What does this proverb imply?

- Both father and mother play wisdom roles.
- The repercussions of wise/foolish decisions ripple through others' lives: parents, grandparents, the larger community.
- Children of any age impact their parents.
- Living wisely brings joy; foolishness brings sorrow.
- Human life includes the experiences of gladness and sorrow, and by extension, other emotions: relief, frustration, pride, etc.
- Each child must make their own wisdom decisions.

Yet this single proverb raises several substantial questions as well:

- What makes a child wise or foolish?
- Are children born wise/foolish or do they grow into being wise/foolish?
- Can a child be nurtured into being wise?
- Is wise/foolish a sliding scale or a rigid dichotomy?

These two lines prompt the reader to ponder and unpack the proverb's truth, seeking to understand more through this entry point into insight.

Beyond the clear structure of individual proverbs, the organization of Proverbs 10-31 presents the reader with a puzzle. Contemporary readers often expect the proverbs to be grouped by topic; while understandable, such expectations arise from modern organizational standards and do not apply to this ancient literature. Instead, proverbs on the same topic are scattered throughout the book. This dispersion of insight forces readers to piece wisdom together themselves, building a nuanced web out of the assembled fragments. This careful thinking reflects the complexity of a wise decision: one must consider the issue at hand, other relevant wisdom, one's personal motives, the fear of the Lord, the individuals involved, the situation's unique needs, etc. The very form of the book of Proverbs forces the reader to engage the wisdom process.

After considering a proverb on its own, the reader can consider the proverb's immediate context: the Y axis. Frequently, proverbs near one another treat different aspects of related topics. Proverbs 26:4-5, quoted earlier in this chapter, serves as the parade example of reading proverbs with proverbs. Should a wise person answer a fool or not answer a fool? The juxtaposition of these two verses clearly answers with "it depends," pushing the reader to formulate a more complex answer than either of the proverbs could give alone. This pairing illustrates the principle that wisdom decisions cannot rest on a single proverb. While the X axis asks the reader to analyze one proverb and offers some insight, the Y axis asks the reader to compare, contrast, and connect wisdom with more wisdom.

In some cases, Proverbs offers an extended treatment of a particular theme, following that theme through several spheres of life. Associating the ideas in connected verses provides a larger framework for seeking wisdom.[66] In other words, the passage contains a conversation of sorts between its proverbs. Proverbs 19:1-7, for example, discusses the connections between the poor, the rich, and friends:

19:1   Better is a **poor person** who walks in his integrity

Than one who is *crooked in speech* and is a fool.

2   Desire without knowledge is not good,

And whoever makes haste with his feet misses his way.

---

[66] Michael Fox refers to such a passage as an "associative sequence," explaining, "Consequently, I try to respect the individuality of each proverb by interpreting it alone as well as considering the new meanings created by context." *Proverbs 10-31: A New Translation with Introduction and Commentary*. New Haven, CT: Yale University Press, 2009: 478. Other helpful examples of this Y-axis reading can be found in Proverbs 10:11-21 (words), 11:24-28 (generosity), 12:13-25 (words), 16:1-9 (sovereignty of *YHWH*), 16:10-15 and 25:1-7 (the king).

3   When a man's *folly* brings <u>his way</u> to ruin,

    His heart rages against the Lord.

4   <u>Wealth</u> brings many new friends,

    But a **poor man** is <u>deserted by his friend</u>.

5   A <u>false witness</u> will not go unpunished,

    And he who breathes out <u>lies</u> will not escape.

6   Many seek the favor of a **generous** man,

    And everyone is a <u>friend</u> to **a man who gives gifts**.

7   All a **poor man's** brothers hate him;

    How much more do his <u>friends</u> go far from him!

    He pursues them with <u>*words*</u>, but does not have them.

The bolded words pertain to the poor and rich, whereas the underlined and italicized words highlight repeated ideas: way, friend, and words. Studying these proverbs together provides a broader wisdom context for understanding the right, just, and equitable way to think about and act toward the poor and the rich. For instance, this passage suggests:

- Poverty and foolishness are not the same.
- A poor person of integrity deserves respect.
- Hasty decisions often prove to be bad decisions.
- Do not be hasty or foolish when responding to the poor.
- Do not judge the poor by their friends or how their family treats them.
- Beware of false witnesses against the poor.

- Do not be swayed by generous people with money.

- Research and acquire a deep understanding of an issue before making decisions.

- Remember that the rich can be fools.

- Fools blame God for the results of their foolishness.

By considering proverbs with proverbs, the reader can piece together the nuances required to think wisely. The puzzle continues to grow in complexity and depth as one finds more topical threads in the same passages. For instance, the passage above also offers insight about rage and hate, friends, and family.

To continue the example above, the reader's next step is to collect other proverbs talking about the poor from the rest of Proverbs—the Z axis. For instance:

- Proverbs 13:23 – poverty can be the result of injustice

- Proverbs 17:5 – mocking the poor taunts God, their Maker

- Proverbs 21:13 – those who do not show mercy to the poor receive no mercy themselves

These three proverbs add perspectives not addressed in Proverbs 19. Each proverb offers a piece of wisdom: considering proverbs with proverbs—the Y and Z axes—adds necessary complexity to the reader's ever-growing web of considerations. Revisiting each axis of the XYZ analysis continues to grow the reader's wisdom, offering more insight, prompting more reflection.

Here the book of Ecclesiastes jumps into this discussion, since Ecclesiastes also contains proverbs.[67] After the frame editor summarizes the Preacher's sermon—all is vanity, *hebel* (Eccl 12:8)—he pivots and describes the Preacher as a man on the wisdom path (Eccl 12:9-10):

---

[67] The NIV translates more verses from Ecclesiastes in proverbial/poetic form than other English versions.

12:9 In addition to being a wise man, the Preacher (*qohelet*) also taught the people knowledge;

and he pondered, searched out and arranged many proverbs.

10 The Preacher sought to find delightful words and to write words of truth correctly.

With his closing words, the frame editor describes *Qohelet* in terms of his proverbial wisdom: seeking, finding, and teaching knowledge, proverbs, and truth. Even though *Qohelet* recognizes the limitations of human wisdom, he is presented as a teacher of wisdom: his words are "delightful" (*hepes*), "just the right words" (NIV), "acceptable words" (NJV).

Qohelet's "delightful" proverb in Ecclesiastes 7:1-6 supplies another helpful illustration for the three-axis reading strategy. The verses reveal what is better in life and what relates to the good versus bad life. Each verse can be read on its own (X-axis), as a thematic collection (Y-axis), and as related to the other statements about the good life and vanity (*hebel*) in the book (Z-axis).

7:1 A good name is **better** than precious ointment,

And the day of death than the day of birth.

2 It is **better** to go to the house of mourning

Than to go to the house of feasting,

For this is the end of all mankind,

And the living will lay it to heart.

3 Sorrow is **better** than laughter,

For by sadness of face the heart is made glad.

> 4   The heart of the wise is in the house of <u>mourning</u>,
>
>   But the heart of fools is in the house of <u>mirth</u>.
>
> 5   It is **better** for a man to hear the <u>rebuke</u> of the wise
>
>   Than to hear the <u>song</u> of fools.
>
> 6   For as the crackling of thorns under a pot,
>
>   So is the <u>laughter</u> of the fools;
>
>   This also is vanity.[68]

This collection of "delightful" proverbs about the "better" life teaches readers to avoid judging circumstances too quickly or superficially. What may initially seem surprising or absurd begins to make sense after some pondering. In this passage, *Qohelet* offers readers another way to look at the good life: backwards, upside down. Proverbs' "better is" sayings offer similar wisdom; for instance, Proverbs 15:16-17 reads:

> 15:16   Better is a little with the fear of the Lord
>
>   Than great treasure and turmoil with it.
>
> 17   Better is a dish of vegetables where love is
>
>   Than a fattened ox served with hatred.

These passages from Ecclesiastes and the book of Proverbs prompt readers to examine the life of the wise beyond its surface[69]. Both books agree: though initially unattractive, a life of virtue makes for better living, even in the midst of negative circumstances.

---

[68] In this context, *hebel* may have the sense of apparent absurdity. *Qohelet* assigns *hebel* to other absurd situations: two people in rivalry (Eccl 4:4), God giving gifts to someone but not allowing them to enjoy them (Eccl 6:1-2), and the righteous suffering (Eccl 8:14).

[69] For more "better is" proverbs, see Proverbs 16:8, 16, 19, 32, and 27:5, 10.

Readers of the OT love the book of Proverbs, even in its complexity. Learning to recognize, understand, and apply wisdom continues to preoccupy the wise even today. The three-axis strategy often proves helpful to readers seeking wisdom in the pages of this eclectic text, pondering the nuances and various applications of wisdom in the context of their own lives.

Toward the New Testament

1. Instruction in Wise Living: Righteousness, Justice, Equity

The NT continues the OT's instruction in wise behavior, echoing Proverbs' language of the nature and pursuit of wisdom. In one of several passages,[70] Paul teaches that Christians should walk (Eph 4:2-3):

4:2	with all humility and gentleness, with patience, bearing with one another in love,
3	eager to maintain the unity of the Spirit in the bond of peace.

Paul's description sounds like Proverbs' wisdom path: humility, patience, love, unity. In his letters, Paul typically follows his theological instruction with practical instructions for living out his teaching.[71] These directives often sound like proverbial wisdom. For example, Colossians 4:2-6 reads:

4:2	Continue steadfastly in prayer, being watchful in it with thanksgiving.
3	At the same time, pray also for us, that God may open to us a door for the word, to declare the mystery of Christ, on account of which I am in prison—

---

70 See also Ephesians 2:10, 4:1; Colossians 1:10, 2:6; and 1 Thessalonians 2:12.

71 For instance, Romans 12-16, Ephesians 4-6, Colossians 3-4, Galatians 6, and 1 Thessalonians 4-5, and 2 Thessalonians 3.

4	that I may make it clear, which is how I ought to speak.
5	Walk in wisdom toward outsiders, making the best use of the time.
6	Let your speech always be gracious, seasoned with salt, so that you may know how you ought to answer each person.

This life sounds like the OT description of a person seeking to embrace Lady Wisdom. 2 Timothy 3:16-17 also sounds like Proverbs:

3:16	All Scripture is breathed out by God and profitable for teaching, for reproof, for correction, and for training in righteousness,
17	that the man of God may be complete, equipped for every good work.

Notice the Proverbs 31-like emphasis on Scripture permeating every area of one's life, for the purpose of doing good to others. From the Gospels through Paul's letters and the epistles, the NT upholds and continues the OT wisdom teachings.

The NT also picks up a second OT wisdom theme: the emphasis on righteousness, justice, and equity. As discussed earlier in this chapter, the OT wisdom texts use one's treatment of the poor and needy as the primary assessment of a wise life. In Matthew 23:23, Jesus rebukes the scribes and Pharisees for "neglecting the weightier matters of the law": justice and mercy and faithfulness.[72] Paul echoes this priority in Galatians 2:10 when he records that James, Cephas, and John "asked us to remember the poor, the very thing I was eager to do." James 2:1-13 rails against those who show partiality to the rich; they

---

[72] Of the four Gospels, Luke deals the most with those on the margins of society, especially the poor. See Jesus' quotation of Isaiah 61:1-2 in Luke 4:18-19, the story of Zacchaeus (Luke 19:1-10), and Jesus' parables unique to Luke: the good Samaritan (Luke 10:25-37), the great banquet (Luke 14:12-14), and the rich man and Lazarus (Luke 16:19-31).

"are committing sin and are convicted by the law as transgressors," on par with murderers (James 2:9-11). James continues, vehemently condemning those who mistreat the poor: "For judgment will be merciless to one who has shown no mercy" (James 2:13). In the NT as in the OT, caring for the poor and needy continues to be a primary charge for Christ-followers.

2. Lady Wisdom and the Son

The Writings cast the kings of Israel and Judah as sons of Adam, men who played the fool and brought on the death and exile of Israel. Even David and Solomon are portrayed as great kings who also embraced folly and sin (1 Chron 21; Neh 13). The editors of the Writings shaped a collection of texts that leaves the reader looking for a wise son of Adam, son of David to come, one who will bring in blessing and not a curse.

The Gospel of Luke paints Jesus as that son: the youth who answers Lady Wisdom's call in Proverbs 1-9. For instance, Luke presents Jesus as the young boy so wise he sits with the teachers of Israel, listening and asking them questions, amazing everyone with His understanding and answers (Luke 2:40-52). God publicly declares to Jesus, "You are my beloved son, in You I am well pleased" (Luke 3:21-22). Luke casts Jesus as the second Adam (Luke 3:23-38), the one who will choose wisdom and not folly. Jesus is the perfect son of Lady Wisdom; His deeds and words flow from the wisdom of God. In Luke 7:35, Jesus discusses the Pharisees' criticism against Himself and John:

> 7:34 The Son of Man has come eating and drinking, and you say, "Look at him! A glutton and a drunkard, a friend of tax collectors and sinners!"
>
> 35 Yet wisdom is justified by all her children.

In this text, Jesus casts Himself as the embodiment of Lady Wisdom. His actions parallel hers: He spends time eating and drinking with tax collectors and sinners, those who need salvation. Like Lady Wisdom, he seeks out and publicly appeals to the wayward to embrace Him and live. Jesus even openly calls Himself "The Wisdom of God" when he introduces His woes against the Pharisees (Luke 11:49).

The Gospel of John also casts Jesus as wisdom. In John 1:1-18, John introduces the Word who creates all things, presenting Jesus as similar to Lady Wisdom at creation (Prov 8). This Word takes on humanity to make God known: Jesus appears as Lady Wisdom made flesh, active in creation and the redemption of that creation. Later, Jesus refers to Himself as the temple, God's house of wisdom (John 2:19). Jesus, son of Adam, is the long-awaited son of David, the wise one to go up and dwell with the Lord in His temple (see Chronicles chapter).

3. Proverbs in the NT

The NT book most resembling Proverbs is the epistle of James. Although not structured as a collection of proverbs, James' topics vary, making it difficult to outline or follow its thought development. The central chapter, chapter 3, devotes considerable text to one's words and the two ways of wisdom and folly. Like Proverbs, James focuses on behavior as evidence of wisdom. James 5:11 also makes the only NT reference to Job and his steadfastness (*hupomone*). If one pairs this reference with the beginning of the letter's discussion of trials producing steadfastness (James 1:3), these two references create thematic bookends for the book as a whole. Echoing the OT Writings, James emphasizes suffering and trouble as the context of wisdom.

Continuing the OT form of teaching through proverbs or parables, in the NT, Jesus speaks in parables to teach his disciples about the kingdom (Matt 13:10-17). Jesus' parables function similarly to the "dark sayings" of Proverbs 1:6. Matthew comments on this pattern by quoting Psalm 78:2 in Matthew 13:34-35:

> 13:34 All these things Jesus said to the crowds in parables; indeed, he said nothing to them without a parable.

> 35   This was to fulfill what was spoken by the prophet:
>
> "I will open my mouth in parables;
>
> I will utter what has been hidden since the foundation of the world."

By speaking in parables, Jesus reveals truth to those who have the wisdom to interpret it correctly. As Proverbs teaches, the wise use wisdom to understand other wisdom. Jesus makes this same point when discussing His parables with His disciples. After teaching His disciples the parable of the sower, Jesus asks (Mark 4:13):

> 4:13   Do you not understand this parable? How then will you understand all the parables?

The parable of the sower appears to be the wisdom the disciples need to decipher the other parables. By explaining this parable to them in Mark 4:14-20, Jesus gives them the key to His other parables: wisdom to understand other wisdom. Jesus, the sage-king, must reveal the truth of the kingdom to his disciples. Matthew adds that this wisdom is old, from the foundation of the world (Matt 13:35). The Wisdom of God, Jesus is come to unveil the mysteries of the kingdom, yet this wisdom is only for the wise. Only those who seek and fear the Lord get understanding.

Further Reading

Dell, Katharine J. *The Solomonic Corpus of "Wisdom" and Its Influence.* Oxford, 2020; online edition, Oxford Academic, 22 Oct. 2020.

Dell, Katharine J., and Will Kynes, eds. *Reading Proverbs Intertextually.* Library of Hebrew Bible/Old Testament Studies. New York, NY: T&T Clark, Bloomsbury Publishing Plc, 2019: 629.

Steinberg, Julius, "Reading Proverbs as a Book in the Writings." *The Oxford Handbook of the Writings of the Hebrew Bible*, Donn F. Morgan, Ed. Oxford Handbooks, 2018; online edition, Oxford Academic, 7 Nov. 2018.

Waltke, Bruce. *The Book of Proverbs in New International Commentary on the Old Testament.* 2 vols. Grand Rapids, MI: Eerdmans, 2005.

Zuck, Roy B., ed. *Learning from the Sages: Selected Studies in the Book of Proverbs.* Grand Rapids, MI: Baker, 1995.

Ruth: Woman Wisdom

Old Testament Background to the Book of Ruth

- Israel in the time of the Judges
    - Repeated idolatry
    - Samson, the climactic last judge: Judges 14-16
    - Civil war and Benjamin's acquisition of women: Judges 20-21
    - "Everyone did what was right in their own eyes; there was no king in Israel": Judges 17:6, 21:25
- The Abrahamic promise – land and seed: Gen 12:1-3, 17:4-6, 22:17
- Preserving the family seed
    - Moab's origins in incest: Gen 19:30-38
    - Tamar and Judah: Gen 38
    - Kinsman redeemer: land - Lev 25:5-10, seed - Deut 25:5-10
- Leaving the land due to famine:
    - Abraham: Gen 12:10-20
    - Isaac: Gen 26:1-6
    - Judah: Gen 43:1
- Moabites banned from the assembly of Israel: Deut 23:3-6

Creation and the Book of Ruth: Adam and Eve Revisited

The book of Ruth connects to creation by replicating and/or answering several patterns first presented in Genesis 1-4. Ruth and Boaz, man and woman of virtue (*hayil* – Ruth 2:1, 3:11), correspond to each other the way the man (*'ish*) and the woman (*'ishah*) in the Garden correspond to each other (Gen 2:18, 23). In each case, the rightly paired man and woman become one flesh, are fruitful, and multiply. Boaz and the fruitfulness of his fields echo *'adam*'s relationship to the ground (*'adamah*), demonstrating not a curse, but the Lord's blessing Bethlehem after the famine. Ruth, woman of virtue (*hayil*), functions as an "anti-Eve," counseling Boaz for the good of all and actively contributing to God's redemption and restoration of Naomi (Ruth 3:6-13, 4:14-15). In Genesis 3:15, the Lord promises the seed of the woman will redeem humanity; in the Ruth story, Obed (*'obed*, "serve") restores and redeems Naomi. By "giving Ruth conception" (Ruth 4:13), the Lord preserves the seed of Judah, the lineage leading to King David. Through this family, God will in time fulfill His creation plan of ruling through *'adam* (Gen 1:26; 1 Chron 17:11-14).

The Book of Ruth: An Outline

The book of Ruth tells the story of Naomi's emptiness and the Lord filling Naomi's life with Ruth's son Obed, grandfather of David:

Chapter 1: Naomi loses everything in the fields of Moab and returns to Bethlehem empty.

Chapter 2: Ruth shows kindness to Naomi and gleans in Boaz' field, evidence of the Lord's lovingkindness (*hesed*).

Chapter 3: Following Naomi's counsel, Ruth asks Boaz to redeem her.

Chapter 4: Boaz redeems Ruth and Naomi; Boaz and Ruth's son Obed fills Naomi's emptiness. The book ends with a genealogy connecting Ruth, Obed, and King David.

Major Themes: Naomi's Redemption, Lovingkindness, and Ruth - Woman of Excellence

1. Naomi's Redemption

The Hebrew word for redemption, *ga'al*, occurs over 20 times in the four chapters of the book of Ruth, focusing the reader on the centrality of this theme. In the first paragraph, Naomi's family moves to Moab, and her husband and sons die, leaving her bereft with two Moabite daughters-in-law (Ruth 1:1-5). Returning to Bethlehem, Naomi bemoans her life as going out full and coming back empty (Ruth 1:21). Her emptiness is resolved in chapter 4, when Ruth's child, Obed, is placed in Naomi's lap (Ruth 4:16-17). Through Ruth, Boaz, and Obed, the Lord redeems Naomi's life.

2. Lovingkindness

Another theme in the book of Ruth pertains to the lovingkindness (*hesed*) of the Lord, Ruth, and Boaz. Lovingkindness, like glue, holds a relationship together. Frequently found in the context of covenants, lovingkindness requires both parties to uphold covenantal fidelity. Even though the book only references the Lord's lovingkindness twice (Ruth 1:8, 2:20), each instance signals a critical turning point in the story. The first marks Naomi's blessing of Ruth the Moabitess and her future (Ruth 1:8). The second occurs when Naomi hears of Ruth gleaning in Boaz' field. Naomi understands this event as a sign that the Lord has not withdrawn His lovingkindness (*hesed*) from her as she had previously thought (Ruth 2:20). Ruth and Naomi's story hinges on this perspective change.

Ruth herself also demonstrates lovingkindness (*hesed*). Ruth's first kindness lies in her loyalty in word and deed to the destitute Naomi; her second act of kindness is asking for protection, security, and redemption from Boaz on the threshing floor (Ruth 3:10). Just as the Lord's lovingkindness signals a turning point for Naomi, Ruth's request to Boaz sets in motion their marriage, Boaz' purchase of Naomi's field, and her redemption. Although lovingkindness is not mentioned with regard to Boaz, Ruth references the grace (*hen*) he demonstrates to her, a vulnerable, foreign woman (Ruth 2:10, 12). Whereas lovingkindness speaks to relational fidelity, grace points to acts of kindness to those in need. First as individuals and then as a couple, Ruth and Boaz epitomize lovingkindness (*hesed*), treating each other and Naomi with grace (*hen*).

3. Ruth, Woman of Excellence

The book named after her presents Ruth as a woman of excellence (Ruth 3:11). "Excellence" (*hayil*) can also be translated "army, wealth, or strength of character." Ruth 2:1 describes Boaz as a man of great *hayil*, a wealthy or virtuous man. *Hayil*'s core meaning is power—power of a king's military, of one's possessions, or of one's character. Boaz' statement in Ruth 3:11 summarizes the overall nature of Ruth's character and all her actions: she is a powerhouse of virtue, and the whole town of Bethlehem has noticed her character. Thus, although the term appears only once in the book, *hayil* describes Ruth's actions throughout the story: she clings to Naomi and her God, labors on behalf of Naomi, requests Boaz' redemption, and finally gives birth to Obed. Ruth's excellence of character has transformed not only her family, but also the town of Bethlehem; ultimately, her influence through King David transforms all Israel and the whole world.

The Sages in Conversation

1. Naomi's Redemption

The theme of Naomi's redemption from emptiness to fullness can be understood more generally as loss to gain. A number of other persons within the Writings experience this same journey: David, Job, and the exiles returning to the land in Ezra-Nehemiah. Conversation between their texts reveals several different aspects of this experience.

David characteristically experiences loss when his enemies gain the upper hand over him, such as in Psalm 3 when he flees from Absalom. Echoing his typical lament psalm, David would say his loss is due to the Lord having apparently forgotten him (Ps 13:1-2, 18:4-5, 16-17, Pss 52-60). But Naomi's loss is different. Caught up in the emotional and financial consequences of the death of her husband and two sons, Naomi cannot see clearly through the Lord's inscrutable workings in the world and her life. Unlike David, she has no human enemies. In chapter 1, she views the Lord as her current adversary, saying He has afflicted her (lit. "do evil," *ra'a'* - Ruth 1:21). By the end of the next chapter, Naomi's perspective has changed; she joins David in reiterating trust in God's lovingkindness and joy in His salvation (Ruth 2:20; Ps 13:5-6).

The sage of the book of Job now enters this conversation. Blameless Job declares that his calamities (lit. "evils," *ra'ah*) are due to the Lord's unjust management of His world. Throughout the book, Job maintains his innocence—responsibility for Job's suffering lies solely at the feet of the Lord. Although Naomi's complaint against the Lord in Ruth 1 sounds similar to Job's, she does not claim innocence or blamelessness in her loss. Though Elimelech may be at fault for leaving the land, the text does not hint at any wrongdoing by Naomi. She would agree with Job that the Lord is responsible for her plight as she charges Him with bringing calamity upon her, but she does not bring her innocence or guilt into the conversation at all. Building on Naomi's silence, Job's perspective addresses the righteous suffering calamities and waiting on the justice of the Lord while maintaining their blamelessness.

This conversation between Job, David, and Naomi underscores a consistent theme in the wisdom texts: suffering. From David in the Psalms through the returned exiles in Ezra-Nehemiah, the Writings are filled with individuals who suffer loss and yet walk in wisdom. Compounding this seemingly unjust suffering, the righteous experience the apparent absence of God[73]; David cries out (Ps 13:1):

> 13:1 How long, O Lord?
>
> Will You forget me forever?
>
> How long will You hide Your face from me?

Job wants to appear before the Lord to present a case for his vindication:

> 23:3 Oh that I knew where I might find him,
>
> That I might come to his seat!

When Naomi tells the women of Bethlehem that "the Lord has witnessed against me," she declares that the Lord has participated

---

[73] For a discussion on the apparent absence of God, see the Esther chapter.

in the judgment against her and abandoned her to suffering and loss (Ruth 1:21). David, Job, and Ruth cry out for the Lord to make His faithfulness known to them; in their suffering, they cannot yet see His lovingkindness (*hesed*). Although the Lord eventually delivers them and reverses their fortunes, He does not do so immediately. The Lord reigns over all creation and knows all the happenings on earth, yet these righteous sufferers oftentimes feel and say the Lord does not hear, see, or care for them. Nonetheless, in their pain, they raise their voices to affirm the Lord's goodness and faithfulness even as it seems He intentionally delays their deliverance. Each provides a model for suffering: until God intervenes, His people must continue to walk the narrow path of wisdom.

Within the larger framework of the Writings, the people of God wait for the coming of His kingdom; during this period, they suffer losses of various kinds and face the temptation to prioritize a quick and easy way to relieve their suffering. However, the wise sufferer also sees the reality that departing from the path of wisdom means taking the path of folly. For example, had Job listened to his foolish friends' advice to repent of his sin to get his good life back, he would have lied, since he was, in fact, blameless. Unbeknownst to Job, his actions carry dramatic implications in the heavenly realm: if Job confesses falsely, he compromises his status as a God-fearer and confirms the adversary's initial accusation against him (Job 1:7).

The sage of Ezra-Nehemiah speaks here, offering the exiles' suffering as another example of loss to gain in the Writings. Israel's tragic exile to Babylon means the loss of the Davidic kingdom and kings, the loss of the temple and the Lord's presence, the breaking of the Sinai covenant, the loss of the land, and the loss of people to foreign captors. These events mark the complete reversal of the Lord's deliverance of His people out of captivity in Egypt under Moses. The Lord's whole agenda for Israel appears to be swept away. Like Naomi and Job, the exiles lost everything: city, temple, land, and people.

What would the believing remnant in exile have to say in this conversation with Naomi, David, and Job? To begin, the exiles would confess the sin and breaking of the covenant that led to their losses (Ez 9:7-14; Neh 9:33-37; Dan 9:7-16). Through his penitential psalms, such as Psalms 32 and 51, David agrees: the exiles suffer because of Israel's repeated choice of folly over wisdom. However, because of the Lord's lovingkindness and grace, He keeps His promises. The exiles can live in expectation that after the 70 years of exile are fulfilled, the Lord will restore His people to their land (Ez 9:8-9; Jer 25:12, 29:10). Within the lines of Ezra-Nehemiah, one can easily imagine the returnees echoing Naomi's realization: the Lord's lovingkindness for His people remains. As promised, He has redeemed their life from calamity.

Naomi, Job, David, and the returnees illustrate the crucial role the wisdom of God plays in the lives of those who experience loss and gain. Each sufferer determines their specific path of wisdom by referring to the wisdom of God in their particular situation. In Naomi's case, Ruth serves as the embodiment of the wisdom of God, the agent through whom the Lord removes Naomi's loss and fills her with a future. In the midst of his suffering, the Lord, wise beyond limited human thinking, speaks to Job, educating him about the Almighty's governance of the creation (Job 28, 39:13-18). David's life centers on the instruction or *torah* of God (Ps 19). Characteristically, David laments about his troubles but in the end, trusts and praises the Lord. As illustrated in Psalm 16:7-9, the Lord's counsel turns David's attention from his trouble to the Lord Himself. As one would expect, then, in Ezra-Nehemiah, the people return to the land and receive instruction from Ezra who held "the wisdom of God in his hand" (Ezra 7:25, Nehemiah 8). In each case, the wisdom of God serves as the focal point for sufferers seeking to determine how to return to or stay on the path of wisdom. Listening to the wisdom of God in times of suffering connects all the narratives.

2. Lovingkindness

Lovingkindness (*hesed*) appears in the Writings in two different ways: the Lord's lovingkindness and humans' lovingkindness toward one another. The former plays a central role in the books of Psalms and Lamentations (Lam 3:22) and will therefore be discussed in the Lamentations chapter. The sages of Ruth and Proverbs often focus on human beings in relationship to one another; their lovingkindness (*hesed*) takes the form of faithfulness and fidelity. In this conversation, the sages of Ruth and Proverbs connect wisdom and lovingkindness, using the lives of Ruth and Boaz to illustrate this essential wisdom quality of faithful love.

Ruth and Boaz demonstrate *hesed* both separately and together. The Hebrew word *hasid*, "saints" or "faithful ones" (NRSV, NLT), is built off the same root as *hesed*; *hasid* therefore contains the idea of being faithful, loyal, kind, and gracious. Simply put, *hesed* characterizes the *hasid* person—lovingkindness characterizes the saint. Conversely, the faithful are characterized by their lovingkindness. Consider how Ruth and Boaz embody the *hasid* of Proverbs 2:6-8:

> 2:6 For the Lord gives wisdom;
>
> From his mouth come knowledge and understanding;
>
> 7 He stores up sound wisdom for the upright;
>
> He is a shield to those who walk in integrity,
>
> 8 Guarding the paths of justice
>
> And watching over the way of his saints (*hasid*).

As this passage states, the Lord gives wisdom to His faithful ones, the upright who walk in integrity. He guides the wise along the path of wisdom. In turn, the wise treat those around them with lovingkindness, as described in Proverbs 3:

> 3:1 My son, do not forget my teaching,
>
> But let your heart keep my commandments,

> 2   For length of days and years of life
>
>   And peace they will add to you.
>
> 3   Let not steadfast love (*hesed*) and faithfulness (*'emet*) forsake you;
>
>   Bind them around your neck;
>
>   Write them on the tablet of your heart.

To keep the teachings and commandments of the Lord, one's heart must be marked by steadfast love and truth (NIV "love and faithfulness," NRSV "loyalty and love"). There is no wisdom without the demonstration of these virtues. These verses form a simple summary of the so-called second tablet of the ten commandments: how God-fearers should treat their neighbor. Thus, when Boaz characterizes Ruth as a woman of excellence/virtue, he proclaims that she is a Law-keeper, that she loves the Lord with all her heart. Given her origins in Moab, this is quite the compliment: Boaz measures Ruth by the God of Israel's standards and finds her virtuous (*hayil*).[74]

Yet like the *hayil* woman, a man of steadfast love and faithfulness (*'emet*) is also rare (Prov 20:6):

> 20:6   Many a man proclaims his own loyalty (*hesed*),
>
>   But who can find a trustworthy (*'emet*) man?

As if in answer to this question, the book of Ruth describes Boaz as a man of loyalty and faithfulness. No other men in the story exhibit such character: not Elimelech, his sons, or the closer relative. Boaz stands out within the town and the Judges' era, setting an example of *hesed* for all Bethlehem. Twice, Ruth calls Boaz gracious (*hen*) (Ruth 2:10, 13).

---

[74] Katherine J. Dell connects Ruth and Proverbs beyond the relationship with Proverbs 31: "The character of Ruth reveals that she is not simply a woman of worth, but she is also a profound exemplar of the values embodied in proverbial wisdom [...]. Other characters in the book too, notably Boaz and Naomi, are a part of this didacticism in that general maxims are also illustrated by their behaviour and by their character interrelationships." "Didactic Intertextuality: Proverbial Wisdom as Illustrated in Ruth." *The Solomonic Corpus of "Wisdom" and its Influence*. Oxford Scholarship Online, 2020.

When everyone was doing "what was right in their own eyes," such a virtuous man must have been both a relief and a rarity.

Again, *hesed* and *hen* are paired in Proverbs 11:16-17:

> 11:16 A gracious (*hen*) woman gets honor,
>
> And violent men get riches.
>
> 17 A man who is kind (*hesed*) benefits himself,
>
> But a cruel man hurts himself.

These verses reinforce one of the main themes of Proverbs: a wise person will enjoy the fruits of their decisions and conduct. In Ruth, the Lord blesses Boaz and Ruth, guiding them into wisdom. The characters in the story see this connection between virtue and the Lord's blessing. For instance, when he hears of Ruth's loyalty to Naomi, Boaz recognizes her kindness and utters a prayer on her behalf: "May the Lord reward your work, and your wages be full from the Lord, the God of Israel" (Ruth 2:12, NASB). As if echoing Boaz, Proverbs 21:21 enumerates the benefits of kindness (*hesed*), linked here with righteousness:

> 21:21 Whoever pursues righteousness and kindness (*hesed*)
>
> Will find life, righteousness, and honor.

Proverbs predicts that persons whose actions exhibit righteousness and kindness will be met with the Lord's blessing. Within the book of Ruth, these blessings manifest themselves in the pairing of the gracious woman (*hen*) with the kind man (*hesed*). Ruth and Boaz are the Lord's blessing to each other; their union leads to Obed, Naomi's fullness and joy.

Yet Proverbs and Ruth both emphasize another principle in the life of the wise: their treatment of the poor. Even in her own poverty, Ruth labors to provide for Naomi, gleaning in the fields so the women can eat. Boaz demonstrates generosity and kindness to Ruth by instructing her to glean on his property, protecting her from men who might prey upon her, and providing her with water and food (Ruth 2:8-9). In so doing, Boaz distinguishes between a person's circumstances and their character. He lives out the wisdom of Proverbs 19:22:

> 19:22 What is desired (*ta'awah*) in a man is steadfast love (*hesed*),
>
> And a poor man is better than a liar.

In Hebrew, "desire" (*ta'awah*) means a yearning, craving, or longing. Even though the poor long for the basic necessities of life, Proverbs and wise Boaz understand *hesed* as a quality more desirable than riches. Boaz sees Ruth's *hesed* toward Naomi and treats her accordingly. In turn, Ruth recognizes Boaz' kindness toward her, a destitute, foreign woman (Ruth 2:10, 13). Ruth and Boaz both act generously, and each in turn experiences the wisdom of Proverbs 14:21: "blessed is he who is gracious to the poor."

Proverbs addresses one last aspect of *hesed* illustrated in the book of Ruth. In Proverbs 16:6, *hesed* and *'emet* are again used together:

> 16:6 <u>By steadfast love</u> (*hesed*) <u>and faithfulness</u> (*'emet*) iniquity is atoned for,
>
> and <u>by the fear of the Lord</u> one turns away from evil (*ra'*).

In this couplet, *hesed* and *'emet* parallel the fear of the Lord, the very heart and soul of wisdom. This verse's unique content should shock the careful reader: in the OT, atonement requires a blood sacrifice, yet this verse states that *hesed* and *'emet* figure in atoning for iniquity.[75] The parallelism is worth examining more closely:

---

[75] Some commentators introduce the sacrificial system into their interpretation of this verse. For instance, Bruce Waltke writes, "The epigrammatic proverb points only to the human virtues that complement the sacrificial system to make atonement (cf. Lev. 1:4, 4:4, 16:21 passim). Unless a person is characterized by unfailing love, the sacrificial system is of no avail (1 Sam. 15:22)." "Chapters 15-31." *The Book of Proverbs*. Grand Rapids, MI: Eerdmans, 2005: 26.

A	<u>By lovingkindness and truth</u>	*iniquity is atoned for,*
B	and <u>by the fear of the Lord</u>	*one keeps away from evil.*

The B line appears to expand the A line: as Lindsay Wilson explains, "iniquity is atoned for … in the sense of helping to purge wrong thinking and doing from our lives."[76] Faithful love toward one's neighbor removes iniquity from one's life not by cleansing sin, but by keeping sin far away. Sinfulness or iniquity are absent when one is kind and gracious to others—that is, when one acts in fear of the Lord. Proverbs 2:11-12a speaks of this same principle:

> 2:11 Discretion will guard you,
>
> Understanding will watch over you,
>
> 12 To deliver you from the way of evil.

What a contrast to the folly and sinfulness of Israel in the book of Judges! With each person doing what is right in their own eyes, Israel flies headlong into evil. The events in the book of Ruth stand out in the era of the Judges; the Ruth narrative includes no record of foolishness or mistreatment between neighbors. In fact, the text emphasizes the opposite repeatedly: neighbors bless each other in the name of the Lord (Boaz 2:4 and 12, 3:10, Naomi 2:20, the men at the gate 4:11, 12; the women of the town 4:14-15). Naomi's Bethlehem appears to be an enclave of God-fearers in the midst of the chaos of Judges' era. The people fear the Lord, treat each other with *hesed*, and in so doing keep sin and its consequences at bay.

Broadening the application of this principle, Proverbs 20:28 expands the impact of *hesed* beyond the town to the whole nation. Though in the time of Ruth and Boaz, there is no king in Israel, the principle of wise governance stands. Just as Boaz and the men of Bethlehem seek wisdom, a wise king understands that lovingkindness and faithfulness preserve his throne, allowing him to administer justice

---

76 Lindsay Wilson. *Proverbs: An Introduction and Commentary*. Downers Grove, IL: InterVarsity Press, 2018: 194.

and righteousness to his people. Emphasizing this key component of "steadfast love" (ESV), both poetic lines contain *hesed* (Prov 20:28):

> 20:28   Steadfast love (*hesed*) and faithfulness preserve the king,
>
> And by steadfast love (*hesed*) his throne is upheld.

As the books of Kings and Chronicles demonstrate, the king who fears the Lord will be preserved. The righteous rule of a *hesed* king stabilizes the nation, keeping evil far away.

This Ruth-Proverbs conversation pairs Solomon's principles in Proverbs and their living illustrations in the book of Ruth. The union of a *hayil* pair, Boaz and Ruth's relationship serves as the catalyst to the resolution of Naomi's emptiness and the coming Messiah. They are true God-fearers on the path of wisdom, treating people with *hesed* and, in turn, enjoy the blessings of the *hayil* life.

3. Ruth, Woman of Excellence

Outside the book of Proverbs, the OT describes only one woman as virtuous (*hayil*): Ruth the Moabitess (Ruth 3:11). This descriptor draws a straight line between Ruth and the virtuous woman parable in Proverbs 31. The sages of the Writings listen to the following conversation between those who describe a woman of excellence: Boaz in the book of Ruth and King Lemuel's mother in Proverbs 31.

Obviously, this woman's most fundamental quality is virtue (*hayil*). Her life of moral excellence demonstrated in her actions is so pronounced that the whole town notices and praises her works in the city gates (Prov 31:31; Ruth 3:11). Both texts agree: as a powerhouse of virtuous living, a person of *hayil* transforms their whole world for good. Just as the Lord created the whole world through wisdom, so also the woman of virtue benefits her whole world, be it Naomi and the town of Bethlehem or the Proverbs 31 woman's family and neighbors.

So what specifically does the wise woman do? First, she "does her husband good and not evil all the days of her life" (Prov 31:12). This woman considers her husband as she makes wise decisions. Lemuel's mother then continues, outlining the works this woman performs for her family, her household, and the poor and needy (Prov 31:13-27). This woman impacts everyone in her sphere of influence for good. Her husband and children praise her: she has surpassed all others in virtue (Prov 31:29). As if to bookend Proverbs, Proverbs 31:30 echoes Proverbs 1:7: a woman who fears the Lord will be praised. The progression of chapter 31 is clear: the virtuous woman seeks to do good to everyone she comes in contact with. Her character is manifest in her actions toward others.

Ruth the Moabitess serves as the epitome of this woman of excellence; she fits this profile perfectly. In Ruth 2:11-12, Boaz praises the work Ruth has done for her needy mother-in-law:

> 2:11 But Boaz answered her, "All that you have done for your mother-in-law since the death of your husband has been fully told to me, and how you left your father and mother and your native land and came to a people that you did not know before.
>
> 12 The Lord repay you for what you have done, and a full reward be given you by the Lord, the God of Israel, under whose wings you have come to take refuge!"

Boaz and Lemuel's mother describe Ruth the same way: she is a virtuous, hard-working woman who transforms her world for good. The household and townspeople all see her value.

Both texts also describe the husbands of these excellent women: these men are recognized and respected in the city gates. Echoing Proverbs 31:31, the elders at Bethlehem's gates praise Ruth, asking the Lord to bless her and, through Ruth, to build the house of Israel as through Rachel and Leah (Ruth 4:11-12). Just as Lady Wisdom built her house of wisdom in Proverbs 9:1, so will wise Ruth build Boaz' house through her actions and their children. The elders' prayers also mention Boaz' virtue, casting Ruth and Boaz as the quintessential power couple of wisdom, doing good and not evil to all those around them.

Yet Ruth is not merely an example of a virtuous woman. The connection between the book of Ruth and the Proverbs 31 parable presents Ruth the Moabitess as an Old Testament wisdom figure comparable to King Solomon. Proverbs 31 is not an add-on to the previous chapters of Proverbs, offering one last nugget of wisdom. As many book endings do, this parable serves as the conclusion of the book of Proverbs, summarizing the teachings of the entire book. Specifically, the excellent woman of chapter 31 embodies Lady Wisdom's instructions (Prov 1-9) and wise Solomon's teaching. Ruth is not just an example—she's an archetype. Ruth demonstrates to every reader, male and female, what wisdom looks like. The texts' implication here is to see Ruth as a template, not just an illustration. When we think of wise persons in the Old Testament, we should think of Ruth as often as we think of Solomon. It is fitting indeed for *hayil* Ruth to be part of the lineage not only of Obed—who redeems Naomi—but David, Solomon, and Jesus of Nazareth, who redeems the whole world.

Toward the New Testament

1. Redemption

The NT takes up the wisdom theme of loss to gain specifically with respect to Christians' spiritual state. 1 Corinthians 1:18-2:16 provides the most concentrated discussion of wisdom and the Gospel in Paul's epistles. Paul contrasts believers' and unbelievers' views of the Gospel using wisdom language (1 Cor 1:18, 30):

> 1:18 For the word of the cross is foolishness to those who are perishing, but to us who are being saved it is the power of God.

> 1:30 But by His doing you are in Christ Jesus, who became to us wisdom from God, righteousness and sanctification and redemption, ...

Just as the Lord redeemed Naomi through Ruth, a woman embodying wisdom, so the Lord acts through Christ Jesus, the wisdom from God; Jesus redeems, sanctifies, and accomplishes God's saving, righteous deeds. Paul's personal testimony also reflects this loss-to-gain recalibration (Phil 3:7-8):

> 3:7 But whatever things were gain to me, those things I have counted as loss for the sake of Christ.
>
> 8 More than that, I count all things to be loss in view of the surpassing value of knowing Christ Jesus my Lord, for whom I have suffered the loss of all things, and count them but rubbish so that I may gain Christ.

These words from Paul echo those of Jesus Himself, speaking of the cost of being His disciple (Matt 16:24-26):

> 16:24 Then Jesus said to His disciples, "If anyone wishes to come after Me, he must deny himself, and take up his cross and follow Me.
>
> 25 For whoever wishes to save his life will lose it; but whoever loses his life for My sake will find it.
>
> 26 For what will it profit a man if he gains the whole world and forfeits his soul? Or what will a man give in exchange for his soul?"

Though the redemption stories in the Writings tell mostly of human calamities and losses—death, famine, and poverty—the NT applies this pattern to salvation from sin. Through the Word made flesh, the Wisdom of God, death becomes life as Christians die to self that we may gain Christ and follow Him.

2. OT Lovingkindness and NT Mercy

The Hebrew words lovingkindness (*hesed*) and grace (*hen*) are so close in meaning that they are usually both translated "mercy" or "to be merciful" (*eleos, eleeo*) in NT Koiné Greek. Hosea 6:6 reads, "For I delight in lovingkindness (*hesed*) rather than sacrifice." Jesus quotes this passage while rebuking the Pharisees: "But go and learn what this means: 'I desire mercy (*eleos*), and not sacrifice,' for I did not come to call the righteous, but sinners" (Matt 9:13). Jesus again quotes this same Hosea passage in Matthew 12:7, apparently using it as a proverb of sorts to summarize a central truth about keeping the Law of God. By repeatedly quoting a familiar text to the Pharisees, Jesus highlights their misunderstanding of the *Torah*, the Law they pride themselves in upholding. Specifically, Jesus casts the Pharisees as breaking the second greatest commandment: to love your neighbor. Instead of showing grace, mercy, and covenantal fidelity toward their neighbors, the Pharisees exhibit their foolishness, lack of wisdom, and sin. It is no wonder these Pharisees wanted Jesus dead.

Jesus again reiterates mercy as a central quality of the wise in the parable of the Good Samaritan (Luke 10:25-37). Within the context of a conversation about the two great commandments, to love the Lord and to love one's neighbor, Jesus re-shapes the discussion to come full circle. He answers the young lawyer's question "Who is my neighbor?" with the parable of the Good Samaritan, finishing by telling the young man to go and show mercy (*eleos*) to anyone in need. Jesus' message is clear: law-keepers fulfill both the first and the second commandments in all their relationships. The primary demonstration of Law-keeping is loving God; the second is showing mercy (*eleos*) to all—the NT version of *hesed*.

3. Mary, Woman of Excellence

The Gospel of Matthew begins by recounting Jesus' genealogy, featuring several women (Matt 1:5-6):

1:5	Salmon was the father of Boaz by Rahab, Boaz was the father of Obed by Ruth, and Obed the father of Jesse.
6	Jesse was the father of David the king. David was the father of Solomon by Bathsheba who had been the wife of Uriah.

Luke 3:23-38 also recounts Mary's genealogy, tracing her lineage through Boaz, Obed, Jesse, and David, all the way back to Adam, the original son of God. Every Old Testament promise concerning the Messiah comes to Israel through Judah, Boaz and Ruth, and King David. These two genealogies draw parallels between Ruth the Moabitess and a new virtuous woman: Mary.

Luke 1 narrates what must have been a shocking event: an angel appears and promises Mary that the Holy Spirit will overshadow her, and she will give birth to Jesus, the Son of God, who will sit on the throne of David forever (Luke 1:31-35). Ruth's faithfulness to Naomi's God and her labor in birthing Obed foreshadow Mary's faithfulness to God and her labor in birthing Jesus. Mary's son, the seed of the woman promised in Genesis 3:15, redeems humanity; like virtuous Ruth, virtuous Mary's work transforms the world for good.

The parallels between these two excellent women run deeper still. Ruth 4:13 reads, "and the Lord (*YHWH*) gave Ruth conception." This expression is unique in the OT for two reasons: first, Ruth 4:13 is the only instance of divine action narrated in the book of Ruth. Only here does God directly intervene in the Ruth narrative; the Lord's direct action highlights Ruth's conception of Obed as a critical moment in the story. Second, "the Lord (*YHWH*) gave Ruth conception" is the OT's most direct expression of God's intervention in childbearing. Though the Lord plays a direct role in the pregnancies of Sarah, Rachel, Rebekah, and Hannah, for example, certainly overseeing these women's conceptions, the specific wording in the text of Ruth emphatically highlights God's agency in Ruth's pregnancy. While

Ruth is not a virgin, her conception of Obed edges closer to Mary's conception of Jesus than to those of Sarah and other OT women.

Mary, servant of the Lord, follows Ruth as a NT woman of excellence; these *hayil* women work within their marriages, homes, towns, and countries to bring good to all. In the culmination of God's promise to Israel, Mary births Jesus the Messiah, the incarnate Wisdom of God, bringing good not only to Israel but ultimately to the whole world.

Further Reading

Bartholomew, Craig G., and Ryan O'Dowd. "Chapter 5: Woman, Wisdom and Valor." *Old Testament Wisdom Literature: A Theological Introduction*. Lisle, IL: IVP Academic, 2011.

Block, Daniel. *Judges, Ruth. New American Commentary*. Nashville, TN: Broadman & Holman, 1999.

Dell, Katharine J. *Didactic Intertextuality: Proverbial Wisdom as Illustrated in Ruth*. New York, NY: Oxford University Press, 2020.

Lau, Peter and Gregory Goswell. *Unceasing Kindness: A Biblical Theology of Ruth*. Lisle, IL: IVP Academic, 2016.

Sutherland, Kandy Queen. *Ruth & Esther*. Macon, GA: Smyth and Helwys Publishing, 2016.

The Song of Songs: Creation's Call to Love

Old Testament Background for the Song of Songs

- Creation, Eden, Adam, and Eve: Gen 1-4
- The voice of Lady Wisdom: Prov 1-9
- Ruth and Boaz: the book of Ruth
- Covenant between the Lord and Israel as marriage:
  - Ezek 16, 23
  - Jer 3, 31
  - Hos 1-3
  - Lamentations
- Other OT texts introduced as songs:
  - Moses: Ex 15
  - Deborah: Judges 5
  - Korah: Ps 45
  - Isaiah: Is 5:1-7
- Solomon's wisdom and folly:
  - 1 Chron 22, 28-29; 2 Chron 1-9
  - 1 Kings 1-11
  - Neh 13

Creation and the Song: Love in the Garden

The Song's garden imagery, flora and fauna references, and the coming together of a man and a woman all harken back to the Garden of Eden. In fact, in Genesis 2, Adam sings the first song of the OT after the Lord brings the woman to him (Gen 2:23):

> 2:23   This at last is bone of my bones
>
> And flesh of my flesh;
>
> She shall be called Woman (*'ishah*),
>
> Because she was taken out of Man (*'ish*).

Adam's singing "at last" (*pa'am*) after his long search among the animals emphasizes his longing for a suitable match, beginning the theme of seeking and finding so prominent in the Song. In his brief song, Adam uses the Hebrew words "man" (*'ish*) and "woman" (*'ishah*), forming a play on words; *'ish* and *'ishah* are a match, and yet different. Genesis 2:24 then comments:

> 2:24 For this reason a man shall leave his father and his mother, and be joined (*dabaq*) to his wife; and they shall become one flesh.

Adam's seeking and finding the woman ends with the two humans becoming one flesh. This Genesis narrative presents the same arc of love as the Song: searching and finding one's love in a garden, leading to sexual union as a physical manifestation of the couple's marriage bond.

A second connection between Genesis 3 and the Song hinges on the woman's words in God's "good" garden (Gen 1-2): she sees the forbidden fruit as a "delight" (*ta'awah*) and "desirable" (*nehmad*) to make one wise (Gen 3:6). Though translated "delight," *ta'awah* carries a stronger meaning—the woman longed, craved, or yearned for the fruit. Although not used in its text, the idea of *ta'awah* is pervasive throughout the Song: from beginning to end, the Song expresses the woman and the man's yearning for and longing to be with each other.[77] Along these same lines, the woman in Song of Songs 2:3 also uses "desire" (*nehmad*), here translated "delight":

> 2:3 As an apple tree among the trees of the forest,
>
> So is my beloved among the young men.
>
> With great **delight** (*nehmad*) I sat in his shadow,
>
> And his fruit was sweet to my taste.

---

[77] The Song also contains several other words translatable as "desire." *Qinah* (Song 8:7) is often translated "jealousy, passion, or zeal." Song 7:10 uses *teshuqah* for the man desiring his darling, the same word Genesis uses for the woman's desire for her husband and sin's desire for Cain (Gen 3:16, 4:17).

The woman of the Song is expressing the same kind of longing for her beloved—a tree and his fruit—as the woman in Genesis 3 felt for the tree of the knowledge of good and evil and its fruit.[78] Read against the backdrop of Genesis 3, the Song casts the beloved as a good creation of God withheld from the woman and the man, just as the good fruit of the tree of the knowledge of good and evil was also withheld from them. By using Genesis 3:6 language, the Song presents the man and woman's lovemaking as good, deeply desirable, but forbidden until the right time, until marriage.[79]

The voice of the woman forms a third significant connection between the Song and Genesis 1-4. In Genesis 3:17, the Lord condemns the man for listening to the voice of his wife instead of His voice. In Eden, the woman plays a wisdom role: her voice prompts the man to make a wisdom choice and act upon it. The Song mimics this scene: the man asks to hear the woman's voice (Song 2:14, 8:13); he then listens to her and responds. However, unlike the woman in Eden, the woman in the Song urges the man toward good. The Song repeats Eden, with a pointedly different outcome.

The Song of Songs: An Outline

Nearly every aspect of the Song of Songs is disputed: its interpretation and meaning, its structure, which person says what, Solomon's role, etc. Acknowledging this larger scholarly conversation, *Voices of the Sages* intentionally limits the Song's context, or con-textuality, to the Writings.[80]

As with any text, genre matters. So far, the wisdom texts have been historical narratives, proverbs, psalms, or a mixture of these genres. Solomon's song fits none of these categories; the Song of Songs is a lyrical, fictional poem. Readers need to keep in mind that the

---

78 This desire itself carries no negative connotations: in Song 2:13 and 5:16, desire is parallel to sweetness (from *mataq*); Psalm 19:10 and 119:103 use *mataq* to describe the sweetness of the *torah* of the Lord.

79 Whether the tree of the knowledge of good and evil would have been given to the man and the woman at some point is not discussed in Genesis.

80 To give a contrasting example, reading the Song with the Prophets leads to interpreting the Song as a picture of the covenantal love between the Lord (*YHWH*) and Israel, just as reading the Song in light of the NT leads to a similar interpretation of Christ and His church.

entire poem is a creation of the author, Solomon. Though Solomon uses recognizable elements in his poem—a woman, a man, garden imagery, Jerusalem—the characters, their voices, the plot, and the setting are all imaginative creations offering readers a window into reality and truth. Solomon has created a fictional world meant to offer a perspective on reality and truth, the world God created. As a lyrical fictional poem, the Song's genre sets it apart from all the other wisdom texts, adding to its uniqueness.

Complicating matters further, the contents and structure of the Song can be viewed as a cycle, a narrative sequence, a chiasm, or a series of episodes/songs, and none of these options are mutually exclusive. The Song does appear to contain several clear components: a superscription, three textual anchors, a center, a climax, and a conclusion. Love speeches between the man ("beloved," *dod*) and the woman ("darling," *rayah*) on a variety of subjects fill out the body of the Song. The progression of the book can be plotted like this:

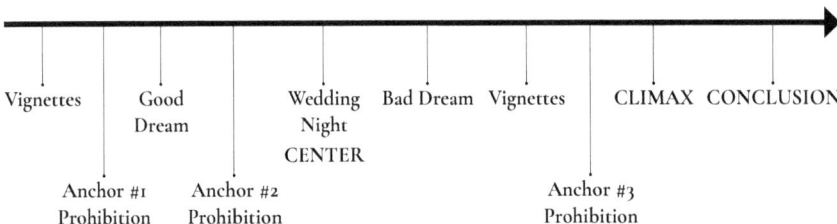

The textual anchor appears three times, each time prohibiting the lovers' consummation of their yearning. Yet chapters 4 and 8, the center and the climax of the text, seem to present moments of consummation. This tension, discussed in more detail below, forms the substance of the text. This reading of the Song can be outlined like this:

<u>The song of songs which is Solomon's (1:1)</u>

Vignettes of Love Speeches (1:2-2:3)

Anchor #1 (2:4-17)

- *Together in the house of wine with his banner of love overhead.*
  Let his left hand be under my head; let his right hand embrace me.

- *Do not arouse or awaken love until it pleases.*

- *The man is coming to her leaping on the hills.*

Good Dream – Seeking her Beloved, Not Finding, then Finding Him (3:1-3)

Anchor #2 (3:4-11)

- *Together in the house of her mother.*

- *Do not arouse or awaken love until it pleases.*

- *Solomon's wedding entourage is coming up from the wilderness.*

CENTER - WEDDING NIGHT (4:1-5:1)

Bad Dream – Rejecting her Beloved, Seeking Him, Not Finding, and Finally Finding Him (5:2-6:3)

Vignettes of Love Speeches (6:4-7:13)

Anchor #3 (8:1-4)

- *Together in the house of her mother.*
  Let his left hand be under my head; let his right hand embrace me.

- *Do not arouse or awaken love until it pleases.*

- *The woman is coming up from the wilderness, leaning on her beloved.*

CLIMAX: UNDER THE APPLE TREE THE WOMAN AWAKENED HER BELOVED (8:5-7)

Conclusion (8:8-14)

A final note: unlike Genesis 1-4, the Song makes no references to children (Gen 1:28, 3:15-16, 4:1-2). This focus change comes as a surprise given the OT's heavy emphasis on seed and descendants. Foregrounding the passionate pursuit of love, the Song for the most part puts marriage in the background and leaves children completely out of the picture.

Major Themes: the Passionate Pursuit of Love, the Consummation of Love, and Love Divine

1. The Passionate Pursuit of Love

The Song brims with the passion of lovers yearning for love. Right from the beginning all the way to the end, the text expresses desire for physical affection and togetherness: "May he kiss me with the kisses of his mouth" and "Hurry, my beloved" (Song 1:2, 8:14). The related theme of seeking and finding also runs throughout the entire book. The woman actively searches for her lover in two dream sequences (Song 3:1-4, 5:2-6:3), and the man pursues the woman, calling out to see her face and hear her voice (2:8-17, 8:13). Often, when their love seems close to fulfillment (2:4, 3:4, 8:3), the Song pivots and prohibits the awakening/arousal of love (2:5, 3:5, 8:4). As a result, the Song portrays love as an ongoing pursuit, cultivating anticipation and desire throughout the text.

2. The Consummation of Love

The passages depicting the pursuit of love exist in tension with other passages in which love appears to be realized. For instance, in Song 1:4, the woman says the king has brought her into his chambers, fulfilling her wish for his kisses. Various other scenes in the book depict the man and woman in places associated with love (a forest 1:17, a house of wine 2:3-4, her mother's house 3:4 and 8:2, vineyards and countryside 7:10-13), but in each of these cases, the text quickly changes the scene without portraying the couple's lovemaking.

On the other hand, two passages do seem to imply consummation. On the heels of Solomon's wedding day procession (Song 3:6-11), Song 4:1-5:1 depicts the man and woman enjoying their wedding night. If the Song is indeed a chiasm, this wedding night scene forms the all-important chiastic center. After the man describes the beauty of his bride (*kallah*, only used in chapter 4), the woman invites him into her "garden" (Song 4:16); he accepts her invitation and later declares that he has come into his "garden" (Song 5:1). In direct contrast to the prohibitions against arousing love, this central sequence appears to portray the lovers' consummation of their love so desired throughout the Song.

The climax provides a second picture of consummated love. In Song 8:5, the woman proclaims that she awakened (*'ur*) the man, using the same verb from the text's prohibition against the arousal (*'ur*) of love; this word choice strongly implies that the previously prohibited love is about to take place. Then, Song 8:6-7 pivots into commenting on this awakening of love, describing the qualities of love (*'ahabah*) apart from lovemaking (also *'ahabah*). These two verses reveal that the ultimate resolution lies not only in the couple's physical lovemaking but in a covenant-like bond of unbreakable love. By the end of the book, the meaning of love (*'ahabah*) has flipped from intensely passionate lovemaking to a deep bond between two lovers. This turn echoes the man and the woman of Genesis 2 clinging (*dabaq*) to each other as one flesh.

3. Human Love, Love Divine

On the surface, the Song certainly treats human love. The Song does not explicitly name God; this omission parallels the book of Esther wherein God's name is absent while His activity is implied. Yet Song 8:6 alludes to God's presence and involvement in human love. Song 8:6 uses the Hebrew phrase "*shalhebet-yah.*" *Shalhebet* means "flame." The word's ending, *yah*, can be translated as an abbreviated form of the name of God, *Yah-weh* ("the very flame of the Lord") or as an indicator of the intensity of the flame ("an almighty flame"). Many translators opt for "the very flame of the Lord," connecting the depths of love and jealousy with the nature of God. As a lyrical fictional poem, the Song appropriately contains several layers of meaning. Though focused on human lovers, the Song casts human love as stemming from divine love: divine love is manifest in creation through the human capacity for and depth of love. As such, divine love can be present in every and any human experience. The Song of Songs, the best human song, is so because it sings about God's love demonstrated in the lovers' love.

The Sages in Conversation

1. The Passionate Pursuit of Love

As discussed in the Proverbs chapter, Proverbs introduces the female wisdom figures of the *Megilloth*. In each of these wisdom texts, women wisdom figures develop different aspects of the wise life: Lady Wisdom offers the Lord's instruction, the virtuous woman of Proverbs 31 impacts her household and city through her good works, Ruth is recognized for her virtue and lovingkindness, the woman in the Song properly engages human passion, and Esther strategizes the deliverance of her people from their enemies. As their conversation will show, the woman in the Song, Lady Wisdom, and Ruth each instruct readers in wisdom through the theme of the pursuit of love.

Before diving into this conversation, the woman in the Song requires more examination. The superscriptions to Proverbs and the Song clearly pair the books: both are the work of the same sage, King Solomon. Nonetheless, Song 6:13 refers to the poem's primary voice as the "Shulammite." Normally, Hebrew indicates people's geographical and ethnic origin by adding "ite" (*-iy*) to the name of the place they come from: Canaanites come from Canaan. Following this pattern, the Shulammite woman should come from Shulem. However, neither the OT nor the archeological records mention such a place.

Given this ambiguity, "Shulammite" (*shulammit*) becomes the key to understanding who this woman is. Her name appears as the Hebrew sh-l-m consonants, the same consonants as in the words "*Shlomo*" (Solomon) and "*shalom*" (peace). *Shulammit* forms the feminine version of *shlomo*. These ideas come together in Song 8:10 when the woman says she has become in Solomon's eyes like "one who finds peace (*shalom*)." Thus, the woman of the Song is not a character in her own right, but the female alter-ego of King Solomon. As such, she, too, speaks wisdom from the Lord. This imaginative creation of Solomon's befits the genre of lyrical, fictional poem. This wise woman's voice tells a parable of sorts, presenting creational wisdom about love to all people, unbound by specific persons, times, or events.

The sages now begin to talk. The primary connection between Proverbs and the Song revolves around the theme of seeking and longing. Both women beseech men to love them: the woman in the Song pursues her lover, and Lady Wisdom pursues both those who need wisdom and those who already love wisdom. Proverbs also uses the same vocabulary as the Song: those who love (*'ahabah*) Lady Wisdom will diligently seek (*shahar*) her and find her (Prov 8:17). As the woman in the Song cries "let his right hand embrace me" (Song 2:6, 8:3), so the father in Proverbs instructs his son to embrace Lady Wisdom (Prov 4:6-8):

4:6   **Do not forsake her**, and she will keep you;

        Love her, and she will guard you.

7   The beginning of wisdom is this: get wisdom,

        And whatever you get, get insight.

8   **Prize her** highly, and she will exalt you;

        She will honor you if **you embrace her**.

These texts describe the wholehearted pursuits of love and wisdom in the same positive terms. Each text also paints the relationship as one of mutual pursuit: the son is to prize and embrace Lady Wisdom the same way the man in the Song comes to his darling seeking love in Song 2:8-17 and 5:2-7.

In yet another similarity, both texts use the common OT phrase "listen to the voice of" (*shamaʿ qol*), often translated as "obey." The Hebrew's implication is that the listener does what the voice demands or requests. In Proverbs, the son, the wise, and those seeking wisdom are to "listen to the voice" of Lady Wisdom, acting accordingly. The Song ends with the woman's voice calling for her beloved to hurry to her; the implication is that he does, in fact, "listen to her voice" and come to her, eager to satisfy their longings of love (Song 8:13-14).[81] Taken together, these similarities between the son/wisdom and the man/woman relationships highlight their pursuits as mutual and wholly encompassing.[82] Inasmuch as Ruth the Moabitess illustrates the life of the woman of virtue (Prov 31), the Song illustrates the passionate pursuit of wisdom (Prov 1-9).

As discussed above, the wise woman in the Song instructs the reader on the goodness of sexual passions. The sage of the book of Ruth begins by explaining yet again the connection between Proverbs and Ruth: Proverbs as a whole speaks of Lady Wisdom, Proverbs 31 offers a parable of a woman of virtue, and Ruth then provides a historical example of such a woman. However, the Writings place the book of Ruth between Proverbs and the Song, prompting readers to also connect Ruth, the woman of virtue, with the seeking and longing woman of the Song. The sages bristle—how can a woman of virtue be so ... overtly sexual? As one can imagine, this possibility rarely surfaces in Sunday school or in sermons at church.

The sage continues. In Ruth 3:1-13, Ruth actively pursues Boaz. Following Naomi's counsel, Ruth puts on her best clothes, perfumes

---

[81] In Song 2:14, the man requests his darling speak to him; he wants to hear (*shamaʿ*) her voice, for it is sweet.

[82] Proverbs and the Song also portray their respective pairs as siblings. Proverbs 7:4 reads:

> 7:4 Say to wisdom, "You are my sister (*ahot*)"
>
> And call insight your intimate friend (*modaʿ*).

In this text, "sister" is parallel to intimate friend (*modaʿ*), better translated "relative." Using similar language, the man in the Song repeatedly calls his darling his "sister" (*ahot*, Song 4:9, 10, 12, 5:1), and the woman calls her lover her "brother" (Song 8:1). Though the juxtaposition with a sexual union may seem odd, this language suggests another kind of bond/oneness between the man and wisdom: they both come from the same womb or family.

herself, and goes to visit Boaz on his threshing floor after his successful barley harvest and ensuing wine drinking. There, in the middle of the night, Ruth uncovers "the place of Boaz' feet" (*margelot*). In Hebrew, a man's feet (*regel*) can be a euphemism for his genitalia. However, the text uses the phrase "the place of his feet" (*margelot*), restraining a euphemistic reading. Uncovering the place of his feet, Ruth awakens Boaz to propose that he serve as her kinsman redeemer (Ruth 3:9). Ruth's action, originating from Naomi, serves as a real-life illustration of the woman awakening the man in Song 8:5. Both lead to marriage and sexual union. This event also echoes the Garden of Eden scene when the Lord puts the man to sleep and fashions the woman from his rib. When she is brought to him, she apparently awakens him (Gen 2:21-22). This parallel will be more fully discussed in the conversation about consummation.

This threshing floor meeting between Ruth and Boaz strongly foreshadows their union. In the morning, Ruth spreads her cloak so Boaz can fill it with barley (Ruth 3:15). He sends her back to Naomi laden with barley seeds; carrying the barley in her cloak, she probably even appeared pregnant. Ruth's appearance so surprises Naomi that she asks, "Who are you?" (Ruth 3:15-16). How could Ruth be gone a single night and come home looking pregnant? These events foreshadow Boaz and Ruth's sexual union leading to the conception of Obed, Naomi's redemption (Ruth 4:13).

Though Boaz's threshing floor is not the garden of the Song, the narrative contains garden-like, Song-like elements: the fruitfulness of the land, Boaz drinking wine, a beautiful and sweet-smelling Ruth, flattering words, the intimate cover of night, and a man and woman ultimately pursuing lovemaking and marriage. Ruth and Boaz's story is a narrative version of the Song distilled of all the passion and poetry: Ruth, woman of virtue, seeks out Boaz, man of virtue, for marriage and sex. Ruth's actions that night create a symbolic opportunity for Boaz to become her kinsman redeemer; he follows through on that symbolism by acquiring Naomi's land, marrying Ruth, and having a child with her to continue the line of Elimelech (Ruth 4:5-13). In this threshing floor scene, Ruth simultaneously embodies the Proverbs 31 woman of virtue and the woman of the Song.

The wisdom message of the Song is clear: the longing for love culminating in sexual union is both natural and a gift from the God of creation. Yearning is good. On the other hand, the Song also teaches that the Lord limits or constrains sexual passion. The garden context and echoes of Genesis 2 imply that the Song's wisdom is creational wisdom. As the man's companions realize in Song 8:13, the woman's words, then, are not exclusively for her beloved but contain a message for all to hear. She calls out, urging 'adam, the pinnacle of God's creative works, to listen to her voice and live well.

2. The Consummation of Love

Though the primary thematic focus of the Song is the longing of lovers, the question remains: do the lovers consummate their longing for one another in the Song? This section first answers this question, and then hosts a conversation between the sages of the Song, Proverbs, Psalms, and Ruth about the symbolism of sex in their various books.

As shown in the outline above, structurally, the Song repeatedly warns the lovers not to awaken love until the opportune time; these temporary prohibitions against carnal knowledge live in tension with the longing and yearning the lovers' experience. Each time consummation seems near, the text reverts to the warning (Song 2:4-7, 3:4-5, 8:1-4). The central section of the book appears to describe the couples' marriage and sexual union, but then the prohibition resurfaces again in Song 8:4, after the wedding night chapter. The events of chapter 4, then, appear too early in the poem to be the resolution of the warning about love.

In the last chapter of the Song, immediately after the final prohibition about awakening ('ur) love, the woman sings (Song 8:5c-e):

8:5   Under <u>the apple tree</u> I awakened (*'ur*) you.

           <u>There</u> your mother was in labor with you;

           <u>There</u> she who bore you was in labor.

Under the apple tree (*tappuah*, also "apricot"), where his mother labored and gave birth to the fruit of her own lovemaking, the woman "awakens" her lover. Given the Song's parallels with Genesis 2, this passage hints that both the man's sleep and the woman who awakens him are from the Lord. The Ruth narrative in Ruth 3-4 also upholds this trend: the man and woman of virtue symbolically begin their union on the threshing floor. In all three passages, the man is awakened by the woman to marriage and sexual union. This passage in Song 8 echoes the sexually charged scene in Song 2:3-4 where the woman enjoys the man's fruit under the apple tree and then proceeds to the house of wine with his banner of love flying over it. Chapter 8 appears to reprise the chapter 2 scene, this time as a response to the prohibition in Song 2:7 and 8:4—the time for consummation has now come.

At this point in chapter 8, the focus of the text changes: the passage shifts to describe the qualities of love itself, not lovemaking. The woman awakens the man to lovemaking in light of the permanent, divine, and unquenchable bond between them (Song 8:6-7):

8:6   Set me as a seal upon your heart,

           As a seal upon your arm,

           For **love** (*'ahabah*) is strong as death,

           Jealousy (*qinah*) is fierce as the grave.

           Its flashes are flashes of fire,

           The very flame of the Lord.

7   Many waters cannot quench **love** (*'ahabah*),

           Neither can floods drown it.

> If a man offered for **love** (*'ahabah*)
>
> All the wealth of his house,
>
> He would be utterly despised.

Thus, the climax of the book flips the focus of the Song: whereas most of the book portrays the woman's passionate desire for lovemaking with her beloved, this climax treats love as the indelible bond between the woman and the man. Song 8:6 speaks to the permanence of this bond: by setting the woman as a seal on his heart and arm, the man and woman's identity become permanently bound up together—the lovers are marked as belonging to one another. Because of its parallelism with "love" (*'ahabah*), the Hebrew word "jealousy" (*qinah*) should be understood in positive terms; though jealousy can destroy, its notions of exclusivity can also be translated "zeal," "ardor," or "passion" (NKJV).[83] This unrelenting, exclusive, all-consuming, divine, unquenchable, priceless love serves as the foundation for the lovers' lovemaking.

Song 8:6-7 resolves the text's prohibition by establishing lovemaking as a response to a love bond as strong as death. Though marriage is not explicitly mentioned in this passage, the emphasis on the permanence of oneness represented by the couple's sexual union allows only one conclusion: the best song is the one the lovers sing within a permanent exclusive bond—marriage. So do the lovers consummate their love in the Song? Yes, they become one by the seal of an unbreakable bond.

After listening to the sage of the Song, the other sages now take up the subject of the meaning of the consummation of love in the Writings. Proverbs uses sex as a metaphor for the wisdom decision. Repeatedly, the text likens choosing Lady Wisdom to fidelity in marriage and embracing Lady Folly to adultery. For instance, Proverbs 5:18-20 describes loving one's wife with the same terms as the Song. Both texts use the words in bold:

---

[83] Deuteronomy 4:24 calls the Lord a consuming fire, a jealous (*qinah*) God who demands Israel's covenantal loyalty. This jealousy reflects each partner's right to an exclusive love commitment.

5:18	Let your **fountain** be blessed,
	And rejoice in the **wife** of your youth,
19	A lovely **deer**, a graceful doe.
	Let her **breasts** fill you at all times with **delight**;
	Be <u>intoxicated</u> always in her **love**.
20	Why should you be <u>intoxicated</u>, my son, with a forbidden woman
	And **embrace** the **bosom** of an adulteress?

This passage could fit right into the Song. The father exhorts his son to remain faithful to his wife, reveling in their love. It is wise to be intoxicated (*shagah*) by lovemaking with one's own wife. This language of intoxication, underlined above, also overlaps with the Song: in Song 5:1, the man and the woman "get drunk" (*shakar*) with their lovemaking. The picture in both passages is one of fully engaged, joyful, life-giving sex.

The opposite is also true: uniting with the wrong woman leads to death. In Proverbs 7:15-19, the adulteress calls to the youth lacking sense:

7:15	So now I have come out to meet you,
	To **seek** you eagerly, and I have **found** you.
16	I have spread my couch with coverings,
	Colored linens from Egypt;
17	I have perfumed my bed
	With **myrrh**, aloes, and cinnamon.
18	Come, let us take our fill of **love** till morning;
	Let us delight ourselves with **love**.

> 19   For my husband is not at home;
>
> He has gone on a long journey;

Again, the language here overlaps with the Song, yet in this scene, the consummation of love is a foolish adulterous affair. Just like Lady Wisdom, Lady Folly also offers intoxicating lovemaking, but the outcome spells disaster (Prov 7:27):

> 7:27   Her house is the way to Sheol,
>
> Going down to the chambers of death.

Both passages instruct the son, and by extension, the reader, about the wisdom decision; in each case, the consummation of love symbolizes the lovers' full commitment to the path they have chosen.

At the end of Proverbs, King Lemuel's mother reiterates Lady Wisdom's instruction about the two kinds of women: those who drain one's strength (Prov 31:3) and the woman of virtue (Prov 31:10-31). Once again, the wisdom choice is likened to a man and a woman's sexual union: humans should passionately pursue and unite with wisdom the same way they pursue and unite with their lovers. Proverbs and the Song concur: sex is the physical symbol of the wisdom decision.

Psalm 45, labeled a *maskil*[84] and a song of love, enters the conversation here; it, too, contains a wedding scene. However, instead of being a song between a woman and a man, this song is Korah's wisdom love song for the Davidic king. Featuring a wedding procession, this time the queen's procession to the king, Korah parallels Solomon's wedding procession in Song 3:6-11. The language shared with the Song is here in bold (Ps 45:7-15):

> 45:7   You [the king] have **loved** righteousness and hated wickedness.

---

[84] *Maskil* is related to the Hebrew word for insight (*sekel*); Psalm 45 thus appears to be a wisdom psalm. The NKJV translates *maskil* as "contemplation."

> Therefore God, your God, has anointed you
>
> With the **oil** of gladness beyond your **companions**;
>
> 8 Your robes are all fragrant with **myrrh** and **aloes** and cassia.
>
> From **ivory** palaces stringed instruments make you **glad**;
>
> 9 **Daughters** of kings are among your ladies of honor;
>
> At your right hand stands the **queen** in **gold** of Ophir.
>
> 10 **Hear, O daughter**, and consider, and incline your ear:
>
> Forget your **people** and your father's **house**,
>
> 11 And the **king** will desire[85] your **beauty**.
>
> Since he is your lord, bow to him.
>
> 12 The **people** of Tyre will seek your favor (*face*) with gifts,
>
> The **richest** of the **people**.
>
> 13 All glorious is the princess (*lit., daughter of the king*) in her chamber,
>
> With robes interwoven with gold.
>
> 14 In many-colored robes she is led to the **king**,
>
> With her virgin companions following behind her.
>
> 15 With joy and **gladness** they are led along
>
> As they **enter** the palace of the king.

---

[85] The Hebrew *'awah* means "a very strong desire"; though not used in the Song, it is a synonym of *teshuqah* (desire) from Song 7:12.

Echoes of the Song ring loudly in this passage. Just as in the Song Solomon comes up from the wilderness with his wedding entourage, so the queen processes to stand by the radiant King. Two other commonalities emerge as well: the centrality of a Davidic figure and the detailed description of an impressive man/king (Song 5:10-16; Ps 45:2-8).[86] These elements each prompt a conversation between Psalm 45 and the Song.

First, Korah's psalms include the small collection of Psalms 42-49; Psalm 45 is its central psalm. The victorious king of Psalm 45 ends his people's affliction (Pss 42-44), ushers in the glorified Zion/Jerusalem (Pss 46-48), and marks the turning point in the collection. He leads the nations to God in Zion (Ps 47:1, 8-9, 48:11). The people who love this king as Korah does join the psalmist as he sings (Ps 45:17):

> 45:17   I will cause your name to be remembered in all generations;
>
> Therefore nations will praise you forever and ever.

Along these same lines, Korah describes the city of Jerusalem as a woman in Psalm 48:1-3 and 12-14, and parallels "Mount Zion" with "the daughters of Judah" in 48:11.[87] References to the nations/peoples run throughout Psalms 46-48; Israel and the nations abide together in the City of God, loving the king. The queen of Psalm 45 seemingly stands as the representative of these peoples who will praise the King forever in Zion. The context of the Korah collection allows readers to understand the couple of Psalm 45 to also represent the future union of the inhabitants of glorious Jerusalem and the Son of David. Just like the Song, the meaning of Psalm 45 derives its depth from the symbolic power of the consummation of love: the union is joyful and permanent.

---

86 The Hebrew *beloved* and the name *David* share the same consonants—*dwd*—and so look identical on the page. When the woman in the Song calls to "her beloved," the text prompts readers to think of him as "her David."

87 For further discussion on the significance of the queen, see Seth D. Postell. "A Literary, Compositional, and Intertextual Analysis of Psalm 45." *Bibliotheca Sacra* 176 (702): 146–63.

These psalms of Korah offer another intersection with the Song, this one taking the reader in a totally different direction: the identity of the man in the Song. The Psalter as a whole points to the coming Messianic King, looking forward to the day He rules in Zion. The King in Psalm 45 is this promised Davidic king, the Son of David come to take the throne in Jerusalem and rule over the Lord's kingdom forever (1 Chron 17:14; Ps 110, 132; Heb 1:8-9).[88] If one reads the Song as a parable housed within the context of the Writings, the man and the woman of the Song represent the coming Davidic King and those who yearn for the Messiah. The couple of Psalm 45 could be likened to the couple in the Song. This reading alters the Song's meaning: the woman's love for the man, King Solomon (Song 3:9), represents the people of the Lord yearning for the glorious coming of their King to rule forever from Jerusalem. This conversation between Korah's psalm and the Song highlights the effect of reading text collections as montages. Juxtaposed with one another, each text influences the reader's understanding of the other one, opening up interpretations beyond those prompted by a single text alone.

This Psalm 45 backdrop does address, to a certain degree, several of the unresolved questions of the Song: for example, the fabrication of the Shulammite and why the man's companions want to hear the woman's voice about the passionate pursuit of love (Song 8:13). This reading also makes sense of the Song's dream sequences. In the good dream, the woman seeks and finds her lover—such is the dream and hope of the wise longing for the King. The bad dream visualizes the worst nightmare of the wise: rejecting their King when He comes to them (Song 5:2-7). In this reading, the sexually charged language of the Song takes on a different tone—the Song's carnal knowledge content suggests depth of spiritual yearning for union with the King.[89] Read together, the Song and the Psalms suggest that the pursuit of love in the

---

88 The book of Ruth's ending Davidic genealogy may point in the same direction—the people hope for the seed of David.

89 Echoing the end of the Song, Revelation 22:20 ends the NT by longing for the coming of the King: "He who testifies to these things says, 'Surely I am coming soon.' Amen. Come, Lord Jesus!"

Song is ultimately realized when the wise "kiss the son" and take refuge in Him (Ps 2:12). The wise—the woman of the Song—love the King, long for Him to come to them, and look forward to forging an unbreakable, eternal bond between King, city, people. The union of the King and the peoples ends in unending praise of the King in Jerusalem.

Given its topic of lovemaking, the Song stands out as unique in the Writings collection, and for that matter, the whole Bible. This text's inclusion in the Word of God reminds readers of the goodness of human love, emotional and physical. Though humans do much singing, the Song of Songs remains the best human song.

3. Human Love, Love Divine

A conversation about divine love in the Song proves difficult given that God is not clearly mentioned. As discussed above, the text only hints at the presence of the Lord in Song 8:6 through the expression *shalhebet-yah*, sometimes translated as "the flame of the Lord." This conversation therefore approaches the topic of divine love from a few more creative angles: the text's creational background, the Lord's lovingkindness (*hesed*), and descriptions of God in the Writings as a whole.

In Genesis 2, the Lord God not only creates the man, the woman, and marriage, but in light of the Song, He also creates passionate sexual longing. After naming all the animals the Lord brought the man, Adam declares that now (*pa'am*) he has found what he was searching and longing for: a partner corresponding to him (Gen 2:18-24). God gives sex to the man and the woman, and all of creation follows suit, multiplying and filling the earth.[90] Even amidst the reality that human sin twists and perverts all of God's good gifts, the Song affirms the goodness of God's gift of sexual passion outside the Garden. In this respect, the Song points to love between husband and wife as evidence of God's love for His human creation. Though absent from the words of the text, God is present in the Song as the

---

90 Genesis 1:26-27 presents God in both the plural and singular. The sexual union of the man and the woman images God's person, emphasizing the holiness of the two becoming one.

Creator of love, through His creation.

Outside the Song, the Writings rarely use *'ahabah* (love) and "beloved" (*dod* or *yadidot*) with respect to human relationships; these terms are usually reserved to describe God and His relationships. As discussed in the Lamentations chapter, the Writings also regularly refer to the "lovingkindness" or "steadfast love" (*hesed*) of the Lord for Israel. *Hesed* echoes the love (*'ahab*) of Song 8:5-7; like the powerful, unbreakable, priceless, exclusive love commitment between the lovers, the Lord's *hesed* describes His covenantal loyalty to Israel. The Psalms in particular mention the Lord's choice of Zion and David in the context of His love (*'ahabah*). For instance, Psalm 47:4 and 78:68 pair the two verbs:[91]

> 47:4 He **chose** our heritage for us,
>
> The pride of Jacob whom he **loves** (*'ahab*).
>
> 78:68 But he **chose** the tribe of Judah,
>
> Mount Zion, which he **loves** (*'ahab*).

As these passages from the Psalter highlight, divine love in the Writings relates to God's choice of His people Israel. Their relationship is held together by the *hesed* of the Lord.

In contrast to the few instances of *'ahab* outside the Song, Chronicles, the Psalter, Lamentations, and Ezra-Nehemiah frequently use *hesed*, centralizing the Lord's fidelity and faithfulness to the promises He made to Israel. The Writings offer "the *hesed* of the Lord is everlasting" as an anthem for wise living in the post-exile (1 Chron 16:34, 41; 2 Chron 7:3, 6; Pss 107, 118, and 136).

As lovers act on their love, so God acts on the basis of His love for His creation. The Song remains unique in its contribution to the Writings but joins the other texts in their portrayal of this God

---

91 For more on the Lord's elective love, see Psalm 89:3 and 132:13; 1 Chron 28:4-10; and 2 Chron 6:5-6, 38, 7:16.

through His goodness and His mighty acts:⁹²

- Chronicles: The Lord brings about His rule through *'adam* and His covenant with David.

- Psalms: The Lord rules over Israel and the nations from Zion.

- Job: The Lord alone understands wisdom and wisely governs His creation.

- Proverbs: The Lord reveals wisdom for living in His creation.

- Ruth: The Lord remembers His lovingkindness to His people.

- Song: The Lord creates love for *'adam*, the man and the woman.

- Ecclesiastes: God appropriately limits human life and wisdom.

- Lamentations: The Lord judges His people and provides hope.

- Esther: God supersedes world powers and delivers His people.

- Daniel: God reveals mysteries about Gentile kingdoms and His eternal kingdom.

- Ezra-Nehemiah: The Lord restores His people from captivity and sin.

In sum, the God of the Writings is the Lord God, Creator of all, who rules Israel and the nations while remaining intimately involved in the daily lives of humans within their creational context.

Compiled and arranged in the post-exile, the Writings remind readers of their hope that the Lord God will usher in His eternal kingdom and a new creation. The love described in the Song offers *'adam*, the man and the woman, a kind of oasis in the midst of the turmoil and trials of life. While the world spins in chaos, love and lovemaking remain a kind of Garden of Eden for God's people in their

---

92 Paul House provides a similar summary of the theology of God for each book in the Writings in *Old Testament Theology*. Downers Grove, IL: IVP Academic, 2012.

troubles. In an act of divine love, the Creator gives his human creation a Song of love to sing, echoing the Garden no matter the current circumstances.

Toward the New Testament

1. The Pursuit of Love

The Song proves unique in both the OT and the NT. Overall, the NT's rich vocabulary pertaining to desire[93] tends to focus on how human desires have been perverted by sin and folly (Matt 5:28; Rom 1:22-27; Gal 5:16; 1 Cor 10:6). In his lengthy chapter on marriage in 1 Corinthians 7, Paul references the burning passion for sex, but Paul appears to treat such passion as a lack of self-control, to be resolved in marriage if one does not possess the gift of celibacy (1 Cor 10:5, 9). Yet not all NT mentions of human love are negative; in 1 Timothy 4:3-5, Paul presents a positive creational perspective of food and marriage. He calls them "gifts,"

> 4:3 that God created to be received with thanksgiving by those who believe and know the truth.
>
> 4 For everything created by God is good, and nothing is to be rejected if it is received with thanksgiving,
>
> 5 for it is made holy by the word of God and prayer.

Desire, love, and marriage, created by God, should not be forbidden or dismissed. From the Garden through the NT, the Creator gives these good gifts to His Creation, for them to enjoy.

2. The Consummation of Love

After the Lord God established love in the Garden, humans developed

---

[93] For a full list, see the 58 entries in Louw-Nida (25.1-58 – desire, desire strongly, and love). Johannes P. Louw and Eugene A. Nida. *Greek-English Lexicon of the New Testament: Based on Semantic Domains*. 2nd edition. Minneapolis, MN: Fortress Press, 1999.

cultural practices and norms around marriage. Though Jesus teaches about marriage, fidelity, divorce, and adultery (Matt 5:27-32, 19:1-12) and addresses the absence of marriage in the resurrection (Matt 22:23-30), NT texts mentioning marriage often pertain to a wedding and a feast. These texts echo the wedding of Song 4, the symbol of the couple's impending physical union. For instance, Jesus tells of a king who gave a wedding feast for his son, but the invited guests refused to come (Matt 22:1-14). In this parable, Jesus is the bridegroom; His triumphal entry in the previous chapter should have been the celebration of Jesus' covenantal union with Israel, but the guests failed to attend (Matt 21:1-17). This tragic feast of Jesus' first coming will turn into a glorious feast at His second coming (Rev 21:7-10, 22:17).

Ephesians 5 contains a number of elements in common with the Song: a man and a woman, love, allusions to the creation of marriage, the beauty of the bride, and the body. These commonalities tie Paul's teachings about the marriage relationship back through the Song to the Garden of Genesis 2. However, at the end Paul adds (Eph 5:32-33):

> 5:32 This mystery is profound, and I am saying that it refers to Christ and the church.
>
> 33 However, let each one of you love his wife as himself, and let the wife see that she respects her husband.

Here at the end of the chapter, Paul seems to change his emphasis: he calls the Genesis teaching about the man and the woman becoming one flesh "a mystery." He then states that the Genesis passage pertains to Christ's relationship to the church. Throughout this chapter, Paul's teachings about human marriage stem from the basis of Christ's relationship with the church, not the other way around. For Paul, Genesis 2:24 serves primarily as a Christological text: the basis of all marriage, and especially Christian marriages, is Christ's love for His bride, the church. No matter how Christians interpret and apply Ephesians 5, the central point of this chapter remains the foundation of Christ's sacrificial love for His church and the church's submission to Him. In this light, the Song reads as a parable about the King and His bride, looking forward to the permanent, joyful union between King and people.

3. Divine Love

God is love (*agape*, 1 John 4:8); the consequences of that love shine through the whole NT (John 3:16). John's simple statement alone teaches the divine origin of love in all its manifestations. However, the broader context of 1 John 4 develops this love still further (1 John 4:7-12):

4:7	Beloved, let us **love** one another, for **love** is from God, and whoever **loves** has been born of God and knows God.
8	Anyone who does not **love** does not know God, because **God is love**.
9	In this the **love** of God was made manifest among us, that God sent his only Son into the world, so that we might live through him.
10	In this is **love**, not that we have **loved** God but that he **loved** us and sent his Son to be the propitiation for our sins.
11	Beloved, if God so **loved** us, we also ought to **love** one another.
12	No one has ever seen God; if we **love** one another, God abides in us and his **love** is perfected in us.

In simple terms, John teaches that love is from God, that humans love because God first loved us, and that love characterizes humans as being from God. No hint of the passionate love from the Song emerges here; instead, this passage connects to the climax of the Song in chapter 8, emphasizing the bond between those who love one another. God's *agape*, His selfless, sacrificial, and unconditional love revealed by Jesus's words and works, is ultimately the source of the powerful, unbreakable love between humans in the Song.

Further Reading

Davis, Ellen F., "The Ecstasy of Intimacy—Song of Songs." *Opening Israel's Scriptures*. New York, 2019; online edition, Oxford Academic: 361-374.

Dell, Katharine J. *The Third Solomonic Book: Does the Song of Songs Have Any Connections to "Wisdom"?* Oxford: Oxford University Press, 2020: 8-26.

Duguid, Iain M. *The Song of Songs*. Tyndale Old Testament Commentaries. Downers Grove, IL: InterVarsity Press, 2015.

Kingsmill, Edmée. *The Song of Songs and the Eros of God: A Study in Biblical Intertextuality*. Oxford Theological Monographs. Oxford: OUP Oxford, 2009.

Longman, Tremper, III. "The Song of Songs: Human Love or Divine Love … or Both." *The Bible Today* 60 (4): 206–13.

Schellenberg, Annette. "'May Her Breasts Satisfy You at All Times' (Prov 5:19): On the Erotic Passages in Proverbs and Sirach and the Question of How They Relate to the Song of Songs." *Vetus Testamentum* 68 (2): 252–71.

Walsh, Carey, "The Wisdom of Desire in the Song of Songs." Donn F. Morgan, Ed. *The Oxford Handbook of the Writings of the Hebrew Bible*. Oxford Handbooks, online edition, Oxford Academic.

Ecclesiastes: The Preacher on Wisdom

Old Testament Background for Ecclesiastes

- Creation, Abel: Gen 1-4
- Human wisdom and divine wisdom: Job 28, 38-41
- Solomon's history with wisdom: 1 Kings 1-11; 2 Chron 1-9
- Solomon's wisdom: Proverbs and the Song of Songs
- Life in the post-exile:
    - Ezra-Nehemiah
    - Haggai
    - Zechariah
    - Malachi

Creation and Ecclesiastes: Elohim, Abel, and the Cyclical Nature of Life

Ecclesiastes' connections back to Genesis emerge clearly from the Preacher's words; he adopts the language and theology of Genesis 1-4 as the backdrop for his sermon.[94] In particular, names provide several direct associations. In contrast to other books in the Writings, Ecclesiastes does not use *YHWH*, the covenant name of God, but instead calls God Elohim, the Creator God of Genesis 1. Ecclesiastes also primarily uses *'adam*, underlining the connection between humanity and the image of *Elohim*.[95] This combination of *Elohim* and *'adam* points to the Creator God's sovereign rule over all human concerns. The creation poem in Ecclesiastes 1:3-11 echoes Genesis 1, but instead of focusing on creation's goodness, this passage addresses the futility (*hebel*) of human life within that creation.

---

[94] For more discussion of Ecclesiastes and Genesis, see Matthew Seufert. "The Presence of Genesis in Ecclesiastes." *The Westminster Theological Journal* 78 (1): 75-92.

[95] Meaning "man" generally or "humanity," *'adam* carries theological implications that *'ish*, "man" specifically, as opposed to "woman," does not.

Surprising those who read in English, Genesis 4 contains another direct connection to Ecclesiastes: futility or vapor (*hebel*) is also the name "Abel." Abel, son of Adam, is born in Genesis 4:2, presents an acceptable offering to the Lord in 4:4, and is murdered in 4:8 by his brother Cain. Abel's brief life reflects the literal meaning of *hebel*, making him the representative of the Preacher's sermon: a vapor, here one moment and gone the next. Genesis then records the Lord saying that Abel's blood cries out from the ground for justice (Gen 4:10), yet God does not seem to heed Abel's cry. What is the Lord doing and why? The death of Abel shapes the Preacher's confusion: the world should work one way, but appears instead to work in a different, confusing way.

Genesis 2 records the Lord God providing for all the man and the woman's needs: companionship, food, a home, the two paths of wisdom and folly, and life itself. This passage also reveals the limitations the Lord God places on human knowledge: He prohibits eating from the tree of the knowledge of good and evil. When the man and the woman cross these boundaries, the Lord God judges them, but His curses are still paired with provision. Moving forward, they will toil by the sweat of their brow yet also have food to eat. They will endure hard labor all their days and in the end die, returning to the dust from which they came, but their children will live, multiplying and filling the earth. When those children die, the cycle will continue. The Preacher's sermon examines this same cyclical pattern of human life, painting death as the ultimate vanity (*hebel*). Echoing the return to dust in Genesis 3, the Preacher ends his sermon with humanity's journey back to the dust of the earth (Eccl 12:1-7). Both passages cast God as the sovereign Creator of all and specifically extend that sovereignty to His arrangements over life and death.

Ecclesiastes: An Outline

Detailed outlines of Ecclesiastes abound. For the purposes of this book, an overview suffices nicely. Ecclesiastes refers to the Preacher from two different perspectives: from the third person (he, him, his) and from the first person (I, me, my). The two third-person sections bracket the first-person section, creating an editor's frame around the Preacher's sermon. These two voices combine to form the whole of the text:

The Editor's Opening Frame: Introductory Summary (Eccl 1:1-11)

> The frame editor summarizes the Preacher's words: "vanity of vanities" (*habel habalim*). He then asks what advantage humans gain from all their labor, answering his own question with a poetic portrayal of the repeated, seemingly profitless cycles of creation's labor.
>
> > *The Preacher's Sermon* (Eccl 1:12-12:7)
> >
> > > Part One: the Preacher's personal experience with *hebel* (Eccl 1:12-2:26)
> > >
> > > Part Two: the Preacher's observations on the times of life (Eccl 3:1-12:7)

The Editor's Closing Frame: Concluding Summary (Eccl 12:8-14)

> The editor evaluates the words of the Preacher, ultimately urging readers to fear God and keep His commandments.[96]

A note on authorship: Ecclesiastes does not identify the editor and reveals only that the Preacher was a wise king of Israel in Jerusalem (Eccl 1:12-16). The Preacher also never identifies himself, only calling himself "Preacher" (*qohelet*). Though this Preacher could very well be King Solomon, *Voices of the Sages* uses his self-attributed title to identify him, leaving discussions of his identity to other scholars.

Major Themes: *Hebel*, the Good Life, and the Limitations of Human Knowledge

> *1. Hebel*

The editor summarizes the Preacher's message rather succinctly: everything is *hebel*. *Hebel* goes on to appear over forty times in

---

[96] The chapter on the book of Job addresses the fear of the Lord more fully.

Ecclesiastes, presenting scholars and translators with much to discuss. *Hebel's* basic root or literal meaning is "vapor" or "breath." Depending on its context, English versions translate *hebel* as "vanity, useless, futile, meaningless, emptiness, or fleeting."[97] The word's scope of meaning forms part of the Preacher's focus: the indecipherability of life. To allow readers to feel the flexibility of the term, this chapter does not translate *hebel* into English. The frame editor and the Preacher offer many examples of *hebel*:

- Pleasure (Eccl 2:1)

- Dissatisfaction with money/wealth (Eccl 5:10)

- The righteous dying and the wicked living (Eccl 7:15)

- The righteous and wicked being treated contrary to expectations (Eccl 8:14)

- Youth and the prime of life (Eccl 11:10)

After many of these statements, the Preacher likens *hebel* to chasing, grasping, or striving after wind (Eccl 1:14, 2:11 and 26, etc). This phrase depicts humans expending energy toward a goal, yet in the end having nothing to show for their labor. Both the editor and the Preacher connect *hebel* to a lack of profit (Eccl 1:3, 2:11). This futility becomes particularly clear in light of the end of a human life: death is the ultimate and universal experience of *hebel*. After all of *'adam*'s labor and striving, their lasting contribution to the world is apparently nothing at all. All *'adam* dies, returning to the dust (Gen 3:17-19; Eccl 12:1-8). This explanation rings true and leaves readers looking for Ecclesiastes' answer to this human problem.

The Preacher's sermon then further examines the *hebel* of life outside the Garden. The ground is cursed and does not cooperate

---

97 Michael V. Fox argues that *hebel* ought to be understood as "absurdity." He writes, "As I see it, *hebel* designates not the mysterious but [...] the manifestly irrational or meaningless" (411). He goes on to explain that "the absurd" is what is contrary to expectations. Expecting reasonableness in the universe, the preacher is frustrated by the absurdity he sees in every area. See "The Meaning of *hebel* for Qohelet" *Journal of Biblical Literature* 105 (3): 409-427.

with human efforts. *'Adam* is stuck in a continuous cycle: work to eat, eat to work, work to eat, and so forth all the days of their lives until they die. Like Abel, humans are *hebel*, here one moment and gone the next, leaving nothing behind. However, the Preacher's worldview is not pessimistic; he presents the realities of human life under the sun outside the Garden as God organized it. All this *hebel* comes from the hand of God. The Preacher then focuses his attention on how to live as *'adam* in all this *hebel*: fear God (Eccl 3:14, 5:7, 12:13).

2. The Good Life

While the Preacher candidly outlines the futility and pain within God's *hebel* world, he also highlights its goodness. The Lord God provided a good life for the man and the woman in the Garden of Delight (*'eden*). When He exiled them because of their sin, He sent them away with good gifts still in hand: children so that the human race would continue, the ability to work and grow food from the cursed ground, clothing, and the bond of marriage so they would not be alone. Within the pain, toil, and death that characterize human life, the Lord God remains merciful. Humans can still enjoy the good life outside the Garden. As Ecclesiastes explains, celebratory events—feasts, for instance—underscore the goodness of life with food, song, fellowship, thankfulness, and joy. Daily life, too, contains good: even a simple meal offers a moment of the good life under the sun. Though some call him a hedonist for his focus on these pleasurable moments (Eccl 2:24-26, 3:12-13 and 22, 5:18-20, 8:15, 9:7-10), the Preacher is neither a pessimist nor a hedonist; he simply recognizes that God has given good gifts to humanity within their *hebel* lives. *'Adam*'s proper response to these gifts is to enjoy them and fear God.

3. The Limitations of Human Knowledge

In the Garden of Eden, the Lord God limited human knowledge by forbidding the man and the woman to eat the fruit of the tree of the knowledge of good and evil (Gen 2:17). In Ecclesiastes, the Preacher focuses in on this reality. The Preacher's "Who knows …?" questions appear time and time again, pinpointing the limits of human knowledge in this *hebel* world. For instance, Ecclesiastes 6:12 reads:

> 6:12   For who knows what is good for man while he lives the few days of his *hebel* life, which he passes like a shadow?

This verse likens *hebel* to a shadow (*tsel*), an image lacking any substance of its own, appearing, disappearing, shifting by the hour. Looking at the events of a human life—birth, death, feasts, holidays, jobs, weddings—the Preacher points out that humans do not know in the moment if these events will ultimately prove good or bad. How many initially joyous weddings or births ultimately lead to sorrow and heartache? Only God knows in real time. According to the Preacher, "God has so worked that 'adam should fear Him" (Eccl 3:14); these limitations drive 'adam to his Creator.

The Sages in Conversation

1. Hebel

Though Ecclesiastes mentions *hebel* the most, *hebel* also appears in other books in the Writings. The parallelism in these verses provides more insight into the word's meaning as the word pairs either amplify or contrast one another:

- Job 7:16 – *hebel* // forever
- Job 21:34 – *hebel* // faithless
- Job 35:16 – *hebel* // without knowledge
- Psalm 31:6 – worthless idols (*hebel*) // the Lord (*YHWH*)
- Psalm 62:9 – *hebel* // lie
- Psalm 78:33 – *hebel* // terror
- Psalm 94:11 – *hebel* // the thoughts, devices, plans of 'adam

- Psalm 144:4 – *hebel* // a passing shadow (*tsel*)
- Proverbs 13:11 – *hebel* // work (*yad*, lit. "hand")
- Lamentations 4:17 – *hebel* // fail

On the whole, the words expanding *hebel* indicate an absence or insubstantiality; like steam, *hebel* contains no substance and rapidly vanishes into nothing. On the other hand, the words that contrast *hebel* emphasize permanence, the hand that produces work, and that which relates to the Lord. This pattern continues as the sages of Ecclesiastes and Psalms engage in conversation, surely over a delicious meal with good wine provided by the Preacher.

David appears to share the Preacher's perspective on *hebel* in Psalm 39; twice, the psalm states "surely all *'adam* is a mere breath" (*hebel*, 39:5, 11). David comments specifically on the brevity of his own life (Ps 39:4-6):

39:4   O Lord, make me know **my end**

And what is the measure of **my days**;

Let me know how **fleeting** I am!

5   Behold, you have made my days a **few handbreadths**,

And my lifetime is as **nothing** before you.

Surely all mankind stands as a **mere breath**! *Selah*

6   Surely a man goes about as a **shadow**!

Surely for **nothing** they are in turmoil;

Man heaps up wealth and **does not know** who will gather [it]!

After initially talking about himself personally, David expands his situation to apply to all *'adam* (Ps 39:5); in this psalm as in Ecclesiastes, all *'adam* are *hebel*, a breath, a shadow, a fleeting nothing, a handsbreadth.

However, both David and the Preacher also appear to understand *hebel* to be the context of human life outside the Garden, not the direct result of a person's sin. This difference matters; if *hebel* is the context of life and not directly caused by one's sin, *'adam* can hope to experience good in this life. In Psalm 39, David pleads with the Lord to alleviate his guilt, reproach, and sorrow for sin, to look away that David may smile (*balag*) before he departs and is no more (Ps 39:8, 12, 13). Though he does not address God's forgiveness, the Preacher repeatedly states that the good life comes from the hand of God (Eccl 2:24-25, 3:13). David and the Preacher agree: the Creator's good gifts allow *'adam* to experience good and joy within the *hebel* of their fleeting life.

Here Moses enters the conversation through Psalm 90. Since, as mentioned above, *hebel* is often contrasted with eternity, the relationship between these two concepts deserves examination. Ecclesiastes 3:11 states:

> 3:11 He has made everything beautiful in its time.
> Also, He has put eternity in man's heart, yet
> he (*'adam*) cannot find out what God has done
> from the beginning to the end.

This eternity stamped on the heart of *'adam* leaves humans dissatisfied with the *hebel* nature of their lives and world.[98] In Psalm 90:1-6, Moses contrasts this transience of human life with the eternity of God (Ps 90:2-3):

> 90:2 Before the mountains were brought forth,
>
> Or ever you had formed the earth and the world,
>
> From everlasting to everlasting you are God.

---

[98] This stamp may be a reference to the image of God in *'adam* from Genesis 1:26.

> 3   You return man (*'enosh*) to dust
>
> And say, "Return, O children of man (*'adam*)!"

Like the grass that initially flourishes but soon withers into dust (Ps 90:5-6), human life is brief. Humans live a mere seventy or eighty years; the "pride" of our life is labor and sorrow (Ps 90:10). Therefore, Moses petitions the Lord (Ps 90:12):

> 90:12   So teach us to number our days
>
> That we may get a heart of wisdom.

These words of Moses expand the Preacher's advice to fear God. Because *'adam* possesses something of God's eternity, the reality that we ultimately only replenish the ground with dust causes humans anxiety—attuned to eternity, *'adam* alone cannot escape *hebel*. In response to this anxiety, Moses and the Preacher point *'adam* to the fear of the Lord. The *hebel* of human life drives *'adam* to learn to number their days, finding eternal significance within this *hebel* life, in working, doing good, and seeking wisdom. With this focus, *'adam* fears God and lives in relationship with their Creator.

As mentioned above, the ultimate *hebel* is death itself. The Preacher concludes his sermon with a funeral procession: people mourn while a human body is led to a cemetery for burial (Eccl 12:7). Immediately following this closing chapter of Ecclesiastes, Lamentations opens with Lady Jerusalem sitting in a ruin, alone, surrounded by death (Lam 1:1). Having broken their covenant with the Lord, Jerusalem and Judah are destroyed and exiled—they are no more. Like flourishing grass, David's kingdom rose to prominence and greatness under Solomon. Solomon ruled in peace over the greatest kingdom of his time, built a magnificent house for the Lord, and hosted surrounding kings and queens seeking his wisdom. Yet David and Solomon's sons did not fear the Lord, leading the people toward Jerusalem's destruction and exile (2 Chron 36:11-21). Lamentations bears witness to the destruction of the Preacher's once great city and kingdom. Imagine the Preacher's reaction, learning from the sage of Lamentations that his city and kingdom were destroyed—seemingly a vapor, *hebel*.

The sages then turn their attention to the people's question: has the Lord rejected his people completely? (Lam 5:22) Will Jerusalem remain dust forever? Lamentations' most famous passage, "great is thy faithfulness" (Lam 3:23), offers hope in the center of the book, but surprisingly, the book's ending prayer makes no reference to this hope. Instead, Lamentations concludes with the death of the kingdom in exile and a petition that the Lord restore his people "as in days of old" (Lam 5:21). The request is present, but hope in the Lord Himself is not explicit in this request. The people seem to ask in disbelief, "Was our kingdom *hebel*, too?" Psalm 89 ends in similar fashion. Although mostly detailing the Lord's covenant faithfulness to David (Ps 89:1-37), the psalm concludes by describing the fall of the Davidic kingdom (89:38-45). Ethan, the psalmist, asks the Lord, "How long will you wait?" and "Where is your former lovingkindness (*hesed*)?" (Ps 89:46, 49), petitioning the Lord to forgive and redeem His servants. After voicing Israel's pain at the now obvious *hebel* of the Davidic kingdom, both texts end by asking the Lord to restore His city and His people. Like widow Jerusalem, Israel sits in the dust, wails, and waits.

The return from exile does not materialize until Cyrus the Persian's decree in 2 Chronicles. When it does take place, this return disappoints: only a remnant goes back to Jerusalem, the Lord's presence does not fill the rebuilt temple, and no Davidic King reigns on the throne. Israel must wait still longer for the eternal king and kingdom promised to David in 1 Chronicles 17. Until then, Lamentations, Ethan the psalmist, and the Preacher concur: Israel and Jerusalem epitomize the truth that *'adam* and his world are indeed *hebel*. Though the other texts in the Writings offer deeper treatments of the Lord's ability to overcome the *hebel* of creation and kingdom, the sages in this conversation struggle to find that hope themselves.

2. The Good Life

Ecclesiastes 3:1-7 teaches that *'adam*'s life vacillates between extremes: love and hate, war and peace, weeping and laughter, etc. The Preacher attributes the good days as well as the bad/evil (*ra‘*) ones to the Lord (Eccl 7:13-14), emphasizing the bittersweet taste of *'adam*'s life amidst all the *hebel* outside the Garden. The Preacher then names God's gifts to *'adam*: work, food, clothing, and marriage (Eccl 9:7-10), the very gifts the man and the woman carried with them as they left the Garden. In the midst of the *hebel* of life, God extends joy and goodness to *'adam* through the blessings of word, food, clothing, and marriage, among others. These good gifts come exclusively from God; any human who enjoys them does so as the recipient of God's blessing (Eccl 2:24-25, 3:13, 5:18-20, 9:7-9). The sages of Job, Psalms, Ruth, Proverbs, and the Song all clamor into this conversation.

Job provides a clear example of a good life. According to the adversary in Job 1, the Lord had blessed the work of Job's hands, increased his possessions, and created a hedge of goodness around His servant (Job 1:10). Job himself confirms these blessings: his days were "bathed in butter," he was respected by men of repute, and in many respects, he held king-like status in his community, enjoying the goodness of life from the hand of the Lord (Job 29:6, 7-11, 21-25). Once Job's sufferings end, the Lord restores Job's good life two-fold (Job 42:10-17), again demonstrating that both good and evil (*ra‘*) come from God.

Psalm 112 extends this good life to those who fear the Lord and delight in His commandments. Using much the same vocabulary as the book of Job, the psalmist depicts the life of the God-fearer: parent of blessed children, manager of wealth, reveling in "light," servant of the poor (Ps 112:2-9). In the book of Ruth, Boaz serves as a living example of such a man, one whose productive fields and abundant harvests come from God. When Boaz marries Ruth, the townsfolk foresee the house he and Ruth will build through their child, earning them wealth and fame in Israel (Ruth 4:11-12). Like Job, Ruth and Boaz, the man and woman of virtue, live the good life from the hand of the Lord.

Proverbs offers a different angle on the topic, contrasting the good life of the wise with the disastrous life of the foolish. Proverbs 31 acts as a summary of Proverbs 10-31, listing the elements of this good life. The wise person, represented by the woman of virtue:

- Enjoys and does good, not evil (Prov 31:12)
- Provides food for all (Prov 31:14-15)
- Profits from labor (Prov 31:16-19, 24)
- Provides for the needy (Prov 31:20)
- Has confidence for the future (Prov 31:21-25)
- Speaks the *torah* of kindness (*hesed*) (Prov 31:26)
- Deserves and receives blessing and praise from the community (Prov 31:28-31)

This list could easily describe Job, Boaz, and Ruth. Though each person's life also contains suffering and pain, amidst the *hebel*, the Lord provides moments and seasons of joy and blessing for His people, particularly in the areas of productivity, wealth, and reputation.

Here the Song of Songs chimes in. As the chapter on the Song discusses at length, the Song describes the woman and the man longing for love. Re-creating Eden with the man and the woman in a garden setting, the Song depicts the love between the man and the woman as one of the best gifts of God—if not the best gift. Again, joy and good are mixed with suffering. The dream sequences in the Song develop the contrast between the joyful and painful aspects of love. In both dreams, the woman searches for her lover. In the first dream sequence, the woman finds him quickly; in the second, after rejecting her lover's advances, she seeks him but is beaten by the night watchmen (Song 5:7). Together, these two scenes cast separation between lovers as one of the most painful experiences of life. The Song sings of lovers belonging together and longing to be one; this unity should not be disturbed. In His goodness, the Lord God has given passionate love between lovers to *'adam* as an oasis of joy within the *hebel* life. In the midst of the pain and toil of life outside the Garden, the man and the woman find solace in each other and rejoice together. According to the Song, marriage links lovers outside the garden back to 'eden, the Garden of Delight.

At the same time, the Preacher recognizes that love and marriage are also *hebel*. Ecclesiastes 9:9 reads:

> 9:9 Enjoy life with the wife whom you love, all the days of your vain (*hebel*) life that he has given you under the sun, because that is your portion (*heleq*) in life and in your toil at which you toil under the sun.

Within the context of the brevity of life, the days of love with one's spouse are *'adam*'s portion, reward, or lot (*heleq*) amidst a brief life of toil. The preacher understands marriage to be a respite, God's gift to humanity, but like everything under the sun, marriage is *hebel*—it lasts only "till death do us part."

Though some read Ecclesiastes as a hedonistic outlier in the OT, the Preacher speaks many of the same truths as his companions in the Writings: *hebel* is the context of living, a fact of *'adam*'s life outside the garden. Yet within that context, the Lord God continues to bless *'adam* with good gifts. While the Writings certainly highlight the Lord's blessing on those who fear Him, these gifts are by no means exclusive—any *'adam* enjoying these gifts is basking in the goodness of the Creator.

3. The Limitations of Human Wisdom

As discussed above, Ecclesiastes traces good and evil (*ra'*) within human life back to the Lord God (Eccl 1:13). English versions often translate *ra'* in Ecclesiastes 1:13 as "grievous, unhappy, tragic, or a sore business." The same word appears in Job 2:10: Job says he should accept both good and evil/ calamity (*ra'*) from the Lord. All human endeavors outside the Garden come tinged with pain and toil; finding and understanding wisdom proves no exception. Ecclesiastes 1:13 specifically casts human exploration into the works of *'adam* as a calamitous/evil (*ra'*) task. According to the Preacher, God has afflicted this evil upon *'adam*; in other words, the searching out of everything done under the sun is a calamity given to *'adam* by God. The Preacher continues (Eccl 1:18):

> 1:18 For in much wisdom is much vexation, and he who increases knowledge increases sorrow.

This vexation comes through in several areas in Ecclesiastes, as the Preacher explains that wisdom was too far and too deep for him. In apparent exasperation, he asks "Who can find it?" (Eccl 7:23-24). The Preacher had hoped to understand everything done under the sun, all the work of God (Eccl 3:11). Like all humans, he remains caught between his desire to understand the larger picture of life and his finite nature. No matter how much we search, humans simply cannot understand the ultimate significance of human or divine deeds (Eccl 8:17, 3:11). Ecclesiastes paints *'adam* as bounded by ignorance:

- Who knows what is good for *'adam* in life? (Eccl 6:12)
- Who can tell what will happen to *'adam* after him under the sun? (Eccl 6:12)
- If no one knows what will happen, who can tell when that thing will happen? (Eccl 8:17)
- *'adam* does not know what awaits him: it could be love or hatred (Eccl 9:1).
- *'adam* does not know his time; like fish taken in an evil net and birds caught in a snare, so the children of *'adam* are snared at an evil time, when evil suddenly falls upon them (Eccl 9:12).

Just as *'adam*'s life and deeds have limited, finite profit (Eccl 2:10), so also *'adam*'s knowledge of the world is limited. God has set up human life so that *'adam* cannot comprehend the work of God or humans "from the beginning to the end" (Eccl 3:11). With eternity stamped on our hearts but without the ability to find all knowledge, humans are driven to turn to God in trust and faith. Ecclesiastes calls this turn the fear of the Lord.[99]

Still treating this topic of the limitations of human knowledge, the book of Job reaches the same conclusion as the Preacher via a different route. Job 28:12-13 contrasts the success of human mining for gold and jewels with humans' inability to find wisdom:

> 28:12 But where shall wisdom be found?
>
> And where is the place of understanding?
>
> 13   Man (*'enosh*) does not know its worth,
>
> And it is not found in the land of the living.

Humans can dig mines and find treasure deep in the earth, but such a search cannot reveal wisdom; it is "hidden from the eyes of the living" (Job 28:21). According to Job 28:23-24, from His unique vantage point outside creation,

> 28:23 God understands the way to [wisdom],
>
> And he knows its place.
>
> 24   For he looks to the ends of the earth
>
> And sees everything under the heavens.

Because He is not bounded by His creation, the Creator can see everything in the world clearly. This passage in Job 28 plays an important interpretive role in the book of Job by helping readers appraise the thoughts of Job, his three friends, and Elihu. These men may have understood pieces of wisdom, but they are unable to fully understand their situation: they cannot step outside the created world to observe

---

[99] For a full discussion on the fear of the Lord, see Chapter 4 on the book of Job.

the heavenly dialogues between the Lord and the adversary recorded in Job 1-2. Because of their status as creatures, these friends of Job begin and end the book cut off from full wisdom and understanding.

Underscoring their finitude even more, Job and his friends do not recognize the limits of their own wisdom; they debate and assess Job's situation full of confidence in their ability to understand why Job is afflicted. Unlike the Preacher, who investigates and then concludes that he is unable to understand (Eccl 1:13-17, 3:10-11, 7:23-25, 8:17), Job learns about his limitations only when the Lord directly teaches Job about them (Job 38-39). The book of Job does not record Job's friends ever learning this lesson; through its silence, the text allows readers to assume Job's friends continued pontificating in their ignorance, until the Lord forgave their folly through Job (Job 42:7-9). In their respective texts, the Preacher and Job stand out as wise men, acknowledging and living within the limitations of their human knowledge, fearing God during their *hebel* life.

Proverbs urges its readers to live similarly to Job and the Preacher, specifically by recognizing their limited knowledge. Many proverbs remind the wise not to be wise in their own eyes (Proverbs 12:15, 14:12, 16:25, 21:2, 26:12, 28:26). For instance, Proverbs 3 reads:

> 3:5   Trust in the Lord with all your heart,
>
> And do not lean on your own understanding.
>
> 3:7   Be not wise in your own eyes;
>
> Fear the Lord, and turn away from evil.

Proverbs also points to one's reaction to reproof as an indicator of wisdom or folly. The one who recognizes his limitations increases in wisdom (Prov 15:31-33):

> 15:31   The ear that listens to life-giving reproof
>
> Will dwell among the wise.

32	Whoever ignores instruction despises himself,
	But he who listens to reproof gains intelligence.
33	The fear of the Lord is instruction in wisdom,
	And humility comes before honor.

A wise person listens humbly, open to being corrected and reproved from wrong, incomplete, or foolish thinking (Proverbs 19:20, 25:12, 27:6). Even wise Agur testifies to his ignorance in Proverbs 30:2-3:

30:2	Surely I am too stupid to be a man.
	I have not the understanding of a man.
3	I have not learned wisdom,
	Nor have I knowledge of the Holy One.

Given the wisdom and insight he offers in Proverbs 30, Agur appears to be using some hyperbole here; however, his warning against foolishly exalting oneself stands (Prov 30:32). The person wise in their own eyes is not wise at all. As the introduction to Proverbs explains, the wise increase in knowledge by listening to wise advice (Prov 1:5). Hating knowledge and instruction/discipline (*musar*) is the mark of a fool (Prov 1:7 and 22, 5:3-14).

The sage of the book of Daniel, having listened patiently, now offers his contribution on the limits of human knowledge. In Daniel 2, Nebuchadnezzar seeks a trustworthy interpretation of his dream and so demands that his wise men tell him both the dream and its interpretation (Dan 2:4-11). Exasperated, his wise men openly declare the limits of their knowledge: no human can know the dream—dreams are the purview of the gods, those who do not dwell with humans (Dan 2:10-11). Even the wisest of humans recognize that they are cut off from certain knowledge. When Daniel is called upon this scene, he, too, affirms that no human can give the king what he asks for. Daniel clearly attributes his knowledge of the dream and its interpretation to his God (Dan 2:27-28). Similar events take place in Daniel 4-5, when the king again calls for Daniel, the Jewish exile with "a spirit of the holy gods" (Dan 5:14-16). What humans cannot know, Daniel knows because of his gift from God Most High (see also Dan 5:8-16).[100]

These sages concur: though *'adam* is able to search out and find some wisdom and knowledge, *'adam*'s status as creation limits humans' knowledge, no matter how laboriously they seek it out. Though *'adam* can search out some truth, wisdom and understanding come only from the Creator.

Toward the New Testament

1. Hebel

The NT also recognizes the *hebel* world God has given humans to live in. According to Paul, God subjected the creation to "futility" (*mataiotes*, Rom 8:20). The NT's answer to the *hebel/mataiotes* world is eternal life; Paul explains that creation will be delivered from this current corruption through the redemption of the body, the glorious resurrection life (Rom 8:21). Paul's letters further develop Ecclesiastes' teachings about eternity in *'adam*'s heart and the future judgment of a person's deeds (Eccl 3:11, 12:14). What Ecclesiastes hints at, Paul explicitly states: the pain and death of this *hebel/mataiotes* world will one day be resolved in the resurrection of Christians and subsequent redemption of all creation. In 1 Corinthians 15, his most developed instruction on the resurrection, Paul urges his readers to apply this truth in their daily lives:

> 15:58 Therefore, my beloved brothers, be steadfast, immovable, always abounding in the work of the Lord, knowing that in the Lord your labor is not in vain.

Paul's concluding point echoes Ecclesiastes: although the life of a Christian is finite, the resurrection guarantees that service to the Lord

---

[100] For an extended discussion of Daniel as the quintessential wise man, see Chapter 11.

will not be in vain. Christians will be judged for our actions, whether good or bad, during our *hebel* life (2 Cor 5:10; 1 Cor 4:5). Paul and the Preacher both focus the reader on this final verdict: in the end, everything will matter.

2. The Good Life

Though creation has been subjected to futility (*mataiotes*), the NT also upholds its goodness. In 1 Timothy 4:1-5, Paul warns the church about false teachers who deny the goodness of creation, marriage, and food. Paul corrects this false teaching:

> 4:4 For everything created by God is good, and nothing is to be rejected if it is received with thanksgiving,
>
> 5 for it is made holy by the word of God and prayer.

Even though the Lord cursed the ground due to *'adam*'s sin in the garden (Gen 3:17), Paul testifies to the goodness of creation. The Preacher and Paul affirm that amidst the *hebel/mataiotes* of life, everything created by God is good—not just marriage and food. Christians should receive and enjoy all of God's creation gifts with thanksgiving; these are God's grace to *'adam*. In the above passage, Paul goes one step further and declares that the Word of God and prayer sanctify these creation gifts. This verse suggests that receiving and enjoying God's creation gifts are part of Christian worship. In 1 Corinthians 10:31, Paul teaches that whatever we do, whether we eat or drink, we should do it all to the glory of God. A Christian life of glorifying and worshipping God includes and embraces even the most mundane aspects of life: eating, drinking, waking, working. Once again, everything in this *hebel* world matters; our offering of worship to God is made up of the entirety of our human life (Rom 12:1).

3. The Limitations of Human Knowledge

The NT emphasizes the three Christian virtues of faith, hope, and love, presenting faith as the opposite of sight (2 Cor 5:7). Within this context, 1 Corinthians 13:12 addresses the limitations of human knowledge:

> 13:12 For now we see in a mirror dimly, but then face to face. Now I know in part; then I shall know fully, even as I have been fully known.

The word translated "dimly" is the Greek word *ainigma*, the linguistic root of the word "enigma." In Greek, *ainigma* carries the sense of a riddle or an obscure, puzzling saying as in Proverbs 1:6. The above verse pairs seeing and knowing as parallel to one another. For now, humans see God or spiritual truths as enigmas, but in the end, we shall know them as we have been known by our Creator. Thus, walking by faith, living with partial knowledge, characterizes not only the wise of the OT but the NT Christian experience as well.

Using language similar to the Preacher's sermon on the *hebel* world and the issue of profit, James 4:13-15 reads:

> 4:13 Come now, you who say, "Today or tomorrow we will go into such and such a town and spend a year there and trade and **make a profit**"—
>
> 14 yet **you do not know** what tomorrow will bring. What is your life? For you are a **mist** (*atmis*) that appears **for a little time and then vanishes.**
>
> 15 Instead you ought to say, "**If the Lord wills**, we will live and do this or that."

In both Ecclesiastes and James, we humans do not know what the future will bring (Eccl 9:1, 10:14), neither do we know whether our labor will bring a profit (Eccl 11:1-7). James even uses the same metaphor as the Preacher: a mist or vapor (*hebel*, *atmis*). In our short lifetime before we vanish into the dust of the ground, Christians must look to the sovereignty of God for an eternally profitable existence.

Further Reading

Fox, Michael V. *A Time to Tear Down and a Time to Build Up: A Rereading of Ecclesiastes.* Grand Rapids: Eerdmans, 1999.

Gibson, David. *Living Life Backward: How Ecclesiastes Teaches Us to Live in Light of the End.* Wheaton, IL: Crossway, 2017.

Goh, Samuel T. S. "The *Hebel* World, Its Ambiguities and Contradictions." *Journal for the Study of the Old Testament* 45 (2): 198–216.

Huovila, Kimmo, and Dan Lioy. "The Meaning of *Hebel* in Ecclesiastes." *Conspectus* 27: 35–49.

Kynes, Will, and Katharine J. Dell. *Reading Ecclesiastes Intertextually.* Library of Hebrew Bible/Old Testament Studies. New York, NY: Bloomsbury T & T Clark, 2016.

Seufert, Matthew. "The Presence of Genesis in Ecclesiastes." *The Westminster Theological Journal* 78 (2): 75–92.

Lamentations: Suffering and Hope

Old Testament Background for Lamentations

- The blessings and curses of the covenant: Deut 28; Lev 26
- The causes of the exile: 2 Kings 17:7-23
- The siege, destruction, and fall of city, temple, and people:
    - 2 Kings 24-25
    - 2 Chron 36
- The fall of Jerusalem in prophecy:
    - Jeremiah
    - Habakkuk
    - Zephaniah
- The fall of Jerusalem in poetry: Book III of the Psalter

Creation and Lamentations: Judgment and Death

At first glance, the book of Lamentations does not seem directly related to Genesis 1-4 and its creation themes. Upon further reflection, several continuities emerge when readers pair the Garden of Eden and the temple, two meeting places for the Lord and His people. Both places feature gold, water, people listening to the *torah* of the Lord, and cherubim guards. These similarities continue as the people of Israel follow in the foolish footsteps of Adam and do not listen to the voice of the Lord. Consequently, the Lord drives them out to the east, exiling them because of their sin. In both cases, the Lord's judgment is death. Both books look to the Lord in the aftermath of their fall from grace: humanity's in Genesis and Israel's in Lamentations.

Lamentations: An Outline

In brief, Lamentations is a poetic, synoptic version of the fall of Jerusalem narrated in Kings and Chronicles. This book, called *'ekhah* in

Hebrew, opens with mourning and hopelessness:[101]

> 1:1 How (*'ekhah*) lonely sits the city
>
> That was full of people!
>
> How (*'ekhah*) like a widow has she become,
>
> She who was great among the nations!
>
> She who was a princess among provinces
>
> Has become a slave.

These lines set the tone for a series of funeral songs or dirges. Four of the five chapters take the form of an alphabetic acrostic, a typical wisdom poem following the sequence of letters in the Hebrew alphabet. Additionally, each chapter contains a different speaker. Outlined, Lamentations can look like this:

Chapter 1: a 22-verse acrostic featuring Lady Jerusalem

Chapter 2: a 22-verse acrostic featuring a prophetic observer

Chapter 3: a 66 (22 x 3) verse acrostic in the voice of an afflicted man

Chapter 4: a 22-verse acrostic again featuring the prophetic observer

Chapter 5: a 22-verse pseudo-acrostic[102] in the voice of a chorus

Layering theme into form and voice, the book of Lamentations forms a chiasm:[103]

---

101 *'ekhah* also begins Lamentations chapters 2 and 4.

102 The 22 verses of Lamentations 5 match the number of letters in the Hebrew alphabet but not their order.

103 Elie Assis offers a detailed study of the parallelisms between chapters 1 and 5: widowhood (1:1, 5:3), the past (1:7, 5:21), weeping (1:16, 5:17-18), loss/pain (1:20, 22, 5:15, 17), mourning (1:4, 5:14-15), unrest (1:3, 5:5), servitude (1:3, 14-15, 5:5, 8, 13), shame (1:6, 5:12), and economic distress (1:11, 5:9). "The Unity of the Book of Lamentations." *The Catholic Biblical Quarterly* 71 (2): 306–29.

Lamentations 1 – The immediate aftermath of the fall of Jerusalem
    Lamentations 2 – The Lord's wrath on Jerusalem described
        Lamentations 3 – The prayer of the afflicted man
    Lamentations 4 – Jerusalem's desolate present vs. glorious past
Lamentations 5 – The later aftermath of the fall of Jerusalem

This chiasm highlights the central theme of the book at its center, chapter 3: Israel's suffering and need of repentance. Within the OT Writings, Lamentations finds its home in the *Megilloth*, a group of books within the Writings introduced by Proverbs and featuring women (see Introduction). The *Megilloth* collection also forms a chiasm;[104] Lamentations and the Song are paired in the progression to and from the fulcrum, Ecclesiastes:

          a. Ruth
            b. Song of Songs
Proverbs   c. Ecclesiastes
            b'. Lamentations
          a'. Esther

The books of Ruth and Esther form an easy couple: both narratives highlight women of wisdom who mediate God's salvation of His people. Lamentations and the Song offer a more surprising duo. Since both books feature chiastic structure with multiple voices, the similarities in form highlight the contrasts between the content of their texts. Whereas in the Song the man and the woman enjoy goodness and joy in their "garden" of delight (*'eden*), in Lamentations Lady Jerusalem sits alone weeping within the destroyed city, her "garden" of death. If the Song is the best human song, then Lamentations is the most tragic.

---

104 See Stone, *Megilloth*, 205.

Major Themes: Lady Jerusalem, the Lord's Judgment, and the Hope of the Afflicted Man

1. Lady Jerusalem

Lamentations 1 presents a first-person perspective on the desolation of Jerusalem and Judah at the hands of the Lord, through her enemies. Despised and destroyed, she turns to onlookers to witness the pain the Lord has afflicted upon her (Lam 1:12, 18). Her cries echo Psalm 22:1-2:

> 22:1 My God, my God, why have you forsaken me?
>
> Why are you so far from saving me, from the words of my groaning?
>
> 2 O my God, I cry by day, but you do not answer,
>
> And by night, but I find no rest.

No comforter approaches her (Lam 1:16, 21); no one comes to her side in her distress (Lam 1:2, 7, 9, 17). She sits in the dust—a widow, deserted and alone. The prophetic observer later seeks to comfort her (Lam 2:13, 4:22), but his efforts fail. She sits, frozen in time,[105] desperately seeking comfort and relief in vain.

Lady Jerusalem then continues with a call for vengeance against her enemies. While she recognizes the Lord's righteousness and her sin against Him and His commands (Lam 1:14, 18, 20), her petition for the Lord to look upon her desolation implies that if He did, He would certainly step in to judge her enemies. She ends her first speech by urging the Lord to deal with her enemies the same way He dealt with her. In her second speech, her tone rises to the level of indignation; she implies that the Lord has gone too far in His judgment (Lam 2:20-22). How could the Lord treat His own people worse than her idolatrous neighbor nations? Lastly, though Lady Jerusalem does recognize the Lord's justice and her many sins, she stops short of seeking forgiveness.

---

105 English versions translate this notion of time by using present and present perfect verbs.

Her words do not speak of a contrite heart, appeal to the Lord's *hesed*, or recount His great deeds of the past. She acknowledges her sin, but as a confession, her words fall flat.

2. The Lord's Judgment

Lamentations 2 changes the focus to the Lord's wrath, beginning with a description of the Lord's destruction of His city (Lam 2:1-10). The verbs in particular create a picture of the Lord completely undoing, overthrowing, and bringing Jerusalem to naught: swallowed (2:2, 5), not sparing (2:2, 8), cut off (2:3), destroying (2:5, 6, 8, 9), causing to be forgotten (2:6), and abandoning (2:7). The Lord actively destroys every facet of Jerusalem's life and society. In His wrath, the Lord has un-created His city, leaving only desolation and death.

Guided by the four voices of the five chapters of the book, readers come to expect the Lord to answer the cries of His people. Much like the book of Job, Lamentations envelops the reader with the people's frustration, loss, and loneliness as they suffer, begging the Lord to speak. However, unlike in the book of Job, in Lamentations, the Lord remains silent. The text refers to some of the Lord's commands indirectly and generally (1:10, 17-18 and 21, 2:17, 3:37-38). For instance, in chapter 3, the afflicted man says, "You came near when I called on you; you said, 'Do not fear'" (Lam 3:58), but he offers no further detail clarifying when the Lord spoke or in what context. The closest Lamentations and her readers get to hearing the voice of God is this second hand, mediated report. And when His people call on Him, the Lord, the destroyer of Israel, remains silent.

This prolonged silence leaves the people and the readers needing clarity from God regarding Lady Jerusalem's future. The choral voice in Lamentations 5 affirms the Lord's eternal reign and petitions for restoration, but also asks if the Lord has rejected Israel forever (Lam 5:19-22). The Lord reigns, but the book ends with the people still waiting for Him to look upon them and speak.

3. The Hope of the Afflicted Man

Complementing Lady Jerusalem's perspective, Lamentations also features the voice of an afflicted man (*geber*, often translated "mighty man" elsewhere). In a pattern similar to the Song, the center of Lamentations, chapter 3, provides the man's response to the plight of judged Jerusalem. His sufferings parallel those of Lady Jerusalem:

- Affliction (3:1 // 1:3-4, 7, 9)
- Wrath (3:1 // 2:2, 4, 4:11)
- Bitterness (3:5, 15, 19 // 1:2, 4)
- Desolation (3:11 // 1:4, 13, 16, 4:5, 5:18)
- The Lord's bow bent against him/her (3:12 // 2:4)

Lamentations 3:52 presents this afflicted man as an innocent sufferer, attacked by his enemies without cause. Nonetheless, he speaks in the first-person plural, "we," shouldering the nation's guilt, calling Israel to examine her ways and return to the Lord. In contrast to Lady Jerusalem, this mighty man follows David's typical lament psalm form: he acknowledges their sins, declares Israel's hope in the Lord's lovingkindness (*hesed*, Lam 3:22), and calls for the people to return to the Lord. Although the afflicted man's hope shines within the bleakness of Lady Jerusalem's desolation, his message remains isolated within the book and does not resurface in the last chapter. Readers are left feeling the tension of Israel's situation: mired in suffering and seeking hope, the people face a cloudy and uncertain future. Has the Lord forsaken His people forever?

The Sages in Conversation

1. Lady Jerusalem

As explained above, Lady Jerusalem's words focus on her rebellion (Lam 1:14, 18, 20), her petition for the Lord to look at her and see her desolation (Lam 1:9, 11, 20), and the fact that she has no comforter

(Lam 1:16, 17, 21). In essence, she tells the Lord, "Yes, I sinned, but look at me in my distress and help me." In this conversation, two sages respond to her: Psalms and Proverbs.

A comparison between Lamentations and David's penitential psalms reveals stark differences, forcing questions about the nature of Jerusalem's "confession." Psalm 38 provides a helpful parallel, as both texts describe in detail the Lord's chastening of David/Jerusalem for their sin as well as their suffering at the hands of their enemies:

David – Psalm 38	Lady Jerusalem – Lamentations 1
The Lord's anger/wrath for sin (38:1)	The Lord's anger/wrath for sin (1:5, 12-15, 17)
Totally undone (38:2-14, 17)	Totally undone (1:1, 4, 6-7, 9, 11, 15, 18-19)
Confession of sin (38:4, 18)	Acknowledgement of sin (1:14, 18, 20)
Hope in the Lord; He will answer (38:15) Petition for salvation (38:21-22)	Nothing
Enemies have the upper hand (38:19-20)	Enemies have the upper hand (1:2-3, 4, 10, 19)

As this chart demonstrates, David explicitly confesses the sin that brought on the Lord's wrath and anger. He then voices his hope in the Lord, his confidence that He will answer, and concludes with a prayer for timely deliverance. Lady Jerusalem, on the other hand, acknowledges her sin and asks for deliverance without referring to Lord's grace, *hesed*, hope, or salvation at any time. Compared to David's words, her request for the Lord to see and comfort her appears rooted in her own suffering, not in His character or promises. This difference is striking. She says, "Lord, avenge me because I suffer" while David sings, "Lord, save me because of who You are." At this point, the conversation between these sages falters: Lady Jerusalem and David both suffer and cry to the Lord for help, but Lady Jerusalem's cries veer more toward Psalm 88, the psalm of death ending with no hope. This perspective bears little resemblance to David's confidence that in His *hesed*, the Lord sees, hears, and will indeed answer His people when they turn to Him.

Now imagine Lady Wisdom responding to Lady Jerusalem. Using her words from Proverbs 1, Lady Wisdom tells Lady Jerusalem she is eating the fruit of her own way because she chose to rebel against the command of the Lord (Prov 1:29-32; Lam 1:18). The only solution for foolish Jerusalem is to turn and repent (Prov 1:23). Lady Jerusalem had repeatedly been urged to do so; she had heard the voice of wisdom many times through the Lord's prophets (2 Chron 36:15-16):

> 36:15 The Lord, the God of their fathers, sent [word] persistently to them by His messengers, because He had compassion on His people and on His dwelling place.
>
> 16 But they kept mocking the messengers of God, despising His words and scoffing at His prophets, until the wrath of the Lord rose against His people, until there was no remedy.

Jerusalem's total rejection of the word of the Lord has left her without options. According to Proverbs, such rebellion inevitably leads to death. Having embraced folly, Jerusalem herself has become a woman of folly, one whose "house is the way to Sheol, descending to the chambers of death" (Prov 7:27). Given her series of choices, Lady Jerusalem's unanswered cry for a comforter seems part and parcel of her suffering. When disaster and anguish come upon fools who have rejected wisdom, Lady Wisdom offers neither help nor comfort; instead, she laughs and mocks (Prov 1:26-27). Though Jerusalem calls out, Lady Wisdom will not answer (Prov 1:28); there is "no remedy" for the fool's suffering. In fact, even acknowledgment of sin leads nowhere. As discussed in Chapter 5, the wisdom in Proverbs does not provide a solution for sin. Perhaps in frustration, Jerusalem's pseudo-confession rapidly turns to imprecations, betraying her anger at the Lord's complete undoing of Jerusalem and implying that He acted unjustly (Lam 2:20-22). The conversation ends here, with Lady Jerusalem still wailing and Lady Wisdom sitting silently beside her, shaking her head at this foolish woman who still "doesn't get it."

2. The Lord's Judgment

Lamentations 2 paints what might be the most powerful portrait of the Lord's wrath in the OT. Though OT narrative texts tell of the Lord's anger and destruction of Jerusalem (2 Chron 36:16), Lamentations' poetic form appears by nature to intensify the picture. The Asaph psalms also focus on the Lord's judgment; in Psalms 73-83, Asaph specifically addresses the fall of Jerusalem. This overlap in theme—destruction of city and temple—prompts a conversation between Lamentations 2 and Psalms 74, 77, 80, and 83, followed by some commentary from the sages of Ecclesiastes, Esther, and Daniel.

In Lamentations 2:1-19, the prophetic observer describes the Lord's horrific judgment on His people and His city; Lady Jerusalem then responds in complaint (Lam 2:20-22). Psalms 74, 77, 80, and 83 follow this same pattern: a description of the destruction of city and temple followed by Asaph's response. At first, Asaph's psalms echo much of the language in Lamentations. For example, in Psalm 74 Asaph asks the Lord to remember Zion's desolation (74:2, 18, 22), to turn His footsteps to the ruins of Zion (74:3), not to forget the afflicted (74:19, 23), and to consider His covenant (74:20a).[106] Like Lady Jerusalem in Lamentations 1, Asaph prays for the Lord to destroy Zion's enemies, asking how long He will allow her adversaries to revile her (74:10-11, 77:7-9, 80:4). However, each of Asaph's psalms also includes a perspective shift: he turns and looks back into Israel's past to remember the great deeds of the Lord. In each case, Asaph affirms the Lord's reign and celebrates instances of the Lord's deliverance of His people: from Egypt at the Red Sea or from Midian with Gideon

---

[106] Echoing the chorus' petition in Lamentations 5:21, Psalm 80:7 and 19 repeat the refrain, "Restore us and cause your face to shine, and we will be saved."

(Ps 74:12-17, 77:14-20, 80:8-13, 83:9-13). In contrast, Lamentations seems unable to look further back than the recent event of the Lord's wrath upon Jerusalem through Babylon. Asaph's perspective offers hope and confidence for the future, but Lamentations' limited view leaves Lady Jerusalem frozen in her present grief and desolation. This may be the point of the book: for readers to get caught up in Jerusalem's suffering and distress, to experience the depth of her sorrow, guilt, and abandonment. While Lamentations casts the Lord as an angry God who destroys and ignores, Asaph's psalms frame the Lord's wrath on Jerusalem within a long history of His *hesed* and miraculous salvation. Asaph's God both destroys and rescues; in wrath He remembers mercy.

At this point in the conversation, several other sages insert themselves. The Writings' juxtaposition of Ecclesiastes and Lamentations forces the reader to ask whether, like everything else in creation, the Davidic kingdom itself is *hebel*. Ecclesiastes ends with a burial procession: every *'adam* dies, their *hebel* life ending with a return to the dust of the earth (Eccl 12:1-7). Keeping continuity of theme, Lamentations opens with funeral songs marking the death of Judah and Jerusalem; though a remnant of Israel is still alive, Lamentations repeatedly likens the exile to death (Lam 1:3, 5, 18, 2:14, 4:22). Just like Ecclesiastes, Lamentations' funeral songs mark the end of the city and the nation, offering a long sigh in response to the question of whether Israel has any future. Imagine the dismay of the Preacher, once a king in Jerusalem, hearing of the total destruction of his realm. He said and knew all was *hebel*, but listening to the details of Lamentations must be agony indeed. This Ecclesiastes-Lamentations sequence forces readers to wonder if even the kingdom is *hebel*: splendid for a brief time, but eventually returned to dust, wiped off the map without a trace.

Thankfully, Lamentations' context in the Writings addresses the question of Israel's future; the books of Esther and Ezra-Nehemiah take up the question Lamentations asks. The book of Esther, a narrative of the deliverance of the Jews during their exile in Persia, never mentions the name of God, yet the plot of the book implies that the Lord preserves His people against all odds while they live under

Gentile power and dominion. In this conversation, the book of Esther explains to Lamentations that the Lord has not totally forgotten or forsaken His people. After His wrath, His lovingkindness, compassion, and faithfulness endure; He delivers His people and punishes those who oppose them. Moving from the present to the future, the book of Daniel explicitly reveals that in the end the Lord will judge these Gentile kingdoms and usher in His eternal kingdom (Dan 2, 7, and 9). The God of Israel will restore His people and renew the days of old, the days of the Davidic king. And finally, concluding the Writings and the reassurance of the sage of Lamentations, the book of Ezra-Nehemiah narrates the people's return from exile to rebuild the city. As He promised through the prophet Jeremiah, the Lord ensures the fall of Babylon and Israel's return to the land (Ezra 1:1; Jer 25:12-36, 29:10-14; 2 Chron 36:22-23). Esther, Daniel, and Ezra-Nehemiah together affirm the Lord's reign and Israel's bright, hopeful future.

As the Writings reveal, Jerusalem's devastation at the hands of Babylon, memorialized in Lamentations, is not the final word.[107] Although these texts offer Lamentations hope in the Lord, all three books also continue to portray life as the co-existence of suffering and hope. This tension will continue until the Lord fulfills His plan to make an end of sin and bring in everlasting righteousness (Dan 9:24).

3. The Hope of the Afflicted Man

The center of the book of Lamentations features the voice of an afflicted man (*geber*). This man speaking in Lamentations 3 appears to be a representative of God's people and a co-sufferer with Lady Jerusalem. Several sages sit down to talk with him about his role, and then cede the floor to a dialogue between Lamentations and the Psalter on the *hesed* of the Lord.

The afflicted man bears a striking resemblance to Job. Lamentations 3:1-18 uses some of the same language as Job does:

---

[107] Books IV and V of the Psalter also answer the question of the future of the kingdom after the fall of Judah: the Lord and the Davidic King reign!

- Lam 3:4/Job 2:4-8 – flesh and skin waste away
- Lam 3:5/Job 19:8 – besieged
- Lam 3:8/Job 30:20 – the Lord shuts out my prayer
- Lam 3:11/Job 16:12 – torn to pieces
- Lam 3:12a/Job 6:4 – bent His bow against me
- Lam 3:14, 63/Job 30:9 – laughingstock/mocking song
- Lam 3:15/Job 7:11, 9:18, 10:1 – bitterness

While this overlap in specific words connects Job and the afflicted man, one additional factor brings them even closer together: blamelessness. They both suffer at the hands of their enemies without cause (*hinnam*, Lam 3:52; Job 2:3). In this respect, the afflicted man is also like righteous Daniel and King David, occasionally presented in the Psalter as an innocent sufferer (Ps 7, 18, 35, 101, 109).

The conversation between Lamentations 3 and the book of Job raises the possibility that the role of the innocent sufferer is the same in each case: to act as a mediator between the Lord and the guilty. Job himself has no sin to confess, so in the end he turns to the Lord's wisdom in the midst of his suffering. After the Lord vindicates His innocent servant Job but while Job is still suffering, the Lord calls Job to mediate on behalf of his three foolish friends (Job 42:7-9). Similarly, the afflicted man bears the wrath and anger of the Lord alongside Lady Jerusalem, not for his own sins but as the representative of the rebellious people of Israel.[108] He then begins his role as a mediator, calling for communal repentance. The afflicted man speaks using "we," the first-person plural (Lam 3:40-42):

> 3:40 Let us test and examine our ways,
>
> And return to the Lord!

---

[108] Though difficult, one could read the afflicted man not as a co-sufferer but as a sufferer paying the price for Israel's sin. In this case, this conversation turns to include the suffering servant of Isaiah 53.

> 41   Let us lift up our hearts and hands
>
> To God in heaven:
>
> 42   "We have transgressed and rebelled,
>
> And you have not forgiven."

After urging the people to repent and turn to the Lord, the afflicted man then connects his sorrow to Lady Jerusalem's rebellion and desolation (Lam 3:48, also 3:49, 51):

> 3:48   My eyes flow with rivers of tears
>
> Because of the destruction of the daughter of my people.

The juxtaposition of Lady Jerusalem's justified destruction and the innocent man's suffering suggests that his sorrow comes upon him not only because he suffered as she did, but because he sees her pain and enters into her grief.[109] Sitting in the dust with Lady Jerusalem, the afflicted man calls the people to corporate confession. In Daniel 9, righteous Daniel offers a similar prayer on behalf of Israel: "we have sinned and done wrong and acted wickedly and rebelled, turning aside from your commandments and rules" (Dan 9:5). Daniel functions much the same way as Job and the afflicted man of Lamentations 3: he himself did not commit these sins, but his community did. In all three texts, a righteous person mediates between a guilty people and a holy God.

The book of Chronicles now speaks, bringing David and Solomon into this conversation treating Lamentations 3. The text gives no further details about the identity of the afflicted man; however, the term *geber* is used throughout 1 Chronicles 11:10-12:30 to describe the infamous warriors who followed and fought for King David. The author's use of *geber* could be a hint to read this man as a Davidic

---

[109] The afflicted man of Psalm 102 also experiences intense suffering from his enemies due to the Lord's wrath (Ps 102:1-11), yet the psalmist makes no reference to his own sin. In yet another parallel with Lamentations, this psalm connects the afflicted man's plight to Zion's situation and foresees her glorious future.

figure, continuing the king/city pairing so prevalent in the OT.

In Chronicles, David and his line are cast as mediators between the Lord and the people. When David brings the Ark of the Covenant into Jerusalem, he takes on the priestly role as he puts on an ephod. Though David is no Levite, the text contains no negative commentary on his actions, suggesting that David's priest-like activity does not violate the Law in this instance. Later, when David sins by taking a census (1 Chron 21), the Lord strikes the people with a plague. The Lord approves David's intercession for his people by answering him with fire. This epic scene involving the angel of the Lord, King David, and the people takes place on the threshing floor of Ornan the Jebusite, the sacred location to become a more permanent mediatorial place: the site of Solomon's temple. At Solomon's dedication of the temple, he repeatedly highlights that those who pray to the Lord dwelling in this temple will find forgiveness for their sins (2 Chron 6:21, 25, 27, 30, 39, 7:14). Both David and Solomon play key roles in creating a house for the Lord and a literal place of forgiveness for Israel; these events set the expectation that the house of David has and will play a representative and mediatorial role in Israel's relationship with God, specifically vis-à-vis the forgiveness of sin. The afflicted man of Lamentations 3 fulfills much the same role: he calls Israel to repentance, leading the people back into right relationship with their Lord.

As discussed above, the afflicted man is the only one in Lamentations who speaks of hope for Israel; the basis of his hope is the *hesed* of the Lord. The chapter on the book of Ruth discusses *hesed* within the context of relationships between persons; here the conversation turns to the Lord's *hesed* in relation to His people. After examining the concept as it is used in Lamentations 3, the sages of Lamentations and Psalms compare their focus on this crucial character trait.

In OT poetry, *hesed* often finds itself in parallel lines with faithfulness or truth (*'emunah* or *'emet*). *'emunah* in particular offers helpful commentary on the significance of *hesed*. Together, *'emunah* and *hesed* pair faithfulness and lovingkindness, highlighting the fidelity between partners in a covenant. The result is a kind of "covenantal glue" that holds parties together in a stated relationship across time. Because He is both faithful and true, the Lord will keep His promises to judge and to save Israel. In Lamentations 2:17, the prophetic observer states that the Lord has kept His word to destroy sinful Jerusalem without sparing and exalt her adversaries over her. Conversely, in chapter 3, the afflicted man leans on another aspect of the Lord's covenantal fidelity: forgiveness and restoration when His people return to Him.[110]

The centerpiece of the book of Lamentations comes from the mouth of the afflicted man in Lamentations 3:21-24:

> 3:21 But this I call to mind,
>
> And therefore I have hope:
>
> 22 The steadfast love (*hesed*) of the Lord never ceases;
>
> His mercies (*rahamim*) never come to an end;
>
> 23 They are new every morning;
>
> Great is your faithfulness (*'emunah*).
>
> 24 "The Lord is my portion," says my soul,
>
> "Therefore I will hope in him."

The mighty man both begins and ends this segment with statements of hope (3:21, 24); between these brackets, he focuses on the Lord's *hesed*, using language from the Lord's revelation of His goodness to Moses after the Golden Calf event (Ex 34:6 – *hesed, raham, 'emet*). The Hebrew form of *hesed* in Lamentations is actually plural, referring not to one but to many instances of *hesed*. Within the history of

---

[110] The afflicted man moderates his level of confidence in his hope in Lamentations 3:29: "there may yet (*'ulay*) be hope" (ESV, NRSV, NIV). The NASB translates the line as "perhaps (*'ulay*) there is hope" and the NLT as "there may be hope at last." This wording suggests that hope is contingent on either the Lord or the people—given the preceding verses, probably on the people turning to the Lord. Lamentations 5:21 appears to confirm this reading: "Restore us to You, O Lord." Interestingly, the Septuagint omits Lamentations 3:29 completely.

Israel, the Golden Calf event constitutes the people's great sin, the worst among many (Ex 32:30). When the afflicted man uses Exodus 34 language, he parallels Israel's sin of rebellion with the Golden Calf event; in both situations, the sin and its consequences are great, and Israel's only option is to call on the name of the Lord to save them. The same God who stilled His wrath and forgave Israel after their sin with the Golden Calf can forgive His people after their unfaithfulness and restore them. Without referring to specific acts of deliverance, the plural forms of *hesed* and mercies (*raham*) point the reader to the OT's record of the Lord's great deeds of forgiveness and salvation. The afflicted man reminds the people: since the *hesed* of the Lord never ceases, there is hope for Israel.

At this point, the afflicted man and Book III of the Psalter begin a dialogue, with the other sages listening in. *Hesed* features prominently in the book of Psalms, appearing over 250 times. Unlike Proverbs, which uses the term with respect to human relationships, the Psalter uses *hesed* to describe the Lord's relationship to the psalmist. Though many individual and communal psalms treat *hesed*, Book III of the Psalter addresses the fall of Jerusalem, providing ideal thematic overlap here.

The first reference to *hesed* in Book III of the Psalter echoes the end of Lamentations. Psalm 77:7-9 raises the same questions as the choral prayer of Lamentations 5:19-22:

> 77:7 Will the Lord spurn forever,
>
> And never again be favorable?
>
> 8 Has his steadfast love (*hesed*) forever ceased?
>
> Are his promises at an end for all time?
>
> 9 Has God forgotten to be gracious (*hannot*)?
>
> Has he in anger shut up his compassion (*rahamim*)?

The questions in Psalms and Lamentations are the same: has the Lord forgotten his people? The repetition of these questions in the Writings offers readers the comfort of a script for these moments of despair. However, unlike the chorus in Lamentations 5, Asaph the psalmist provides a next step: hope in the Lord's *hesed*. As the psalm continues, Asaph recounts past instances of the Lord's deliverance of Israel, reminding readers of the Lord's faithfulness to His covenant with His people. The psalmist and the afflicted man convey the same message: the Lord has turned to Israel and delivered her before. Since His *hesed* (plural) never cease, He will do so again.

In turn, David follows this same pattern in his lone psalm of Book III, Psalm 86. Notice echoes of the language of Exodus 34:6 and the afflicted man as David sings (Ps 86:5, 13, 15):

> 86:5 For you, O Lord, are good and forgiving,
>
> Abounding in steadfast love (*hesed*) to all who call upon you.
>
> 13 For great is your steadfast love (*hesed*) toward me;
>
> You have delivered my soul from the depths of Sheol.
>
> 15 But you, O Lord, are a God merciful and gracious,
>
> Slow to anger and abounding in steadfast love (*hesed*) and faithfulness (*'emunah*).

With this psalm, the shaper of the Psalter adds David's individual experience with the Lord's *hesed* to Asaph's exhortations. Since Book III focuses on the fall of Jerusalem, the words of David seem at first an odd choice. However, this inclusion parallels David's experience in his distress with the distress of his people later on, offering the king's words as another model of distress and hope. Amidst Asaph's treatment of the fall of Jerusalem, the king's song also leads the people to trust in the Lord.

Yet Psalm 89, the last psalm in Book III, follows Lamentations' pattern of moving from hope to questions. A psalm of Ethan, Psalm 89:1-4 sets the positive tone for the first section, through verse 37:

> 89:1 I will sing of the steadfast love (*hesed*) of the Lord, forever;
>
> With my mouth I will make known your faithfulness (*'emunah*) to all generations.
>
> 2 For I said, "Steadfast love (*hesed*) will be built up forever;
>
> In the heavens you will establish your faithfulness (*'emunah*)."
>
> 3 You have said, "I have made a covenant with my chosen one;
>
> I have sworn to David my servant:
>
> 4 'I will establish your offspring forever,
>
> And build your throne for all generations.'"

Adding to Psalm 86's description of the Lord's *hesed*, Ethan's words emphasize that the Lord's promises to David remain inviolable even if the house of David does not keep His commandments (Ps 89:30-37). Such is the covenant between the Lord and David. Though He promises to punish their transgression, the Lord will not remove His *hesed* from Israel or defile (*halal*) His covenant with David (Ps 89:33-34). This is reassurance indeed! However, after this emphatic declaration of the Lord's faithfulness to David, the next part of Psalm 89 surprises the reader (Ps 89:38-39):

> 89:38 But now you have cast off and rejected;
>
> You are full of wrath against your anointed.

> 39   You have renounced the covenant with your servant;
>
> You have defiled (*halal*) his crown in the dust.

The sages all lean forward, waiting for the Psalter to continue. As Ethan describes the situation, he reverses verse 34's statement that the Lord will not violate or defile (*halal*) His covenant with David. How can this be? In his final words, Ethan cries (Ps 89:46, 49-50):

> 89:46   How long, O Lord? Will you hide yourself forever?
>
> How long will your wrath burn like fire?
>
> 49   Lord, where is your steadfast love (*hesed*) of old,
>
> Which by your faithfulness (*'emunah*) you swore to David?
>
> 50   Remember, O Lord, how your servants are mocked.

Like the chorus of Lamentations 5, Ethan asks whether the Lord's wrath will last forever and begs the Lord to remember His people. Yet like David and Asaph, in his despair Ethan appeals to the Lord's *hesed*, the covenantal glue binding Him to His people. While validating Lamentations' moment of despair, Book III of the Psalms concludes by offering a larger context and direction for the grief and loss of Lamentations: hope in the *hesed* of the Lord.

Books IV and V of the Psalter respond to the situation at the end of Book III. Book IV focuses on the Lord's eternal reign and includes David's teaching on the Lord's forgiveness for those who fear Him, the wise (Ps 103:11, 13). Book V concludes the Psalter by focusing on the theme of the Lord's redemption of His people and His restoration of the king and kingdom (Pss 107, 110, 132). *Hesed* features prominently in Book V: the refrain at its literary seams declares that the Lord is good and His *hesed* is everlasting (Ps 107:1, 118:1, 136:1). And should this truth be overlooked, the antiphonal Psalm 136 repeats, in the B line of every one of its 26 verses, "His *hesed* is everlasting." Israel does indeed have a future! Amen!

Toward the New Testament

1. Lady Jerusalem and the Messiah

One of the great lessons from the book of Psalms is not to reject the anointed king, the son of God (Ps 2); David's psalms specifically state that those who reject, persecute, afflict, and attack the Lord's anointed will suffer the judgment of the Lord. When Jesus, the Messiah and Son of God, comes onto the scene in the NT, He presents Himself as the promised King of Israel. Tragically, the people of Israel reject, afflict, and kill Him; the Gospels spell out the same consequences for Israel in the NT as in Lamentations: the fall of Jerusalem.

In Matthew 23:34-24:2, Jesus indicates that His people will kill Him, as they did some of the prophets in the OT. Jesus laments over the city, hoping Jerusalem would welcome Him, but knowing they will not (Matt 23:37). In Luke's version of Christ's triumphal entry into Jerusalem (Luke 19:41-44), Jesus sees His city and weeps over her; his reaction is the same as the afflicted man and the prophetic observer in Lamentations. Jesus echoes their language in Luke 19:43-44 (also Luke 21:20-24), describing the coming fall of Jerusalem:

> 19:43 For the days will come upon you, when your enemies will set up a barricade around you and surround you and hem you in on every side
>
> 44 and tear you down to the ground, you and your children within you. And they will not leave one stone upon another in you, because you did not know the time of your visitation.

As Jerusalem rejected her Lord in Lamentations, so she rejects her Messiah in the Gospels.

In Luke 21:24, Jesus echoes Daniel's prophecies about the era of Gentile world dominion and persecution of Israel; He states that Jerusalem will be trampled underfoot until the times of the Gentiles are fulfilled. Yet Jesus also voices hope that Israel will return to Him.

In the future, the people will proclaim, "Blessed is He who comes in the name of the Lord" (Matt 23:39). Unlike the first triumphal entry that ended in His crucifixion, at His second coming, the people will welcome Jesus and kiss the Son as their Messianic King (Ps 2:12).

2. Jesus, the Afflicted Man

The NT presents Jesus as the king of Israel; He both represents His people and stands in as a substitution for them. The events at the beginning of the Gospel of Matthew, for example, show that before His ministry to Israel begins, Jesus' life repeats the story of Israel:

- Jesus comes out of Egypt (Matt 2:13-15)

- Jesus "goes through" the Jordan river in baptism (Matt 3:13-17)

- Jesus spends 40 days in the wilderness (Matt 4:1-11)

These actions parallel Jesus and Israel: He represents the nation of Israel in the text. Three years later, Jesus' ministry to His people ends at the cross. Hanging on that tree, charged with being King of the Jews (Matt 27:37; John 19:19-21), Jesus also serves as a substitution for God's chosen people. Blameless Jesus suffers in the place of guilty and afflicted Israel; as their ultimate Passover sacrifice, He opens a path for their deliverance. All four Gospels highlight Jesus fulfilling Isaiah 53's portrayal of the suffering Servant, quoting from that passage (Matt 8:17; Mark 15:28; Luke 22:37; John 12:38). Again, Jesus the suffering Servant not only represents Israel, but takes her place and dies for her sin. The NT does not quote from Lamentations 3; however, as this chapter discussed earlier, reading the afflicted man of chapter 3 as the Davidic king dovetails nicely with Christ's work on the cross. As the innocent but afflicted man suffered with Lady Jerusalem and led her to repentance, so the innocent Son of *'adam*, Son of David, Son of God suffers and dies for Lady Jerusalem, reconciling her to God forever. Christ's substitutionary death on the cross is the ultimate instance of God's *hesed*. This reading appears consistently in church liturgy; the church has historically read Lamentations at the Tenebrae services during the Passion Week. Lamentations and the afflicted man find a fitting place in reflections on Jesus' death, burial, and resurrection.

3. The Lord's Faithfulness

The coming of Jesus testifies to the fact that the Lord has not rejected His people forever: He will indeed restore and renew her as in days of old. The NT uses the Greek word *eleos* to translate the Hebrew *hesed*. In the opening chapters of the Gospel of Luke, Jesus' arrival is cast as a testimony to the Lord's *eleos/hesed*. First, at the annunciation, the angel Gabriel tells Mary Jesus' role in the fulfillment of the Davidic promise and kingdom. After many years of silence, the Lord has not forgotten His promises to Israel (Luke 1:32-35):

> 1:32 "He will be great and will be called the Son of the Most High. And the Lord God will give to him the throne of his father David,
>
> 33 and he will reign over the house of Jacob forever, and of his kingdom there will be no end."
>
> 34 And Mary said to the angel, "How will this be, since I am a virgin?"
>
> 35 And the angel answered her, "The Holy Spirit will come upon you, and the power of the Most High will overshadow you; therefore the child to be born will be called holy—the Son of God."

From this moment on, Mary knows exactly who her child is: the Messiah, the eternal King of Israel. In her response, often called her "Magnificat," Mary speaks of how the birth of Jesus signals the reversal of the fortunes of the weak and strong, demonstrating the Lord's *eleos/hesed* to His covenantal promises (Luke 1:50, 54-55):

> 1:50 And his mercy (*eleos*) is for those who fear him
>
> From generation to generation.[111]
>
> 54 He has helped his servant Israel,
>
> In remembrance of his mercy (*eleos*),
>
> 55 As he spoke to our fathers,
>
> To Abraham and to his offspring forever.

The reason for this birth is ultimately the *eleos* of God. Similarly, Zacharias also attributes the birth of the Messiah to the Lord's *eleos/hesed* in his Benedictus. His poetic response prophesizes of the Lord's redemption of His people through a horn of salvation in the house of David. Like Mary, Zacharias references *eleos* when he blesses the Lord God of Israel, who spoke through His prophets (Luke 1:71-72):

> 1:71 That we should be saved from our enemies
>
> And from the hand of all who hate us;
>
> 72 To show the mercy (*eleos*) promised to our fathers
>
> And to remember his holy covenant ...

A few verses later, Zacharias speaks of John's ministry as the forerunner of the coming Messiah. Again, the *eleos* of the God of Israel is the impetus for these events; Zacharias foretells the coming of John the Baptist, who will prepare the way for the Lord (Luke 1:78-79):

> 1:78 Because of the tender mercy (*eleos*) of our God,
>
> Whereby the sunrise shall visit us from on high
>
> 79 To give light to those who sit in darkness and in the shadow of death,
>
> To guide our feet into the way of peace.

---

111 Mary quotes Psalm 103:17 here: "But the steadfast love (*hesed*) of the Lord is from everlasting to everlasting on those who fear him."

Both Mary and Zacharias immediately connect the birth of the Messiah to the *eleos/hesed* of the God of Israel. This child is coming to be King because God has not forsaken His people; His *hesed* of old is manifest again.

The Last Supper also marks a critical moment in the Lord's *hesed/eleos* toward His people. In the upper room, Jesus explains that His impending death founds the New Covenant; communion is an act of anticipation of the future Messianic feast in the eternal kingdom of God (Matt 26:26-29; Mark 14:22-25; Luke 22:17-20). The Lord's table serves as a consistent reminder that God has not utterly rejected His people or His promises to Abraham, David, and Israel. In Romans 11, Paul explains that in light of her rejection of Jesus, God has left a remnant of Israel who believe and hardened the rest in unbelief (Rom 11:1-10). Yet Paul also anticipates that after this partial hardening of Israel, Gentile salvation will be complete and all Israel will be saved (Rom 11:25-26, also 9:1-13). In the end, both Israel and Gentiles will together proclaim the words at the center of Lamentations: Great is Your faithfulness!

Further Reading

Aitken, James A. "The Inevitability of Reading Job through Lamentations." In Katharine J. Dell and Will Kynes. *Reading Job Intertextually*. Library of Hebrew Bible/Old Testament Studies. New York, NY: T&T Clark, 2013: 204-16.

Bailey, Wilma and Christina Bucher. *Lamentations, Song of Songs*. Believers Church Bible Commentary. Huntington, IN: Herald Press, 2015.

Ellington, Scott, "Lamentations and Canon: Conversations in the Dark." Donn F. Morgan (ed.), *The Oxford Handbook of the Writings of the Hebrew Bible*, Oxford Handbooks, 2018. Online edition, Oxford Academic, 7 Nov 2018.

Goswell, Greg (Gregory Ross). "Assigning the Book of Lamentations a Place in the Canon." *Journal for the Evangelical Study of the Old Testament* 4 (1): 1–19.

Esther: The Absence of the Presence of the Lord

Old Testament Background for Esther

- Joseph's role in Egypt: Gen 37-50
- The exile of Judah: 2 Kings 24-25; 2 Chron 36
- King Jeconiah (Jehoiachin) exiled by Nebuchadnezzar: 2 Kings 24:8-17; 2 Chron 36:9-10
- King Ahasuerus and the post-exilic Jews: Ezra 4:6
- Backstory of the Amalekites, Haman's people: 1 Sam 15; Exodus 17; Deut 25:17-19
- Daniel in a Gentile court: Daniel 1-6
- God's promise to Abraham and his seed: Gen 12:1-3
- Enmity between the seed and the serpent: Gen 3-4
- The Septuagint's additions to Esther, especially Addition C

Creation and Esther: Ruling and the Seed

Like Lamentations, at first glance, the book of Esther and Genesis 1-4 treat different topics. Nonetheless, upon closer examination, two specific threads link Esther back to creation. In Genesis 1:26, the Lord God makes 'adam in His image and tasks them with ruling (*malak*) over creation. As the Creator governs His creation, so His image bearer is to rule over creation, reflecting 'adam's relationship with the Creator. The OT later uses the same language about Nebuchadnezzar: the Lord gave Nebuchadnezzar the rule (*malak*) over the earth, humans, and beasts (Jer 27:1-8). Still this same language emerges clearly in the Esther narrative: the Hebrew words for "king" (*melek*), "queen" (*melakah*), and "to rule" (*malak*) all derive from the same Hebrew root and occur over 200 times in the book of Esther. This linguistic connection prompts the reader to understand the story of Esther as events taking place in a Gentile kingdom under the rule of King Ahasuerus, a Gentile who rules as a delegate of the Lord (Dan 2, 7).

The second link between Esther and Genesis 1-4 pertains to the term "seed" (*zera'*). Throughout the OT, "seed" carries theological meaning regarding the promised seed of David, Judah, and Abraham. *Zera'* is flexible enough to refer to many descendants or a single offspring. "Purim" and "seed" (*zera'*) each occur three times within five verses in Esther 9:27-31, explaining the reason for the holiday. *Zera'* then closes out the book (Est 10:3):

> 10:3 For Mordecai the Jew was next unto King Ahasuerus, and great among the Jews, and accepted of the multitude of his brethren, seeking the wealth of his people, and speaking peace (*shalom*) to all his seed (*zera'*). (KJV)

Esther chapters 9 and 10 ensure the reader finishes the Esther story crystal clear on its main point: Purim celebrates the deliverance of the seed (*zera'*) of Israel.

This connection between seed and destruction/deliverance begins in Genesis, when the Lord God declares that the seed of the woman will suffer enmity with the seed of the serpent (Gen 3:15). However, in Genesis 12:3, the Lord states that He will curse the one who curses Abraham and his seed (*zera'*); He positions Himself squarely on the side of preserving His chosen people. The effects of the Lord's protection surface in the book of Esther: Haman's wife Zeresh warns him that if Mordecai is of Jewish[112] "seed" (*zera'*), Haman will not overcome him, but will fall before him (Est 6:13). Though the Lord is never mentioned in the text of the Esther narrative, His provision for and deliverance of Israel form the cosmic context for the events in this story. Against this backdrop, the book of Esther becomes far more than just a specific, local dispute between the Persians and the Jews in the days of Ahasuerus. The story of Purim offers another illustration

---

[112] The word for "Jew" in the book of Esther is *yehudi*, from "Judah" (*yehudah*). Although the returning remnant comes from all the tribes of Israel, the narrative of Ezra-Nehemiah focuses on the temple and the city of Jerusalem in Judah. Consequently, in the post-exile, the people of Israel were and still are called the people of Judah: "Jews."

of the creational conflict begun in Genesis 3:15 and God's redemption of humanity and creation playing out across the OT into the NT.

The Book of Esther: An Outline

Like most books in the Writings, the author of the book of Esther remains anonymous. This story's events occur during the time of the Persian Empire, after the fall of Babylon and at least 50 years after Cyrus King of Persia allows Israel to return from exile to Jerusalem (Ezra 1:1-4). The Jews in the Esther story opted to stay in Persia and did not return to the land and Jerusalem. While Esther and Mordecai are the story's most significant characters, Ahasuerus appears to be the main focus of the book. Given that Esther's words and deeds serve as the main catalyst for the deliverance of the Jews, the story bears her name.

The narrative can be outlined as follows:

- **Chapters 1-5:** Part 1, culminating in Esther's first banquet

- **Chapter 6:** The Turning Point - Mordecai honored by the King and Haman

- **Chapters 7-10:** Part 2, beginning with Esther's second banquet

This chiasm highlights the role of Esther's two banquets and the story's surprise twist in chapter 6. As a narrative, the text also follows the classic rising and falling action pattern. Each chapter furthers the complex plot, thrilling readers with suspense and tension:

- **Chapter 1:** King Ahasuerus gives a lavish banquet. When he calls for his queen Vashti, she refuses to enter the banquet hall; her refusal results in her dismissal and a royal edict regarding wives and their husbands.

- **Chapter 2:** The king seeks a replacement for Vashti through a beauty competition. Esther, a young Jewess, is taken into the competition, wins it, and becomes queen. Her uncle Mordecai uncovers a plot to kill the king and reports it, preventing an attempt on King Ahasuerus' life.

- **Chapter 3:** Mordecai refuses to bow down to honor Haman, the king's advisor, so Haman devises a plan to exterminate all the Jews in the empire. He sets the day of their destruction by casting lots (*purim*).

- **Chapter 4:** Mordecai and Esther learn of Haman's scheme. Risking her life, Esther decides to intercede for her people.

- **Chapter 5:** Esther hosts the king and Haman at a banquet; there, she requests a second banquet. Haman returns home full of pride and erects a gallows for Mordecai.

- **Chapter 6:** That very night, the king cannot sleep. He orders his servant to read aloud from the book of records and learns of Mordecai saving his life. To reward him, the king instructs Haman to honor Mordecai. Haman does so in humiliation.

- **Chapter 7:** That evening, during her second banquet, Esther reveals Haman as the enemy of the Jews. Furious, King Ahasuerus has Haman hung on the gallows he had prepared for Mordecai.

- **Chapter 8:** The king promotes Mordecai to Haman's position, and, at Esther's suggestion, issues a new decree allowing the Jews to defend themselves against those seeking to destroy them.

- **Chapter 9:** The day of destruction arrives. Organized, the Jews defend themselves and defeat their enemies. Via letters to the Jews throughout the kingdom, Mordecai and Esther establish the two-day feast of Purim for the seed of Israel.

- **Chapter 10:** Mordecai's greatness is recorded in the Chronicles of the Kings of the Medes and the Persians. Second only to King Ahasuerus, Mordecai is remembered for seeking the good and peace (*shalom*) of his seed (*zeraʻ*).

Major Themes: Kings and Kingdoms, Esther - Woman of Wisdom, and the Absence of God

1. Kings and Kingdoms

As mentioned above, the book of Esther focuses on the Gentile king (*melek*) Ahasuerus and his rule (*malak*) along with his queen (*melakah*) Esther. The Writings house this narrative in the second half of the collection, the section focused on the Davidic kingdom. This placement prompts a comparison between the kingdoms of Ahasuerus and the exiled house of David (Est 2:6).

The text of Esther juxtaposes the glory of Ahasuerus with the humiliation of David's kingdom. Esther 1's description of the greatness of Ahasuerus takes the same shape as the Writings' description of the greatness of Solomon and his temple:[113]

Ahasuerus in Esther	Solomon in Chronicles
Sat on his royal throne (Est 1:2)	Sat on the throne of the Lord (1 Chron 29:23)
He displayed the riches of his royal glory and the splendor of his great majesty (Est 1:4).	The Lord gave him royal majesty unlike any king before him (1 Chron 29:25).
Ahasuerus gave a banquet lasting seven days at the citadel in Susa in the court of the garden of the king's palace (Est 1:5).	Solomon consecrated the court before the house of the Lord, observed the feast for seven days (2 Chron 7:7-8).
A description of the king's palace (Est 1:6)	A description of the tabernacle (Ex 26:1-6) and the temple (2 Chron 3:14)
Golden drinking vessels and royal wine (Est 1:7)	All drinking vessels were gold (2 Chron 9:20)

---

[113] For more on this comparison, see Samuel Wells and George Sumner. *Esther and Daniel in Brazos Theological Commentary on the Bible*. Ada, MI: Brazos Press, 2013: 26-28 and Chloe Tse Sun. "Temple: Garden and Palace." *Conspicuous in His Absence: Studies in the Song of Songs and Esther*. Lisle, IL: IVP Academic, 2021.

Since Jerusalem under Solomon marks the high point of Israel's history, these parallel descriptions compare the greatness and glory of Ahasuerus with the glorious OT scenes culminating in Solomon's temple, city, and kingdom. Then, Esther 2:6 mentions the exile of Judah's King Jeconiah (Jehoiachin) at the hands of Nebuchadnezzar. Israel's glory has been destroyed; even the rebuilt Jerusalem and temple remain a shadow of their former selves (Ezra 3:12-13). The glory of the house of David appears to have been passed on to Ahasuerus the Persian. Though the book of Esther focuses on the conflict between Haman and the Jews, the larger context of the Writings casts the book as part of a continuous narrative of divinely ordained Gentile kings and kingdoms reigning while Israel waits on the renewal of the Davidic line and the Lord's eternal kingdom (Dan 2).

2. Esther: Woman of Wisdom

As noted in the Introduction, the book of Esther is part of the *Megilloth*, a subcollection of wisdom texts featuring women; this placement seems appropriate given Queen Esther's role in the deliverance of her people. The book of Esther functions as the second bookend for the MT *Megilloth*; the texts of Esther and Ruth form a pair:

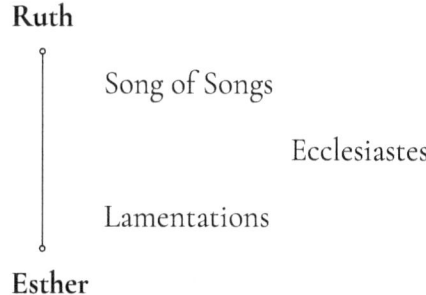

The *Megilloth*'s focus on wise women figures shapes the dialogue between these two books. Like Ruth, Esther is the catalyst for the events in her story, the linchpin holding the book together. In this sense, Esther is akin to Lady Wisdom within creation (Prov 8), the virtuous woman and her household (Prov 31), and Ruth and Bethlehem: these women all do good to those around them. However, the women in these other texts clearly seek and live out the wisdom of God—the book of Esther records no such thing. The storyline attributes Esther's success not to the Lord but to King Ahasuerus' decisions in Esther 5-7. In this respect, Esther's story illustrates Proverbs 21:1:

> 21:1 The king's heart is a stream of water in the hand of the Lord;
>
> He turns it wherever he will.

Readers finish the book of Esther with no sense of Queen Esther's relationship with the God of her people. She could be a devout follower of the Lord or a fairly acculturated Jewish Persian. This conundrum seems to be part of the point of the book: the Lord works wherever and through whomever He pleases to carry out His plans for His people.

3. *The Absence of God*

The most notable feature of the book of Esther remains God's absence from the text. The OT and the Writings in particular contextualize this text as another chapter in the long history of God's relationship with His people—God's role in the Esther story is as significant as His role in Lamentations 2, for example, where He is the subject of almost every verb in every line of poetry. In Esther's time, the Lord remains the faithful covenant God of Israel; His role has not changed. For unknown reasons, the author of the book of Esther abides by certain self-imposed narrative limitations: no mention of God, no mention of Esther's relationship with God, etc. Nonetheless, just as the reader of Lamentations sees the hand of God in the actions of the Babylonians who destroy Jerusalem, so the reader of Esther should see the hand of God behind each turning point in Queen Esther's story.

The only other book in the OT with no explicit reference to God is the Song of Songs. Together, these texts may very well be highlighting perspectives on the life of the righteous when God appears absent. This feeling of His absence surfaces in several other places in the life of the wise in the post-exile:

- The temple is rebuilt, but God is not present in the Holy of Holies (Ezra-Nehemiah).

- There is no Davidic king to reign from the throne of the Lord. The kingdom appears to be *hebel* (Ezra-Nehemiah; 2 Chron 36).

- The people return from exile yet still live as "slaves on their own land" (Neh 9:36).

- The people suffer crises and grief (Dan 6, 7, 11; Esther; Ezra-Nehemiah; Lam 5).

Living within these realities, Jews in the post-exile could certainly feel that the Lord has forgotten them. Even after their 70-year punishment has ended, the chorus' question from Lamentations 5 remains in the air: has the Lord utterly rejected His people forever?

The text of Esther suggests different ways readers can think about the absence of the Lord. God can be absent:

- Textually: a text makes no reference to God (Esther, the Song). God does not appear in the words of the text.

- From the characters' and/or the narrator's perspectives: the characters in the story do not speak of God or His presence; from their vantage points, God is absent. Sometimes, the narrator reveals He works providentially behind the scenes of human events (Esther, Ruth 2, 4, Dan 1, Job 1-2).[114]

- From the center of human power, the kingdom: the Kingdom of the Lord, represented on earth by the reign of the house of David, has been swept away and replaced by Gentile rule and dominion (Dan 2, 7). This earthly absence is real (Ps 89, Lam, Ez-Neh, Esther).

- Experientially: in their distress and suffering, the righteous

---

114 Though not in the Writings, Joseph serves as the prime example of a wise person who suffers without any word from the Lord. Only the narrator reveals that during that time, the Lord was with Joseph (Gen 39:19-23).

experience a sense of abandonment; they do not feel the presence of the Lord in their life. In these cases, God's absence is apparent but not actual (Job, Lam, Lament psalms).

In combination with the books of Esther and the Song, these passages provide validation and direction for those who see or feel the Lord's absence. The Writings continue to push readers to seek the wisdom of God during the difficult moments of His absence or silence.

The Sages in Conversation

1. Kings and Kingdoms

The second half of the Writings treats the kingdom of David amidst the nations during and after the exile. In time, King Cyrus, whose decree allows Israel to return to the land and rebuild, is succeeded by Darius and Ahasuerus, also called Xerxes, king during the book of Esther (Ez 4:5-6). At this point, a question naturally arises: if the exile is over, why are the Jews still in Persia? Given Mordecai's position in the royal court, the Jews had prospered in exile, to a certain degree becoming integrated into Persian culture and society; returning to Jerusalem to rebuild was apparently not an attractive option. As mentioned above, the text of the book of Esther makes no mention of Israel's God, the covenant, or the Lord's promises to His people.[115] Though Mordecai refuses to bow to Haman, he offers no substantive explanation for this choice. The now-Persian Jews may have understood Israel's covenant with her God to be irreparably broken and therefore irrelevant to their present circumstances. The kingdom of the Lord is either over—*hebel*— or uninviting compared to the prosperity of the Persian kingdom. This topic of kings and kingdoms draws the sages of Psalms, Daniel, and Lamentations into conversation.

The book of Psalms has much to say about the conflict between the Davidic king and the nations, contextualizing the events in the

---

115 See the Septuagint (LXX) additions to Esther, especially Addition C. This addition contains prayers of both Mordecai and Esther, centralizing the Lord's covenant with His people and their Abraham-like faith.

book of Esther within the Lord's plan for earthly kingdoms. As part of the introduction to the Psalter, Psalm 2 sets the stage for the book's treatment of this topic, opening with the nations and kings of the earth plotting to eliminate the Lord's anointed (*mashiah*), His king and His Son (Ps 2:1-3). These kings share Haman's goal: the extermination of Israel. After scoffing at this ridiculous plot, the Lord angrily states that His King has already been installed in Zion (Ps 2:4-6). In turn, the Son proclaims the decree of the Lord: He will receive the nations as His inheritance and shatter them like earthenware (Ps 2:7-9). The nations may be mighty now, but they, too, are *hebel* in the hand of the Lord. The psalm then concludes by exhorting the kings and rulers of the earth to wise up (*sakal*) and receive instruction (*yasar*): serve the Lord with fear and trembling, "kiss (*nashaq*) the Son" or perish in His anger (Ps 2:10-12). By mentioning the future of these earthly kings and nations, Psalm 2 clarifies the future for readers of the book of Esther: the house of David and his kingdom are suffering adversity for a time, but it will not always be so. The Lord has already decreed the reign of the Davidic Son over the nations. Esther's account of the deliverance of the Jews fits into the Writings as a testimony of God's preservation of Israel's seed for the coming Messiah, His Son, the salvation of Israel and the nations who turn to love the Lord.

Korah the psalmist also develops this extended perspective in Psalms 42 to 49. The individual and communal laments of Psalms 42-44 deplore the fact that the Lord has rejected His people, scattered them among the nations, and let them become a laughingstock (Ps 44:9-16, also Lam 1). Although the people have maintained their covenant fidelity in exile (Ps 44:17-22), the Lord continues to hide His face and appears to have forgotten their affliction (Ps 44:22-26); feeling abandoned, Israel petitions God to rise up and help them. If Esther and Mordecai cried to the Lord during the events of the book of Esther, their prayers probably sounded something like these psalms.

Psalm 45 answers this petition for help: the King comes, defeats His enemies, and rules forever (Ps 45:3-6). The King then marries His bride (see the chapter on the Song of Songs), and the psalm ends with the peoples giving the King thanks forever (Ps 45:17b). Psalm 45 sings of a total shift in Israel's situation: the nations had the upper hand in Psalm 44, but by the end of Psalm 45, the King reigns forever in glory, fulfilling the Lord's promise to David (1 Chron 17:11-14). While the book of Esther does not end with the Lord reigning in glory, Esther's salvation of her people marks a similar great shift: just as the Lord saved the Jews under Ahasuerus, so will He permanently save Israel in the future. Psalms 46-48 tell of the glory of Jerusalem/Zion as her King reigns forever:

- The city of God is glad; the Lord is exalted among the nations (Ps 46:4, 10).

- All peoples are subdued but also called to praise God (Ps 47:1-3, 8).

- Zion is beautified; praises to the Lord reach to the ends of the earth (Ps 48:2, 10).

The book of Esther thus provides a small-scale glimpse of the power and authority of the Lord over the nations: He will deliver His people in the present and in the future. For readers of the Writings, the book of Esther offers hope as the people wait, suffering as sheep to be slaughtered (Ps 44:22b). As Esther served as the catalyst for the salvation of her people from Haman, so the Davidic Messiah will serve as the catalyst to permanently deliver His people from suffering into joy and praise. Any nation, people, or king who refuses to "kiss the Son" will, like Haman, perish in the Lord's anger; the remnant of Israel and the nations who love the Lord will praise God and His King in Zion.

At this point in the conversation, the book of Daniel speaks up, comparing insights on these earthly kings and the God of Israel with the book of Esther. Both texts showcase the greatness of Gentile kingdoms paired with the Lord's ability to save His people through a glorious Gentile ruler. While the book of Esther does so without naming the Lord, the book of Daniel explicitly and repeatedly states that the God of Israel is greater than the greatest of all human kings.

Even a casual reader of both texts notices the consistent pomp and extravagance of the kings of the Medes and Persians. The book of Esther opens with Ahasuerus "display[ing] the riches of his royal glory and the splendor of his great majesty for 180 days," culminating in a seven-day banquet for "all the people who were present in the citadel of Susa, from the greatest to the least" (Est 1:4-5). As explained earlier in this chapter, the description of this scene echoes Chronicles' description of Solomon and his temple. Daniel 3 and 5 describe similar displays of glory and wealth by Nebuchadnezzar. After Daniel interprets the great king's dream, in which Babylon was the statue's head of gold, Nebuchadnezzar appears inspired by his vision and erects a solid gold statue of himself. He then holds a lavish dedication ceremony for his statue, gathering all his administrators and musicians to worship his image. Daniel 3 repeats the long lists of invitees twice, lists all the different musical instruments three times, and refers to the king's image seven times. The text feels heavy with repetition and detailed insistence, making the chapter's message abundantly clear: Nebuchadnezzar commands all this glory and extravagance—is he not the greatest king?

The Daniel 3 story continues with Shadrach, Meshach, and Abednego defying Nebuchadnezzar, being thrown into the fiery furnace, and surviving certain death by direct intervention from their God. Thwarted, Nebuchadnezzar acknowledges the Lord's authority over his own commands (Dan 3:28):

> 3:28 Nebuchadnezzar answered and said, "Blessed be the God of Shadrach, Meshach, and Abednego, who has sent his angel and delivered his servants, who trusted in him, and set aside the king's command, and yielded up their bodies rather than serve and worship any god except their own God."

Nebuchadnezzar's words echo similar statements of his in Daniel 2:47,

4:1-3, and 4:34-37.[116] By the end of his interactions with Daniel and his God, Nebuchadnezzar understands the Lord's dominion over all earthly kingdoms: no one—including Nebuchadnezzar himself—can defy the sovereignty of the God of Israel. His authority is complete and eternal. Though the book of Esther features no such pronouncements, the events in Susa showcase the Lord's ability to intervene in Gentile affairs and save His people. The Gentile king ultimately carries out the will of the God of Israel. Paired together, the books of Esther and Daniel showcase the Lord's repeated salvation of His people, demonstrating His superiority over human rulers and kingdoms.

This pattern of the Lord's glory overshadowing the Gentile king's glory continues in Daniel 5 with Belshazzar's banquet. In an explicitly degrading and idolatrous act, Belshazzar and his banquet guests drink out of the holy vessels taken from Solomon's temple. The subsequent writing on the wall speaks to the Lord's authority to judge and remove kings and kingdoms (Dan 5:21): prideful Belshazzar is slain that very night (Dan 5:30-31). Here the sage of the book of Proverbs interjects (Prov 16:18):

> 16:18 Pride goes before destruction,
>
> And a haughty spirit before a fall.

All the sages nod in agreement. God repeatedly checks the arrogant. The book of Daniel consistently states and showcases that Gentile kings govern only by ordinance of the God of Israel. All the arrogant pomp of Nebuchadnezzar and Belshazzar becomes mere charade when compared to the power of the God of Israel.

While extravagant, Esther's King Ahasuerus does not seem to wrestle with this exalted view of his person to the same degree. Though he, too, holds ostentatious banquets to display the majesty of his kingdom, he survives both an assassination plot and Haman's plan to destroy the Jews. The text portrays Ahasuerus as a façade, a showy

---

[116] For more discussion of Nebuchadnezzar, see the Daniel chapter.

ruler following the advice of his trusted advisor of the moment. The true villain in the Esther story is Haman, the proud and wicked enemy of the Jews, not Ahasuerus the king. However, the Esther narrative provides its own example of this Gentile ruler coming under the ultimate rule and authority of the Lord. Esther 1:19 and 8:8 refer to "the laws of the Medes and the Persians ... which cannot be changed." Such language insists on the authority of the decrees, solidifying their finality. King Darius the Mede himself was forced to uphold his own law in Daniel 6, throwing his best advisor to certain death in a lions' den. These legal obligations limit the power of the greatest kings on the earth. Since even the king cannot revoke a law once written, Ahasuerus must decree another law to counteract the impending massacre of the Jews (Est 8:8). These legal contortions demonstrate the Lord's authority over even the rare power boundaries of the kings of Media and Persia. These kings may be unable to revoke their laws, but the Lord suffers no such hindrance in defense of His people and their fidelity to Him.

This topic of kings and kingdoms features a third point of interest. The book of Esther develops a theme of reversal of fortunes, dramatic or unexpected—sometimes ironic—shifts for a character or group of people. For instance, Esther 9:1 reads:

> 9:1 Now in the twelfth month, which is the month of Adar, on the thirteenth day of the same, when the king's command and edict were about to be carried out, on the very day when the enemies of the Jews hoped to gain the mastery over them, the reverse occurred: the Jews gained mastery over those who hated them.

Along with this massive reversal, Esther's story contains several others: Esther the orphan becomes queen, Haman is hanged on the gallows he had prepared for Mordecai, Mordecai is given Haman's position and property, and the plot to destroy the Jews becomes the feast of Purim, celebrating the Jews' victory over their enemies. Esther 9:22

again emphasizes this profound reversal for the Jews: Purim celebrates their sorrow being replaced by gladness, mourning giving way to a joyous feast.

Lamentations also features reversals of fortunes, but unlike in Esther, in Lamentations Israel's fortunes turn from joy to sorrow. In Lamentations 5:15, the chorus wails:

> 5:15 The joy of our hearts has ceased;
>
> Our dancing has been turned to mourning.

Having experienced a reversal of their own, Lady Jerusalem, the afflicted man, and the prophetic observer all speak imprecations against the enemies of Jerusalem. The final words of each of their speeches call for the Lord to intervene, reverse their situation, and punish their oppressors. Lady Jerusalem calls out to the Lord (Lam 1:21e-22):

> 1:21 Oh, that You would bring the day which You have proclaimed,
>
> That they may become like me.
>
> 22 Let all their wickedness come before You;
>
> And deal with them as You have dealt with me
>
> For all my transgressions;
>
> For my groans are many and my heart is faint. (NASB)

The afflicted man continues in Lamentations 3:64-66:

> 3:64 You will repay them, O Lord,
>
> According to the work of their hands.
>
> 65 You will give them dullness of heart;

>   Your curse will be on them.
>
> 66   You will pursue them in anger and destroy them
>
>   From under your heavens, O Lord.

And the prophetic observer finishes with the same imprecations (Lam 4:21-22):

> 4:21   Rejoice and be glad, O daughter of Edom,
>
>   You who dwell in the land of Uz;
>
>   But to you also the cup shall pass;
>
>   You shall become drunk and strip yourself bare.
>
> 22   The punishment of your iniquity, O daughter of Zion, is accomplished;
>
>   He will keep you in exile no longer;
>
>   But your iniquity, O daughter of Edom, he will punish;
>
>   He will uncover your sins.

Though each mourner clearly voices the same call for vengeance, Lamentations never resolves these calls for vindication. The Lord offers no answer—has He not heard, or does He not care? Perhaps, as the book concludes, He really has rejected His people forever (Lam 5:22).

The sage of the book of Esther's response probably surprises Lamentations. Instead of destroying her enemies, restoring the people, and renewing their days of old (Lam 5:21), the Lord delivers the Jews through a Gentile king counseled by Queen Esther, a Jewess. The answer to the chorus' prayer in Lamentations 5 does not arrive with a mighty, glorious, renewed kingdom of David. Instead, God works quietly behind the scenes, delivering the Jews while also leaving the Persian kingdom intact. Lamentations' vengeance must wait until the kingdom of God visibly and dramatically breaks into the world at the end of time, as prophesied by Daniel. While the sage of the book of Esther joyously engages in a yearly Purim feast, the sage of Lamentations is probably sitting frustrated in a corner, still muttering the same imprecations.

2. Esther: Woman of Wisdom

As noted above, the Writings pair the books of Esther and Ruth, the only two books named after women, as companion volumes: they both narrate a woman as a central agent of change. As explained in the Introduction, Proverbs sets a trajectory of women of wisdom in the Writings; the books of Esther and Ruth bracket this collection of women-oriented texts. Esther and Ruth themselves parallel Lady Wisdom and the woman of virtue (Prov 1-9, 31):

- The works of the woman of virtue do good to all; she is praised in the gates (Prov 8:21-31, 31:31). Similarly, the men at the gates of Bethlehem praise Ruth (Ruth 4:11-12), and the author of the book of Esther highlights Esther's deeds and words throughout the text.

- Ruth, Esther, and Lady Wisdom each serve as an agent of deliverance or salvation. Lady Wisdom delivers from the way of evil and the strange woman (Prov 2:12-16). Ruth and Esther play key parts in preserving the seed of Israel, looking to the coming Messiah: Ruth transforms Naomi's emptiness into the fullness of Obed and the Davidic line, and Esther transforms her people's imminent destruction into victory.

- Lady Wisdom and the woman of virtue provide counsel and wisdom (Prov 1:20-33, 8:14, 31:26). Likewise, Esther counsels Ahasuerus (Est 7:3-6, 8:1-7, 9:13-14) and Ruth counsels Boaz (Ruth 3:9-13).

These parallels cast Esther as a woman of wisdom in the same vein as Lady Wisdom, the woman of virtue, and Ruth. However, upon closer examination, the text's portrayal of Esther's actions and character generates more questions than answers. Even though Esther's plan successfully delivers the Jews from destruction, the text does not directly relate her success to any specific insight or wisdom of hers. For example, Esther's words to Mordecai contain no hint of a thoughtful plan (Est 4:16):

> 4:16   Go, gather all the Jews to be found in Susa, and hold a fast on my behalf, and do not eat or drink for three days, night or day. I and my young women will also fast as you do. Then I will go to the king, though it is against the law, and if I perish, I perish.

Esther seems desperate—desperate enough to risk her life, yet unsure of her next move beyond going to the king. Twice, the king asks her what she wants, and twice, she invites him to a banquet. While this approach may be crafted to please Ahasuerus and set the scene for a larger request, the text does not read that way; in contrast to Ruth and Naomi's calculated plan for Ruth to go to Boaz's threshing floor, Esther seems to be feeling her way to a solution in real time. Doing so certainly requires aplomb, but the true hinge moment of the Esther story arises from the Ahasuerus' insomnia, an event that does not involve Esther at all. Thus, while the text casts Esther as a brave woman, faithful (*hesed*) to her people, the resolution of the Jews' crisis relies on the king's decisions, at times influenced by Esther and Mordecai, but directed from behind the scenes by the God of Israel.

Neighbors in the Writings, the books of Esther and Daniel beg readers to compare their two central figures.[117] The contrasts between them prove glaring:

Esther	Daniel
Hides her identity at Mordecai's instruction (Est 2:10)	Known as a member of the royal family of Judah (Dan 1:3-4)

---

117 A comparison between Esther and Joseph also proves insightful. See Gary E. Schnittjer's comments in *Old Testament Narrative Books: The Israel Story*. Brentwood, TN: B&H Academic, 2023: 186-190.

Esther (cont'd)	Daniel (cont'd)
Eats the king's food and has sex with the king (Est 2:8-17)	Refuses the king's food (Dan 1:8)
No recorded prayers, even when fasting (Est 4:16)	Prays throughout the book, even when illegal (Dan 6)
Compelled at a young age into the king's service and participates in the competition to be the next queen (Est 3)	Compelled at a young age into the king's service and immediately establishes a line of conviction he will not cross by refusing the king's food (Dan 1:8-21)
No mention of wisdom	Repeated affirmations of the wisdom from God throughout the book Daniel renowned across generations as a wise man
Assumes a Persian identity, intentionally hiding her Jewish heritage and name, Hadassah (Est 2:7)	Given a Babylonian name, Belteshazzar (Dan 1:7), but referred to by his Jewish name, Daniel (Dan 5:11-12)

A stark contrast, indeed! With no rights or recourse, faced with the same looming punishment—death—Esther and Daniel follow two opposite approaches to life in Persia/Babylon. Daniel's explicit and consistent allegiance to the God of Israel no matter the consequences highlights the cavernous silence of the text of the book of Esther. One certainly wonders why the author of the book of Esther chose to omit all details regarding her faith. However, the most salient question emerging from this comparison returns to Esther as a wisdom figure. If Esther directly contrasts the model wise man Daniel, why is she included in the canon of women of wisdom?

The authors of the Septuagint (LXX) Esther shared this discomfort with the text's portrayal of Esther. To fill the void in the narrative, the Septuagint edition of Esther expands the MT text by adding passages such as Esther's prayers to the Lord. This selection from the C Addition to the LXX book of Esther illustrates this point; the text in bold closely parallels the book of Daniel. Filling the silence, Esther prays to the Lord:

> C:26 You have knowledge of everything, **and you know that I hate the glory of the lawless and abhor the bed of the uncircumcised and of any foreigner.**
>
> 27 **You know my predicament—that I abhor the sign of my proud position that is upon my head on days when I appear in public. I abhor it like a menstrual cloth, and I do not wear it on the days when I am in private.**
>
> 28 **And your slave has not eaten at Haman's table, and I have not honored the king's banquet nor drunk the wine of libations.**
>
> 29 Your slave has not rejoiced since the day of my change until now, except in you, O Lord, God of Abraham.
>
> 30 **O God who has power over all things, hear the voice of those who despair, and save us from the hand of evildoers.** And save me from my fear![118]

The Septuagint intentionally develops Esther's inner thoughts and convictions, shaping her to mirror Daniel; in this version of the story, Esther addresses the Lord, voices her hatred for Persian extravagance, and leans on her faith in the God of Abraham. In fact, in the LXX, both Esther and Mordecai speak in no uncertain terms about God, the patriarchs, the Exodus, the promises, and the covenants. The silence is filled.

---

118 Pietersma, A. and Wright, B. G., Eds. *Esther. A New English Translation of the Septuagint (Primary Texts).* K. H. Jobes, Trans. New York, NY: Oxford University Press, 2007: Esther C:25-30. The LXX Esther also adds Mordecai's words in Addition C:2-7.

Yet this perspective simply does not emerge from the Hebrew biblical text, the MT. While Esther remains within the *Megilloth* grouping of women of wisdom, the text does not reveal what, exactly, makes her wise. Even the basic prerequisite for wisdom—fearing God—is absent. This peculiar silence within the context of the Writings leaves readers with one certainty: in His sovereignty, the Lord can and does use all kinds of people to accomplish His will, from the great Persian king to the orphaned Jewish girl.

3. The Absence of God

As explained earlier in this chapter, the book of Esther prompts readers to analyze God's absence from its narrative. This study brings other books from the Writings into conversation with Esther, as they, too, allow for the absence of God. The sages of Chronicles, Psalms, the Song, Proverbs, Lamentations, Daniel, and Ruth crowd around, sharing insights about the absence and presence of God in their texts. Esther, Chronicles, and the Psalter begin by talking about the absence of the Lord's kingdom.

Before Nebuchadnezzar sacked Jerusalem, the prophet Jeremiah predicted a 70-year exile for Israel (Jer 25:11-2, 29:10). After reading the prophet's words, Daniel prays to the Lord to restore Jerusalem and His kingdom (Daniel 9). The Lord answers by sending Gabriel to outline His long-term plan to restore Israel forever: the 70 weeks of Daniel. During this same timeframe in Daniel's life, Cyrus of Persia comes to power and issues the decree allowing the Jews to return to Jerusalem and rebuild. These developments must have shocked readers of Jeremiah; instead of the Lord restoring the glorious kingdom of Israel now, the Medes and Persians control the region and reign securely.

2 Chronicles 36:23 and Ezra 1:1-4 both cast the Jews' return from exile as at least an initial fulfillment of the Lord's promises to restore Jerusalem. The events in Esther take place during this ambiguous time: the exile is over, some Jews have returned to the land, rebuilt Jerusalem

and the temple, and yet the kingdom is by no means restored. The book of Ezra-Nehemiah describes the situation during this time, highlighting several dimensions of the Lord's absence:

- The absence of a Davidic king and kingdom. Zerubbabel, from the Davidic line, serves as governor of Judah but Jerusalem and Judah still fall squarely under Persian rule (1 Chron 3:19; Hag 1:1).

- The absence of the Lord's presence in the temple. Sacrifices are restored, but the glory of the Lord does not dwell in the Holy of Holies (Ezra 6:15-16; 2 Chron 7:1-3).

- The absence of the entirety of the nation of Israel, God's chosen people. A remnant of Israel has returned to the land, but many Jews remain elsewhere (Est, Dan).

- The absence of the blessings of the Lord. The remnant does not prosper; they live as slaves in their own land, persecuted by their enemies and greatly distressed at the hands of their Persian overlords (Ezra 4-5; Neh 4, 6, 9:36-37).

This return from exile is no restoration of the glorious days of David and Solomon. During the events of the book of Esther, the Jews in the land and those in exile must have been puzzled about this fulfillment, looking for God's blessings on their efforts and finding ... little. Psalm 126 sings of this distress: after narrating the people's joy at their return from exile (Ps 126:1-3), the psalm quickly repeats the language of the return from exile and asks for further restoration (Ps 126: 4-6):

> 126:4   Restore our captivity, O Lord,
>
> As the streams in the South.
>
> 5   Those who sow in tears shall reap with joyful shouting.
>
> 6   He who goes to and fro weeping, carrying his bag of seed,

> Shall indeed come again with a shout of joy,
> bringing his sheaves with him. (NASB)

In language reminiscent of the emotional reversals of Esther's Purim narrative and Lamentations, Psalm 126 underscores that though the exile is over, Israel's joy at returning to the land has turned to sadness and mourning. While the people live in faith that the Lord reigns in heaven (Pss 92-100), their songs and narratives describe deliverance and joy (Dan 2-6; Esther 9:20-32; Neh 12) but also persecution, distress, and affliction (Ez-Neh; Esther 3-8). As they wait for the permanent return of the Davidic king at the end of time (Dan 2, 7), the people are left to petition the Lord to end their continuing exile from His Presence (Ps 126:4-6; Lam 5:19-22).

Perhaps God's absence from the text of Esther reflects the Persian focus of the text. Since Ahasuerus does not recognize the authority—perhaps even the existence—of the Lord, His name remains absent from the story. From Ahasuerus' human perspective, the God of Israel would be merely another god of yet another conquered people. Since the kingdom of the Lord is effectively absent from the face of the earth, Israel and her God are irrelevant to Ahasuerus, the focus of the Esther story.

A second area of the Lord's absence in the Writings is His silence, His lack of response to His people. This perceived absence features prominently in the Writings: the people in the texts often cry out repeatedly for the Lord to answer them. The books of Psalms and Ruth offer excellent specific examples; in Psalms 10, 13, 22, and 28, David's questions demonstrate a clear sense of abandonment:

> 10:1 Why, O Lord, do you stand far away?
>
> Why do you hide yourself in times of trouble?
>
> 13:1 How long, O Lord? Will you forget me forever?
>
> How long will you hide your face from me?

2	How long must I take counsel in my soul
	And have sorrow in my heart all the day?
	How long shall my enemy be exalted over me?
22:1	My God, my God, why have you forsaken me?
	Why are you so far from saving me, from the words of my groaning?
2	O my God, I cry by day, but you do not answer,
	And by night, but I find no rest.
28:1	To you, O Lord, I call;
	My rock, be not deaf to me,
	Lest, if you be silent to me,
	I become like those who go down to the pit.

As discussed in the chapter on the Psalter, these laments of David typically turn from abandonment to hope, ending with expressions of trust, confidence, and praise. In the book of Ruth, Naomi follows a similar emotional arc. Returning from Moab, she greets her townspeople with these words (Ruth 1:20b-21):

1:20	Do not call me Naomi; call me Mara, for the Almighty has dealt very bitterly with me.
21	I went away full, and the Lord has brought me back empty. Why call me Naomi, when the Lord has testified against me and the Almighty has brought calamity upon me?

Naomi's statement goes further than David's; she aligns herself with Job by pointing to the Lord as the cause of her suffering. Her statement focuses on the absence of the signs of God's presence: His blessing and provision for her life. Later, when Naomi learns that Ruth gleaned in the field of Boaz, her perspective changes; she recognizes that the Lord had not abandoned her and exclaims, "May he [Boaz] be blessed by the Lord, whose kindness (*hesed*) has not forsaken the living or the dead!" (Ruth 2:20). For Naomi, the Lord's kindness to her serves as a manifestation of His presence.

This perceived absence of the Lord arises throughout the Writings, allowing for the reality that even God-fearers such as David, Naomi, and Job feel the absence of the Lord at certain times. These texts offer readers examples to imitate during the delay between one's petition to the Lord and His deliverance. Even and especially when people feel the Lord has abandoned them, the Writings call for God-fearers to be patient, cling to the Lord, and walk in wisdom.

Such cries would fit well between the lines of the Esther narrative. Facing annihilation, Esther, Mordecai, and the Jews of Susa could have voiced the same question as the last verses of Lamentations (5:19-22), asking if the Lord has abandoned them forever, petitioning Him to turn to them and save them from their enemies. Yet Esther contains no mention or hint of such prayers. The closest the text comes to talking about God surfaces in chapter 4, when Mordecai tells Esther (Est 4:13b-14):

> 4:13 Do not think to yourself that in the king's palace you will escape any more than all the other Jews.
>
> 14 For if you keep silent at this time, relief and deliverance will rise for the Jews from another place, but you and your father's house will perish. And who knows whether you have not come to the kingdom for such a time as this?

With these words, Mordecai affirms his belief that "relief and deliverance" for the Jews are indeed on the horizon, regardless of Esther's actions. Mordecai, openly a Jew himself, speaks with certainty of the salvation of the Jewish people yet does not mention the Lord.

His vague statement, referencing something akin to fate, remains puzzling. Compared to other God-fearers' words in the Writings, Mordecai's words fall short of an expression of biblical faith.

A third area of God's absence or presence in a text focuses on characters' and narrator's perspectives. The sages of the books of Ruth and Proverbs offer their texts for this discussion. Unlike the book of Esther, the book of Ruth contains several overt references to the Lord. As expected, the characters talk about the Lord, at times changing their perspective of Him and His actions. Naomi's thoughts quoted above serve as an excellent example. In contrast to Naomi, Ruth, and Daniel, the text of Esther presents no evidence that Mordecai and Esther are God-fearers; their words do not mention God, the patriarchs, the promises, or the covenants. They demonstrate lovingkindness (*hesed*), care, and fidelity to their people, but this *hesed* could be nationalistic loyalty, love for one's fellow Jews.

The narrator's voice, however, shapes the reader's understanding of the whole story, carrying far more weight than the statements of the characters in the midst of the story. In this respect, the book of Ruth mirrors the book of Job: the narrator shapes the way the reader understands Job's situation far more than Job's words themselves. The narrator of the book of Ruth refers to the Lord one single time: the Lord "gave Ruth conception" (Ruth 4:13). This statement attributes the major redemptive event of the story—the continuation of the seed of Judah to King David—to a specific and pointed action of the Lord's. The narrator's sentence expands readers' understanding of God's hand at work in the story; if the Lord gave Ruth conception, is He not also involved in the other major events of her life? The narrator thus prompts readers to understand major events in the text as the providential hand of God: Elimelech's death, Ruth's faithfulness, Ruth walking into Boaz' field.

The sage of Proverbs now adds to this conversation about the Lord's hidden providence. While Proverbs calls readers to make the wisdom decision to fear the Lord and become one with His wisdom, the book also teaches about His sovereign providential work. For instance, the book's central chapter, Proverbs 16, describes the Lord's involvement in human decisions and deeds (Prov 16:1-2, 4, 7, 9, 11):

> 16:1 The plans of the heart belong to man,
>
> But the answer of the tongue is from the Lord.
>
> 2 All the ways of a man are pure in his own eyes,
>
> But the Lord weighs the spirit.
>
> 4 The Lord has made everything for its purpose,
>
> Even the wicked for the day of trouble.
>
> 7 When a man's ways please the Lord,
>
> He makes even his enemies to be at peace with him.
>
> 9 The heart of man plans his way,
>
> But the Lord establishes his steps.
>
> 11 A just balance and scales are the Lord's;
>
> All the weights in the bag are his work.

After these verses emphasizing the Lord's direction over people's hearts and their ways, Proverbs 16 pivots to address the choice of wisdom over folly, underscoring the importance of human decisions (Prov 16:16-17):

> 16:16 How much better to get wisdom than gold!
>
> To get understanding is to be chosen rather than silver.
>
> 17 The highway of the upright turns aside from evil;
>
> Whoever guards his way preserves his life.

At the exact center of the book of Proverbs, these verses reiterate the importance of the wisdom decision in the midst of a chapter emphasizing the Lord's providential control, even in the smallest of events. Proverbs 16 goes on to end with verse 33:

> 16:33   The lot is cast into the lap,
>
> But its every decision is from the Lord.

These examples from Proverbs articulate a dynamic the Writings appear quite comfortable with: the horizontal reality of humanity's wisdom/folly decisions intersects with the vertical reality of the Lord's providential oversight. How the providence of God and individual human decisions work together or against one another is a mystery, yet the Writings, and specifically Proverbs, consistently pair the two without explaining their intersection. With this background, readers of the book of Esther would see the hand of the Lord at work in Ahasuerus' decisions, even within the silence of the text itself.[119]

Lastly, the Lord can simply be absent from the words of the text. Both the book of Esther and the Song of Songs omit any mention of God from their pages. Though it may contain a hint of the name of the Lord (see Chapter 7), the Song focuses on the human, Garden of Delight ('*eden*) experience of love between a man and a woman. Like so many of Solomon's proverbs, this wisdom text concentrates on life at the horizontal level, on the plane of human existence. Since the love presented in the book is creational, any human, God-fearer or not, can experience this creational blessing from the Lord. The backdrop of creation shapes readers' context for the Song: God created love and marriage, the focus of the book. The same is true of the book of Esther. As discussed earlier in this chapter, creation sets expectations regarding rule and rulers for the rest of the OT. Ahasuerus' rule comes from the Lord, who orchestrates this king's decisions as He sees fit. The Lord is present in the content of the text without being present in its words.

God is absent in every one of these ways within the text of Esther. Silence on the matter reigns, requiring readers to look to other

---

[119] For more connections between Esther and Proverbs see Shemaryahu Talmon. "'Wisdom' in the Book of Esther." *Vetus Testamentum* 13 (1963): 419–455.

books in the Writings to see God's presence and sovereignty between the lines of this thrilling tale.

Toward the New Testament

1. Kings and Kingdoms

The church lives between Jesus' first and second comings, demonstrating faith, hope, and love until Christ returns to establish His eternal earthly kingdom. At his trial before Pilate, Jesus echoes the OT's words on the source of Gentile authority (John 19:11):

> 19:11 Jesus answered him, "You would have no authority over me at all unless it had been given you from above."

This delegation of rule does not change at Jesus' ascension; God still gives Gentile kings and kingdoms the authority to rule over the nations of the earth. The NT makes clear that the church must submit to and obey these governing powers (Rom 13:1-5; Tit 3:1; 1 Pet 2:13-17). In the first century, the Gentile power in question was Rome. The Romans' titles for their emperors signal the dual political and religious dimensions of their role, setting up an easy comparison with Jesus as King-Priest. While these Roman, Latin names themselves are not in the NT, their meanings certainly are:

- *Imperator*, supreme commander // ruler of the kings of the earth (Rev 1:5, 17:14, 19:16)
- *Pontifex* maximus, high priest // high priest according to Melchizedek (Heb 5)
- *Augustus*, exalted one // highly exalted one to whom every knee will bow (Phil 2:9-11)
- *Princeps*, first citizen // firstborn (Rom 8:29; Col 1:15)

In not-so-subtle ways, the NT paints Jesus as rightly occupying the place claimed by the Roman emperor. The early church's persecution arose from their refusal to participate in emperor worship, even if the consequences led to suffering and death. Their example serves as a reminder to the church: Gentile kings and governments exist only for a time and as the God of Heaven wills. In the end, the rule of "Babylon" will fall; no Gentile ruler will prevail when the Messiah comes to rule the earth forever (Rev 14:8, Rev 18-19).

2. *NT Women of Wisdom*

The NT continues the *Megilloth*'s theme of women of wisdom. Mary, the mother of Jesus, plays the role of a new Eve, a new Ruth, and a new woman of virtue (see discussion in the Ruth chapter). Through Jesus, the promised seed of the woman (Gen 3:15), Mary influences her world for good: like Obed, Jesus will redeem and restore the life of Israel (Ruth 4:14-15) and ultimately transform all creation (Prov 8:22-31, 31:10-31). The NT goes on to record many other women serving as agents or catalysts in Jesus' ministry and the work of the apostles. Women played significant roles in several areas:

a. Proclamation of the Gospel

- Mary Magdalene, Joanna, and Susanna supported Jesus' ministry financially (Luke 8:1-3).

- Mary Magdalene announced the resurrection to the disciples (Matt 28:5-10; Mark 16:1-14; Luke 23:55-24:12; John 20:1-18).

- Priscilla and Aquila explained the Gospel to Apollos (Acts 18).

- Timothy's grandmother, Lois, and mother, Eunice, taught him from the Scriptures about salvation in Christ Jesus (2 Tim 1:5, 3:14-15).

b. Evangelization of their own people

- Lydia was the first convert in Thyatira and a central figure in the salvation of others (Acts 16:14-40).

- The Samaritan woman called the people of her city to come

and hear Jesus' words (John 4:28-29, 39-42).

c. Participation in the work of the apostles

- Phoebe, Priscilla, Mary, and Junia helped Paul in various ways, sometimes at their peril (Rom 16:1-7). Phoebe, a servant/deacon (*diakonos*), may have delivered Paul's epistle to the Romans.

- Syntyche and Euodia shared Paul's struggle for the Gospel as fellow workers (Phil 4:2-3).

- Tabitha/Dorcas is described as a woman of virtue doing good to all: "this woman was abounding with deeds of kindness and charity which she continually did" (Acts 9:36, 9:36-43).

These NT women echo the OT's Lady Wisdom, the woman of virtue, Ruth, and Esther; agents of salvation, their deeds impact their world for good.

3. The Absence of God

On the cross, Jesus Himself joins those who speak of the absence of God when He quotes Psalm 22:1, "My God, My God, why have You forsaken Me?" (Matt 27:46; Mark 15:34). This moment dovetails with Jesus becoming sin and bearing God's judgment for the sin of the world (2 Cor 5:21; Rom 3:25-26, 8:3; Heb 2:17). It appears that at this moment, Jesus is separated from God, theologically and/or experientially. When Jesus later commits His spirit into the hands of His Father (Luke 23:46), the union between Father and Son has been restored; Jesus' sacrifice for sin has been accepted. "It is finished" (John 19:30).

Jesus' ascension adds another twist to the discussion of the absence of God and His kingdom. After His resurrection, Jesus gathers the disciples together and instructs them to wait for the Holy Spirit to come upon them. The disciples ask Jesus if He will restore the kingdom to Israel (Acts 1:6); Jesus answers by explaining that the Holy Spirit will empower them to be witnesses of His death, burial, and resurrection (Acts 1:8). He then ascends to heaven. This sequence must have stunned and confused the disciples: Jesus comes back from the dead, just to leave them with no restored earthly kingdom? The events of Pentecost ensue: God sends the Holy Spirit to dwell within them, empowering Christians to serve as witnesses to Christ's life through their life (Rom 8:20; Gal 2:20; Phil 1:19; Col 1:27). While Jesus and His kingdom are absent from the earth between Christ's first and second comings, God is present through His indwelling Spirit.

In light of this absence, Christians have recited and sung from the book of Psalms for millennia. Many published versions of the NT include the Psalter, speaking to the relevance of these texts for the church, those who live in the period between Jesus' two advents. Questions of why, when, and how long constitute much of the prayer life of the church. One day, the glorious kingdom of God will return to earth under Jesus the Messiah. Until then, the church is called to walk in wisdom, cultivating faith, hope, and love.

Further Reading

Goswell, Greg (Gregory Ross). "The Place of the Book of Esther in the Canon." *Trinity Journal* 37 (2): 155–70.

Melton, Brittany N. *Where is God in the Megilloth? A Dialogue on the Ambiguity of Divine Presence and Absence.* Old Testament Studies, 73. Leiden: Brill, 2018.

Melton, Brittany and David Firth, Eds. *Reading Esther Intertextually. Library of Hebrew Bible/Old Testament Studies.* New York, NY: Bloomsbury T&T Clark, 2022.

Stone, Timothy J. "Esther's Frame within the Writings." Donn F. Morgan, Ed. *The Oxford Handbook of the Writings of the Hebrew Bible,* New York, NY: Oxford Handbooks, 2018.

Sun, Chloe Tse. *Conspicuous in His Absence: Studies in the Song of Songs and Esther.* Downers Grove, IL: Intervarsity, 2021.

Daniel: The Power and Wisdom of the God of Heaven

Old Testament Background to the Book of Daniel

- Jeremiah's prediction of Judah's exile: Jer 25:1-11, 29:1-32
- Sabbatical year and jubilee: Lev 25:1-7
- The exile of Judah and Jehoiakim: 2 Kings 24:1-5; 2 Chron 36:1-8
- The empire of Babylon (*babel*): 2 Kings 20-25; 2 Chron 32-36; Is 13-14, 47-48; Jer 50-51
- The tower of Babel (*babel*): Gen 10:10, 11:1-9
- Joseph serving in Pharaoh's court: Gen 37-50
- Forgiveness and the temple: 2 Chron 6
- 7 days of creation, ending with the Sabbath: Gen 1:3-2:3
- God's creation of *'adam*: Gen 1:26-30

Creation and Daniel: The Rule of Babylon

The book of Daniel connects back to Genesis through God's charge to humanity (*'adam*) to rule over His creation. After God creates *'adam* in His image, He tasks them with ruling over all the animals and the earth (Gen 1:26). After the Fall, God chooses Israel and the kingdom of David to serve as His representative rulers (Ex 19:5-6; 1 Chron 17:9-14). When the Lord exiles the kingdom of Judah, He delegates the rule of the earth to a series of Gentile nations; in Daniel 2:37-38, Daniel's words to Nebuchadnezzar echo God's words to *'adam*:

> 2:37 You, O king, the king of kings, to whom the God of heaven has given the kingdom, the power, and the might, and the glory,

> 38 and into whose hand he has given, wherever they dwell, the children of man, the beasts of the field, and the birds of the heavens, making you rule over them all, ...

Both here in chapter 2 and again in chapter 4, Daniel explains that the great king's authority comes from the God of heaven. Nebuchadnezzar has been given dominion and rule over all: humans, lands, and animals. As the king's dream reveals, this era of Gentile rule begins with Nebuchadnezzar, the head of gold, and will ultimately be overturned only by the kingdom of God (Dan 2). Daniel's vision of the four beasts in chapter 7 echoes this arrangement: the succession of earthly kingdoms will each be ruled by Gentile kings, followed in the end by a son of Adam ruling all the nations for God (Dan 7:13-14; Gen 1:26). The book of Daniel and the Writings foretell Israel's continued persecution and deliverance until the Son of Man (*'adam*) returns and rules the earth forever.

The Book of Daniel: An Outline

Daniel chapter 1 presents young Daniel as the consummate wise person, one who understands visions and dreams. This thread holds the whole book together: throughout Daniel 2-12, the text narrates Daniel's ability to receive insight (*sekel*) and understanding (*binah*) into the meaning of his and other people's visons.

The book of Daniel was written in two different languages: Hebrew and Aramaic, the common language of the Gentile world during Daniel's time. The Aramaic section of the book, Daniel 2-7, records the visions and narratives focusing on Gentile kings, kingdoms, and their relationship to God and His kingdom. In Daniel 7, Daniel himself begins experiencing visions and receives wisdom to understand them. Daniel 8-12, written in Hebrew, turns its focus to the future of Israel and the empires of Persia and Greece. After the introduction of chapter 1, both the Aramaic and Hebrew sections of the book form chiasms:

Daniel 1 – Introduction: Daniel taken into exile and given wisdom

ARAMAIC LANGUAGE SECTION

Daniel 2 – Nebuchadnezzar's dream of Gentile rule and the coming kingdom of God

Daniel 3 – Nebuchadnezzar's image and the three young men in the furnace

Daniel 4 – Nebuchadnezzar judged for his pride and restored

Daniel 5 – Belshazzar judged for his pride and assassinated

Daniel 6 – Daniel delivered from the lions' den

Daniel 7 – Daniel's vison of the beasts and a son of man[120]

HEBREW LANGUAGE SECTION

Daniel 8 – Daniel's visions of Persia and Greece

Daniel 9 – Daniel's prayer and vision for temple, people, and city: 70 "weeks"

Daniel 10-11 – Daniel's visions of Persia and Greece

Daniel 12 – Conclusion: Go your way until the end!

The book ends with Daniel seeking further wisdom and understanding about his final vision, without receiving any. Instead, he is instructed to continue on the path of wisdom until the end.

---

[120] Daniel 7 serves as a hinge chapter, tying in to both the Aramaic section (Dan 2-7) and Daniel's own visions (Dan 7-12).

Major Themes: Daniel the Wise, God's Creation Decrees Realized, and 70 "Weeks" of Exile

1. Daniel the Wise

Any biblical book's textual "neighborhood," or context, shapes the way readers categorize that book. The Christian Bible houses the book of Daniel with other prophecy books, after Ezekiel and before Hosea. Jesus Himself mentions Daniel as a prophet in Matthew 24:15. However, within the Hebrew OT, Daniel's textual neighborhood is the Davidic kingdom section of the Writings; this placement within the Lamentations-to-Ezra-Nehemiah sequence emphasizes the text's Davidic and wisdom themes.

The book of Daniel opens with the fall of the Davidic kingdom and Israel being exiled by the Babylonians; certain youths from the royal family (lit. "seed of the kingdom," Dan 1:3) are taken to Babylon to serve King Nebuchadnezzar. By focusing on Daniel and his three companions, the narrative underscores that although the Davidic kingdom is no more, the seed of Judah and David live on in exile. Daniel 1 continues, describing Daniel as:

- skillful in all wisdom, endowed with knowledge, understanding learning (1:4)

- endowed by God with learning and skill in all literature and wisdom (1:17)

- understanding all visions and dreams (1:17)

- ten times wiser than all the magicians and enchanters in all the kingdom in every matter of wisdom and understanding about which the king inquired (1:20)

In no uncertain terms, Daniel is here described as the wisest of the wise men; the rest of the book showcases his ability to interpret visions and dreams in particular.

2. God's Creation Decrees Realized

In Genesis 1, God created 'adam in His image to rule over the fish, birds, cattle, and everything that moves on the earth (Gen 1:26). God decreed that 'adam (male and female) should be fruitful, multiply and fill the earth, and subdue it (Gen 1:28). After the fall of 'adam, this divine decree still stands; 'adam, the Creator's image bearer, will rule the earth through the seed of the woman (Gen 3:16), of Abraham (Gen 12:1-3), of Judah (Gen 49:8-12), and ultimately of David (1 Chron 17:11-14). However, beginning with the exile, God appoints Gentile nations to power until His eternal kingdom comes to earth. Daniel 2, 3, 4, and 7 specifically present Gentile kings as ruling the earth through the authority given them by the God of heaven:

- In Daniel 2, Daniel reveals the mystery of King Nebuchadnezzar's dream: Gentile kingdoms are portrayed as a man ruling the earth. These earthly kingdoms end with the coming of God's eternal and heavenly kingdom.

- In Daniel 3, Nebuchadnezzar sets up a golden image of himself and requires peoples and nations of every language (Gen 10) to worship the king's image as a god. The Most High God subverts this event, demonstrating His superiority over the king's authority and commandments.

- In Daniel 4, King Nebuchadnezzar dreams of himself as a tree visible to all the earth, with beasts, birds, and all living creatures underneath its branches. The tree is then cut down and bound. According to Daniel's interpretation, this dream again reminds Nebuchadnezzar that the Most High God rules over 'adam and bestows earthly rule on whomever He wishes (Dan 4:33-35).

- In Daniel 7, four great beasts come out of the sea and rule the earth in succession. However, in the end, one like a son of man (Aram. 'enash) receives eternal rule over the earth; all peoples and nations of every language serve Him forever (7:13-14).

As the Lord repeatedly tells Nebuchadnezzar through Daniel, Gentile kings and kingdoms rule the earth by divine appointment between the exile and the coming of the Son of Adam. In this interim period, God's people will suffer times of distress, but they must go their way on the path of wisdom until the end (Dan 12:12-13). When God's plan for creation is realized, the wise will inherit God's kingdom and be raised from death to glorious, everlasting life (Dan 12:1-3).

3. 70 "Weeks" of Exile

When the prophet Jeremiah announces the Babylonian exile, he also reveals that after 70 years, the Lord will fulfill His promise to restore Israel (Jer 25:11-12, 29:10-14). Cyrus's decree allowing the people to return to the land marks the fulfillment of this promise. Given its importance, the Writings record the Cyrus decree in two places: at the very end of the first book of the Writings and at the very beginning of the last book of the Writings (2 Chron 36:33; Ezra 1:1-4). These two books form a backdrop, a historical context, for the remaining books in the Writings between them:

Chronicles, **Cyrus Decree** > *Psalms - Daniel* < **Cyrus Decree**, Ezra-Nehemiah

When reading the Writings, readers are meant to understand the content of the books between the bookends as pertinent to life after the exile is over, after Cyrus' decree. This does not mean all the texts in the Writings were originally written after the exile. Curators of the Writings selected and grouped texts written before, during, and after the exile into a collection especially relevant to God-fearers after the Davidic kingdom is destroyed and the exile is technically over. As Ezra-Nehemiah illustrates, the "post-exile" was a time of distress for the Jews, of slavery on their own land (Ez 9:7, 9; Neh 9:36-37). The Writings repeatedly highlight the faithful suffering while remaining on the path of wisdom: David, Job, Naomi, Jerusalem, Esther and her people, the people of Ezra and Nehemiah's day. In the book of Daniel, Daniel and his three friends suffer under Gentile rule but still walk in wisdom, remaining faithful to God.

Daniel's vision of the 70 "weeks" forms a unique contribution to the OT and the Writings. This vision reveals that although the Most High God will indeed fulfill His promise to destroy Babylon and bring the people back to the land, the exile will be extended by 70 "weeks." Daniel 2 and 7 both present four phases of Israel's exile until the coming of the kingdom of God. The expression "post-exile" is thus somewhat inaccurate in that God continues His people's exile by giving the rule of the earth to Gentile kingdoms. A more accurate but awkward way to name this era is the "post-exile exile."

The Sages in Conversation

1. Daniel the Wise

As previously explained, Daniel is presented as the consummate wise person in exile. The text uses four specific wisdom terms to describe his character or virtue (*hayil*):

- Daniel was skillful (*sakal*) in all wisdom (*hokmah*), endowed with knowledge (*yada'*), understanding (*binah*) learning (Dan 1:4).

- God gave the four youths learning (*yada'*) and skill (*sakal*) in all literature and wisdom (*hokmah*). Daniel also had understanding (*binah*) of visions and dreams (Dan 1:17).

Upon hearing this list, the sage of the book of Proverbs perks up. Proverbs 1:2-6 uses the same four terms to describe the purpose of Proverbs:

1:2	To know **wisdom** (*hokmah*) and instruction,
	To **understand** (*bin*) words of **insight** (*binah*),
3	To receive instruction in **wise dealing** (*sakal*),
	In righteousness, justice, and equity;
4	To give prudence to the simple,
	Knowledge (*yada'*) and discretion to the youth—

> 5   Let the wise hear and increase in learning,
>
>   And the one who **understands** (*bin*) obtain guidance,
>
> 6   To **understand** (*bin*) a proverb and a figure,
>
>   The words of the wise and their riddles. (NASB)

This overlap in wording shapes Daniel as a living example of the son of Proverbs 1-9: the youth who makes the decision to embrace Lady Wisdom. Young Daniel arrives in Babylon already possessing some wisdom; the Chaldeans then educate and train him for three years in preparation for his service to King Nebuchadnezzar (Dan 1:4). Daniel 1:17 then adds that the Lord gave Daniel and his three friends wisdom—Daniel was both gifted and a learner.

As the text continues, Daniel shows his wisdom through his words and deeds, beginning with his refusal of the king's choice food and drink (Dan 1:8-16). At first glance, against the backdrop of the OT's dietary laws, Daniel appears to reject this food and drink to avoid defiling himself.[121] However, a closer look at the text suggests another interpretation:

- The food in question is described as "the king's choice food" and the wine as the wine "which [the king] drank." The issue with the food and drink relates to the king—Babylonian gods and Mosaic Law are never mentioned.

- Mosaic Law forbids certain foods but not drinking wine.

- Daniel's solution still involves his consumption of Babylonian foods and water. These replacement foods would not automatically abide by Mosaic dietary law.

---

121 Although the word "defile" (*ga'al*) refers to ceremonial defilement, the verb is also used of sin in general (Is 59:3; Lam 4:4; Zeph 3:1).

Later in the book, Daniel 11:26 uses the same phrase, "eating the king's choice food," to refer to persons loyal to the king. These textual details point to Daniel refusing the king's choice food and wine because those elements symbolize allegiance to King Nebuchadnezzar.[122] Though he serves in the king's court, as Joseph did in Egypt, Daniel repeatedly voices his devotion to the God of Israel. Apparently, Daniel cannot maintain his allegiance to the Lord while eating the king's food and drinking his wine—so Daniel chooses the Lord. Furthermore, this young man finds a way to maintain his convictions without getting his supervisor in trouble for Daniel's personal decisions. Such a plan is wise indeed. Even as a youth, Daniel appears to be living out Proverbs 1:7: "the fear of the Lord is the beginning of wisdom."

The text goes on to describe Daniel as a man seeking to stay on the path of wisdom all his days; he serves many Gentile kings well. As the years go by, the text records no mistakes, faults, or sins of Daniel's. Descending from the royal seed of Judah, Daniel is the kind of wise son of David the Writings long for.

But Daniel embodies the wisdom of Proverbs 1:2-6 in yet another area: the sphere of "riddles" or "dark sayings" (*hidah*). Often surprising contemporary readers, riddles (*hidah*) appear throughout the OT: kings need help solving riddles (Dan 5), Korah and Asaph call their psalms riddles (Ps 49:1, 78:2), even Samson answers questions in riddle form (Judges 15). According to Proverbs 1:6, the wise use wisdom:

> 1:6   To understand a proverb and a saying (*melisah*),
>
> The words of the wise and their riddles (*hidah*).

In this proverb, "riddle" is parallel to "saying," a word also translated "enigma" (NKJV). Though Daniel 1 portrays Daniel and his three friends as all possessing the virtues of wisdom, only Daniel understands visions and

---

[122] Greg Goswell summarizes his discussion of Daniel's ethics, saying, "What we have discovered in the book of Daniel, therefore, is a species of kingdom ethics, with loyalty to God as King the virtue repeatedly on display in the actions of the protagonists." "The Ethics of the Book of Daniel." *Restoration Quarterly* 57:3 (2015): 142. Daniel 3 and 6 display this same loyalty.

dreams (Dan 1:17). He initially demonstrates this ability to explain enigmas by telling King Nebuchadnezzar both his dream and its interpretation (Dan 2:17-23); he does so again in Daniel 4, and again in chapter 5. Years later, when none of the wise men of Babylon can translate the writing on the wall, the queen[123] advises King Belshazzar to call for Daniel, describing him with the wisdom terms in bold (Dan 5:11-12):

> 5:11 There is a man in your kingdom **in whom is the spirit of the holy gods.** In the days of your father, **light and understanding and wisdom like the wisdom of the gods were found in him**, and King Nebuchadnezzar, your father—your father the king—made him chief of the magicians, enchanters, Chaldeans, and astrologers,
>
> 12 because **an excellent spirit, knowledge, and understanding to interpret dreams, explain riddles, and solve problems were found in this Daniel**, whom the king named Belteshazzar. Now let Daniel be called, and he will show the interpretation.

When the king needs wisdom, the queen, here a woman wisdom figure herself, points to Daniel. With this unusual ability to explain riddles (Aram. *'ahidah*), Daniel completes the description of wisdom in Proverbs 1:1-6; among all the wise men of the OT, he stands out as the exemplar of the son of wisdom. It seems fitting that, as the rest of the book of Daniel reveals, God chose this particular wise man to experience and record insights into the future of His people. One can imagine the sage of Proverbs nodding approvingly, eyes glowing with pride, at the description and role of this wise Daniel.

Within this conversation about riddles, the book of Daniel introduces a new wisdom term to this discussion between sages: "mystery" (Aram. *raz*). In Daniel 2, Babylon's wisest men tell the king

---

[123] The NCV translates "queen mother" here.

no man on earth could reveal both the dream and its meaning; only the gods can do that (Dan 2:10-11). These wise men are correct; the resolution to this crisis comes from a god: Daniel's God. After Daniel and his three friends petition the God of heaven for compassion concerning this mystery (*raz*, Dan 2:18), Daniel blesses the God of heaven. Notice the wisdom language in bold (Dan 2:20b-23):

> 2:20 Blessed be the name of God forever and ever,
>
> To whom belong **wisdom and might**.
>
> 21 He changes times and seasons;
>
> He removes kings and sets up kings;
>
> He gives **wisdom to the wise**
>
> And **knowledge** to those who have **understanding**;
>
> 22 He reveals **deep and hidden things**;
>
> He knows what is in the darkness,
>
> And the light dwells with him.
>
> 23 To you, O God of my fathers,
>
> I give thanks and praise,
>
> For you have given me **wisdom and might**,
>
> And have now **made known** to me what we asked of you,
>
> For you have **made known** to us the king's matter.

In this prayer of thanks, Daniel attributes his insight directly to God, the One who gives wisdom and power to those who have understanding. How the Lord does so is not explained: in these first six chapters, God never speaks to Daniel the way He speaks to the prophets. In later chapters, Daniel receives explanations of his visions from angelic guides, but here, he simply attributes his wisdom and might to God. The Gentiles in the stories agree: they repeatedly describe Daniel as possessing "the spirit of the holy gods" (Dan 4:8, 9, 18, 5:11, 14).[124] All parties acknowledge the same truth: the interpretation of dreams and visions—mystery—is the realm of divine wisdom.

Though Joseph interprets dreams and Zechariah's visions include an angelic guide (Gen 37-50; Zech 1-6), the Writings do not provide any real conversation partners on the topic of "mysteries" about the future. This sphere is uniquely Daniel's. However, the sages of Job and Psalms connect this idea of mystery to wisdom. In Daniel 2:22, Daniel describes the mysteries the Lord reveals as "deep" (Aram. *'amiq*), "hidden" (Aram. *setar*), existing in the "darkness" (Aram. *hashok*). The sage of the book of Job chimes in here: Job also learns of the wisdom and power of God, specifically in His sovereignty over creation (Job 12:13-24). Only the Almighty "reveals the deep things of darkness and brings deep shadows into the light" (Job 12:22, NIV). In the book of Job, the Lord Himself broadens out riddles and dark sayings to include humanity's attempt to understand the wisdom of the creation.[125] Humans seek answers to this mystery but cannot find them. Only God knows where wisdom is found; it is hidden from the eyes of all the living (Job 28:21).

The book of Psalms also touches on this notion of the mystery of the past. In Psalms 49:4 and 78:2 respectively, Korah and Asaph describe their psalm as a parable (*mashal*) and riddle (*hidah*): "dark sayings" (NASB) or "hidden things" (NIV). Asaph's psalm provides a poetic recounting of the history of Israel; his riddle focuses on the meaning of Israel's history. The psalm's lesson is two-fold: first, God's people have failed to believe the Lord; they repeatedly sin and rebel against Him. Second, the Lord is compassionate, forgiving, patient, and merciful (Ps 78:38-39, the center of the psalm). These two themes

---

124 In Genesis 41:38, Pharaoh uses the same kind of language when he refers to Joseph as "one having the Spirit of God" (or "a divine spirit" NASB).

125 This limitation echoes *Qohelet*'s unsuccessful search for the overall scheme of creation (Eccl 7:25, 27).

should not surprise the reader; the dual threads of Israel's rebellion and the Lord's compassion run through the entire OT (see Neh 9). What does surprise the reader is Asaph's conclusion to this riddle: the advent of David, a man of integrity (*tom*) and skill (*tebunah*) to shepherd Israel. How are readers in the post-exile to understand this psalm, since David is dead and the kingdom is no more? Is the coming of King David in Psalm 78 a picture of another "King David" to come?

Korah ends his brief collection, Psalms 42-49 of Book II, with a psalm directed to all inhabitants of the earth: a psalm of wisdom (*hokmah*) and understanding (*tebunah*), a proverb (*mashal*) and a riddle (*hidah*) (Ps 49:3-4). Korah's song shifts the riddle to one's personal life; when God-fearers find themselves in the midst of adversity, unable to see clearly through their suffering, Korah refocuses them on the ultimate end of fools and the wise. Understanding the meaning of life as it unfolds often proves difficult (see also Ps 88). Instead of offering a direct resolution to this common conundrum, Korah advocates taking the long view of human lives: in the end, the wise will be redeemed (Ps 49:15). Korah's psalm provides the wisdom of a divine perspective through which to see, if not unravel, the knots of daily life.

The sages involved in this short conversation fall silent, united in both their approval of Daniel the wise and their ongoing perplexity at the mysteries of the past, present, and future. Though He gives the wise glimpses of insight, only the Lord fully understands such riddles. These deep and hidden truths remain beyond human comprehension, in the dark.

2. God's Creation Decrees Realized

As mentioned earlier in this chapter, the thread of the authority to rule runs throughout the visions and dreams of the book of Daniel. Progressively, the Lord unveils His plan for the earth after the fall of Jerusalem. In this conversation, the sages of Daniel, Chronicles, and the Psalter gather around to discuss the outworking of the Creator's decree to '*adam* to reign as His image-bearer.

Surprising His people, God gives the rule of the earth to Gentile kings who do not worship Him or image Him properly. Before the exile, the Lord ruled through the Davidic line from His temple in Jerusalem. At the exile, He transfers His authority to Nebuchadnezzar of Babylon and three successive Gentile kingdoms. Nebuchadnezzar's dream of the image of a man in Daniel 2 sketches out world history until God's coming eternal kingdom: the stone of the dream. During his interpretation, Daniel uses "rule" language, echoing Genesis 1:26-28, below in bold (Dan 2:37-38):

> 2:37 You, O king, are the king of kings. The God of heaven has given you **dominion** and power and might and glory;
>
> 38 in your hands he has placed mankind and **the beasts of the field and the birds of the air**. Wherever they live, he has made you ruler over them all. You are that head of gold. (NIV)

Daniel goes on to give a precise interpretation only of the head of gold (Dan 2:38),[126] phase one of Israel's exile. Phases two, three, and four—the chest, thighs, and feet of the man—represent three unnamed kingdoms following Babylon; the fourth is destroyed by the stone, the eternal kingdom of God (Dan 2:44-45). Through this vision, Daniel learns that only after all four phases of Israel's exile will the Lord reign forever over the earth. Though Daniel 2 leaves out any verbal reference to 'adam, the statue's form—a man—predicts the earth will be ruled by a series of divinely designated, Gentile 'adam. Admittedly, the kingdom of God does not take human form in this vision; as a matter of fact, the stone is "cut out without hands" (Dan 2:34). The emphasis here appears to be on the contrast between the Gentile kingdoms and the heavenly kingdom of God that will fill the whole earth.

---

[126] The visions in Daniel 8 and 10-11 mention the Medes and Persians as well as Greece. Though all Daniel's vision appears to treat the end times, the book of Daniel does not explicitly explain the relationship of these later visions to those in Daniel 2 and 7.

Nebuchadnezzar fails to learn the full lesson of his dream; though he acknowledges Daniel's God as a revealer of mysteries (Dan 2:47), he then displays his continued arrogance by erecting a golden image of himself for all peoples and nations to worship. Given the dream he just had, Nebuchadnezzar appears to be overtly rejecting Daniel's prediction that his rule will come to an end—the whole statue, not just its head, is gold. With this statue, King Nebuchadnezzar of Babylon declares his unmatched greatness. The fiery furnace incident ensues; Daniel's God leaves Nebuchadnezzar unable to enforce his own commandments—his execution of Shadrach, Meshach, and Abednego is publicly foiled by "one like a son of god" (Dan 3:25). Once again, the king fails to learn his lesson; though he declares that no other god can deliver like Shadrach, Meshach, and Abednego's God (Dan 3:29), he still resists putting himself under the authority of the King of Heaven.

Nebuchadnezzar ultimately learns this lesson in Daniel 4, after yet another dream. Containing the creation elements of trees, abundance, beasts of the field, and birds of the sky, this dream predicts Nebuchadnezzar's judgment for his arrogance. As foretold, the great king of Babylon lives like an animal for seven units of time—probably years. Only then does he acknowledge the Lord's rule over all creation, including himself (Dan 4:34b-35); he blesses, praises, and honors the Most High God:

> 4:34 For his dominion is an everlasting dominion,
>
> And his kingdom endures from generation to generation;
>
> 35 All the inhabitants of the earth are accounted as nothing,
>
> And he does according to his will among the host of heaven
>
> And among the inhabitants of the earth;
>
> And none can stay his hand
>
> Or say to him, "What have you done?"

Nebuchadnezzar finally declares what all humans should understand: the Almighty rules over all creation. Any and all authority on earth stems from His will (Dan 4:25); as He decreed in the beginning, the Most High God rules through the 'adam of His choosing.

After the Lord clearly establishes His authority over the Gentile rulers of the time—Nebuchadnezzar, Belshazzar, and Darius—the book of Daniel turns its attention more specifically to the future of Israel. Still treating the topic of rule and authority against the backdrop of creation, beginning in Daniel 7, an angelic interpreter helps Daniel understand his own visions. In this vision, the created world is all mixed up. Instead of the beasts being formed from the ground (Dan 1:24), they emerge from the sea (Dan 7:2-3). Instead of 'adam ruling as image-bearers over the beasts of the earth (Gen 1:26), the beasts have dominion over the earth and 'adam. Ultimately, order is restored by "one like a son of man" (Aram. 'enash) who receives from the Ancient of Days an eternal kingdom: all peoples and nations will serve this human being (Dan 7:13-14). Daniel's angelic guide then adds (Dan 7:16-17):

> 7:17 These four great beasts are four kings who shall arise out of the earth.
>
> 18 But the saints of the Most High shall receive the kingdom and possess the kingdom forever, forever and ever.

According to the dream and its interpretation, both the human figure of Daniel 7:13 and God's saints receive the kingdom. It seems that this human figure represents or embodies the saints of God. This statement in Daniel 7 reveals a significant piece of new information: the angel predicts that in the future as in the days of the Davidic kingdom, a righteous 'adam will rule over the earth with His redeemed people. At this time, the Creator's decree of Genesis 1 will be fulfilled forever.

The sage of Chronicles leans into the conversation here, offering connections between Daniel, Genesis 1-3, and the narrative arc of David and Solomon:

- In Genesis 1:26, an 'adam made in God's image rules on earth for Him. In Chronicles 17:11-14, the Lord chooses an 'adam, David and his seed, to rule on the Lord's throne and build Him a house. Daniel 7 predicts a coming 'adam to reign as the image bearer of the Lord.

- In Genesis, God creates and then rests (Gen 1, 2:1-3). In Chronicles, David defeats his enemies, subdues the earth, and enjoys God's rest (1 Chron 18-20, 22:18). The 'adam of Daniel 7 follows this same pattern: he conquers the fourth Gentile kingdom and brings eternal rest to the earth.

- Following the pattern of the Garden as a meeting place for 'adam and the Lord, Solomon builds the temple, the Lord's dwelling place, where His people come to worship Him. In Daniel 7, when the 'adam figure reigns, Israel and all the nations of the earth worship the Lord and dwell with Him under His rule in His eternal kingdom.

God's plan in Genesis 1-3 revolves around 'adam subduing the earth by subduing the serpent in the Garden and ushering the creation into the rest of God. The Lord passes the mission on to Israel, David, and his seed. When the house of David falls and the Lord exiles Israel, God-fearers are left to hope for a future righteous son of Adam and of David to come.

The sage of the Psalms offers a last connection here. Composed long after the folly of the man and woman and their banishment from the Garden, Psalm 8 echoes the dominion language of Genesis 1:26-28 and Daniel 7:14. David the psalmist sings of God's creation of 'adam to rule the earth (Ps 8:4-8):

8:4	What is man that you are mindful of him,
	And the son of man (*'adam*) that you care for him?
5	Yet you have made him a little lower than the heavenly beings
	And crowned him with glory and honor.
6	You have given him dominion over the works of your hands;
	You have put all things under his feet,
7	All sheep and oxen,
	And also the beasts of the field,
8	The birds of the heavens, and the fish of the sea,
	Whatever passes along the paths of the seas.

This psalm is not a dream, not a vision like Daniel's experience. Yet read within a post-exilic context, David's psalm "envisions" a future time when a son of *'adam* will rule all of creation for the Lord. Who is this son of *'adam*? The Psalter and the Writings answer emphatically: the coming seed of David, the Messiah! In the end, He will fully realize God's creation decree (Ps 2, 72, 110), ending creation's subjection to vanity (*hebel*).[127]

The book bearing his name casts Daniel as both a giver and a recipient of wisdom. Through Daniel, the Gentile kings of the earth, the Jews, and the text's readers gain insight into the Lord's creation plan for Israel and humanity. The Writings contextualize Daniel's visions in the narratives of the Davidic Kingdom: the Son of *'adam* is the seed of David, the Messiah who will subdue the kingdoms of the world and usher in the kingdom of God. The seed of the woman, the Son of David, the Son of *'adam*, will crush the seed of the serpent and reign

---

[127] Probably puzzling readers before Christ, Daniel 12:1-2 predicts a resurrection at this time, as well.

forever in peace. Read in their Writings context, the prophecies of the book of Daniel link Adam to David and Solomon and the coming Messiah through this theme of the rule of the earth. Daniel's visions tie together the past, present, and future of Israel and the nations through the reign of the *'adam* of God.

3. 70 "Weeks" of Exile

The 70 "weeks" of Daniel remain a confusing topic even today. Before hosting a conversation between texts, the sage of the book of Daniel summarizes Daniel 9's content pertaining to these "weeks."

After reading the scroll of Jeremiah prophesying the 70 years of Jerusalem's "desolations," Daniel confesses the nation's sin and prays for the Lord to restore the temple, the city of Jerusalem, and the people (Dan 9:3-19).[128] In this petition, Daniel articulates his expectations for restoration: the people return to the land, the Lord returns to His sanctuary in the temple, and a Davidic king rules from Jerusalem. In essence, Daniel prays for the Lord to restore the Davidic Kingdom as promised in the Book of Consolation, Jeremiah 30-33. Within this short section of Jeremiah, the prophet teaches about the New Covenant, when the Lord writes His *torah* on the hearts of His people (Jer 31:31-34), binding the Lord and Israel together forever in David's kingdom.

Following Daniel's prayer, the Lord sends the angel Gabriel to give Daniel insight (*sakal*) and understanding (*binah*) about the timing of this restoration: Israel's 70 year exile will be extended to 70 "weeks," presumably "weeks" of years, adding a total of 490 years (Dan 9:22).[129] This extension coincides with the four phases of exile revealed in the visions of Daniel 2 and 7. According to Gabriel, the events of these 70 weeks directly address Daniel's prayer for city, people, and temple. In Daniel 9:24, Gabriel says:

---

128 At the dedication of the temple, Solomon mentions that if the exiles repent and pray toward Jerusalem and the house of the Lord, the Lord will forgive His people (2 Chron 6:36-39).

129 The use of the term "weeks" (*shabu'im*) echoes creation, adding another layer to this book's creation and Sabbath themes.

> 9:25 Seventy weeks have been decreed for **your people** and **your holy city**,
>
> to finish the transgression,
>
> to make an end of sin,
>
> to make atonement for iniquity,
>
> to bring in everlasting righteousness,
>
> to seal up vision and prophecy
>
> and to anoint **the most holy** *place*.[130] (NASB)

Using the same vocabulary as Daniel's confession, Gabriel reveals that the 70 weeks will fully deal with Israel's transgression, sin, and iniquity (Dan 9:11, 16, 13). The Lord will then usher in the New Covenant and everlasting righteousness, forgiving His people and remembering Israel's sin no more (Jer 31:33-34).

Gabriel's explanation divides this time period into several segments (Dan 9:25-27):

- 7 weeks take place from the decree to restore and rebuild Jerusalem until the coming of an anointed one, a prince (Dan 9:25a).

- During the next 62 weeks, Jerusalem will be rebuilt in times of distress (Dan 9:25b).

- After the 62 weeks, an anointed one is cut off and the people of the prince to come destroy the city and the sanctuary; war continues until the end (Dan 9:26).

---

[130] The word *"place"* is not present in the original Hebrew text. Several versions simply translate the phrase as "the most holy" (NIV, KJV, NKJV). The Hebrew expression *qodesh qodashim* means "a/the most holy one/thing." Daniel refers to the Lord's holy mountain earlier in his prayer (Dan 9:16, 20), suggesting *"mountain"* as an appropriate addition. This choice would dovetail with the Psalms' refrain that in the end, the Lord will dwell on His holy mountain in the City of David, and the wise will ascend the hill to dwell with Him and His king (Pss 2, 15, 24).

- For one week, the coming prince will make a strong covenant with many (Dan 9:27a).

- In the middle of this one week, the prince ends sacrifices and offerings; abominations and desolation ensue before he is destroyed (Dan 9:27b).

Though Gabriel's explanation provokes more questions than it answers, these 70 "weeks" consistently focus on the city and sanctuary/temple, again specifically answering Daniel's concerns in his prayer. Gabriel's interpretation then stops suddenly, and Daniel receives other visions. The book closes with Daniel asking follow-up questions, seeking more clarity about the meaning of his visions—to no avail. The angelic interpreter tells Daniel to "go his way" because the meaning of the words is sealed until the end of time (Dan 12:9, 13). Apparently, even with his questions, Daniel has received sufficient insight from his visions to walk in wisdom until the end: the kingdom of God.

After listening to this summary, the sages of Chronicles and Ezra-Nehemiah speak up, as they, too, refer to Jeremiah's prophecy concerning the 70-year exile. Unsurprisingly, the three books all mention:

- The end of the Babylonian exile after 70 years.

- The people of Israel, the city of Jerusalem, and the house of the Lord.

- Other Gentile kings after Babylon is defeated: Darius the Mede in Daniel, and Cyrus of Persia in Ezra-Nehemiah and Chronicles (Dan 9:1; Ezra 1:1; 2 Chron 36:22).

- A decree to rebuild Jerusalem and the temple.

Amidst this overlap, each text also brings unique content to the discussion. As explained in depth in Chapter 2, the book of Chronicles begins with Adam, created in God's image to rule the earth, and records a narrative of the history of Israel focused on the house of David and the temple/house of the Lord. Events are explained in light of God's promises to David that his seed will build a house for the Lord and sit on His throne forever. However, in the last chapter, Judah is exiled to Babylon for 70 years. Chronicles concludes with Cyrus the Persian ruling the earth under the authority of God (2 Chron 36:23) and decreeing Israel free to return to the land. Readers finish Chronicles confused and tense—returning to the land is all well and good, but how can this Gentile rule the earth for the Lord? Chronicles' abrupt ending thus lives in tension with the book's explicit hopes for a son/seed of David to reign in Jerusalem, a new Adam. Reading the Writings beginning with Chronicles prompts readers to search the rest of the books in the Writings for answers about the future of Israel, Gentile kingdoms, and the kingdom of God.

Chronicles also consistently highlights the temple, the priests, and the Levites, beginning in the genealogical section of 1 Chronicles and running through David's preparation for the temple on to the end of the book. This focus on the priests and Levites briefly brings the book of Leviticus into the conversation. Uniquely, Chronicles ties Jeremiah's prophecy to a reference to the Sabbatical year in Leviticus 25 and 26. When presenting the curses that will befall Israel if they break their covenant with the Lord, Leviticus specifically addresses the relationship between Israel's exile and the missed Sabbath years of the land (Lev 26:34-35):

> 26:34 Then the land shall enjoy its Sabbaths as long as it lies desolate, while you are in your enemies' land; then the land shall rest, and enjoy its Sabbaths.
>
> 35 As long as it lies desolate it shall have rest, the rest that it did not have on your Sabbaths when you were dwelling in it.

2 Chronicles 36:20-21 echoes this Leviticus passage:

> 36:20 He [Nebuchadnezzar] took into exile in Babylon those who had escaped from the

> sword, and they became servants to him and to his sons until the establishment of the kingdom of Persia,
>
> 21 to fulfill the word of the Lord by the mouth of Jeremiah, until the land had enjoyed its Sabbaths. All the days that it lay desolate it kept Sabbath, to fulfill seventy years.

Against the backdrop of Levitical law, Chronicles casts the exile as the foreseeable consequence of Israel's breaking the Sabbath. This passage also foreshadows Gabriel's explanation that the 70 years of exile are extended to 70 years of Sabbaths: 490 years.

Opening where Chronicles left off, the book of Ezra-Nehemiah begins with a reference to Jeremiah and the long version of the Cyrus decree. This last book in the Writings narrates the people's return to the land to rebuild the house of the Lord and the city of Jerusalem (Ezra 1-6; Neh 1-6). The text of Ezra-Nehemiah portrays the return from exile as a second exodus, complete with Gentile support for the travelers and their project, the building of a sanctuary for the Lord, the giving of instruction to the people, and the Jews' subsequent rebellion against their God. Ezra-Nehemiah ends with yet another story of the unfaithfulness of Israel; readers finish the collection of the Writings depressed and disappointed by Israel's consistent patterns of sin and rebellion. Has Israel learned nothing from her exile?

Unexpectedly, the sage of the book of Job speaks up here, claiming his text contains two subtle allusions to exile. In his suffering, Job eventually hears the voice of the Lord and finds peace (*shalom*) through God's rather intimidating instruction (Job 42:1-6). Job 42 then narrates the Lord's restoration of Job's good life (Job 42:10):

> 42:10 And the Lord turned the captivity (*shub shebut*) of Job, when he prayed for his friends: also the Lord gave Job twice as much as he had before. (KJV)

Though most English versions translate the Hebrew expression *shub shebut* as "restored the fortunes" of Job, the OT uses *shub shebut* elsewhere, especially when referring to Israel's return from exile (see Ps 126). Job 42 marks the only time this expression is used about an individual, painting Job's suffering and the evils that the Lord brought on him as a kind of exile. The sages nod, pondering the implications of this parallel.

The sage of the book of Job continues. Job 42:12 mentions that the Lord blessed Job's "latter end" (*'aharit*) more than his beginning. The term "latter end" is found most often in prophetic texts speaking of the end times when the Lord finally fulfills His promises to Israel—Daniel 2:28 and 10:14 for instance. Here, in Job 42, the Lord restores the captivity of Job and doubles Job's possessions.[131] After this, the Lord also extends the years of Job's life, giving him 140 years of good life after his suffering: 2 times 70 years. Subtly, Job foreshadows the wise whom the Lord brings out of exile to inherit the kingdom in the end times.

The sages fall silent, caught between their hope for Israel's restoration and the disappointing ending of Ezra-Nehemiah. How can Israel be restored while the Gentile kingdoms rule the earth? The answer is a mystery. The sage of Daniel leaves all God-fearers with Daniel's own directive: go their way until the end, walking the path of wisdom until the full restoration of Israel in some distant future.

Toward the New Testament

1. *The Mysteries of the Kingdom*

As discussed above, Daniel 5:10-12 calls Daniel's visions "parables" (*mashal*) and "riddles" (*hidah*). In Matthew 13, Jesus begins to teach the crowds in parables, using them to explain "mysteries of the kingdom" (Matt 13:11). Meant to hide truth from rejectors and reveal truth to seekers, Jesus' parables echo the book of Daniel in multiple ways.

---

[131] Isaiah 61:7 and Zechariah 9:12 foretell that Israel will receive double blessings in her restoration.

Both Daniel and Jesus use the term "mystery" to describe their wisdom sayings about the coming kingdom of God (*raz* in Dan 2:19; *mysterion* in Matt 13:11). Matthew offers an additional comment on Jesus speaking in parables (Matt 13:35):

> 13:35 This was to fulfill what was spoken by the prophet:
>
> "I will open my mouth in parables (*parabole*);
>
> I will utter what has been hidden (*krupto*) since the foundation of the world."

Matthew's comment quotes Psalm 78:2 to describe Jesus' teachings.[132] Yet Jesus includes explanations for His disciples, most notably with the parables of the sower and the tares (Matt 13:18-23, 13:36-43). In Mark 4:13, Jesus also offers wisdom to understand wisdom: He paints the parable of the sower as the key to understanding the rest of His parables. Like those who reject Lady Wisdom's words, those who reject Jesus do not receive the revelation of the parables' meaning and are left in the dark (Matt 13:14-15 quoting Isaiah 6:9-10). Lastly, Jesus makes two allusions to the book of Daniel in Matthew 13, each time using a line directly from its text:

- in the parable of the mustard seed: "the birds of the air come and nest in its branches" from Daniel 4:12.

- in the parable of the tares: "the righteous will shine forth as the sun" from Daniel 12:3.

These allusions tie OT and NT parables and riddles together, likening them to each other. Instead of being distinct, they flow into one another.

In turn, the apostle Paul regularly calls several aspects of the Gospel "*mysterion*," a mystery.[133] For instance, in Romans 11:25-27, he speaks of Gentiles and the future kingdom:

---

[132] Psalm 78:2 reads: "I will open my mouth in a parable (*mashal*); I will utter dark sayings (*hidah*) from of old."

[133] Rom 16:25; 1 Cor 2:7, 15:50-51; Eph 1:9, 3:3-4, 9, 5:32, 6:19; Col 1:26-27, 2:2, 4:3; 2 Thess 2:7; 1 Tim 3:9, 16.

11:25   Lest you be wise in your own sight, I do not want you to be unaware of this mystery (*mysterion*), brothers: a partial hardening has come upon Israel, until the fullness of the Gentiles has come in.

26   And in this way all Israel will be saved, as it is written,

"The Deliverer will come from Zion,

he will banish ungodliness from Jacob";

27   "and this will be my covenant with them

when I take away their sins."

Echoing the language of Daniel's visions, Paul links Israel's rejection of Jesus to their continued exile and hardening in unbelief (Rom 11:1-15). Nonetheless, when God's plan for Gentile salvation has been fulfilled, all Israel will be saved and enter the New Covenant (Isaiah 27:9, 59:20; Jer 31:31-34). In contrast to Daniel, whose visions spoke of the judgment of the Gentiles leading to Israel receiving the kingdom, Paul surprises readers with his mystery of Gentile salvation preceding Israel's.

2. Creation Realized at Jesus' Second Coming

Building on God's revelations to Daniel, God's revelations to John contain the most detailed portrait of God's creation plans coming to fruition:

- Babylon falls (Rev 18; Dan 5).

- Jesus comes from heaven and judges the nations (Rev 19; Dan 2 and 7).

- Books are opened at the great white throne judgment (Rev 20:11-15; Dan 7:10).

- The new heavens and earth arrive (Rev 21:1-22:9; Dan 2 and 7).

To some degree, Revelation parallels events depicted in Daniel's visions: the rule of Gentile kingdoms symbolized by Babylon, the arrival of God's heavenly kingdom paired with the judgment of the nations, and the establishment of God's eternal rule through the Son of *'adam*. Building on Daniel 7's reference to "a" son of *'adam*, the Gospels present Jesus as "the" Son of *'adam* who will rule over all (see Luke 1-3).

Daniel 7 and Psalm 8 play a central role in the NT's presentation of Jesus' rule over all humanity and the whole of creation, earthly and heavenly.[134] When Jesus rose from the dead, He emerged from the grave as the first fruits of the resurrection; the full harvest of that resurrection takes place at His second coming when those in Christ are resurrected (1 Cor 15:20-23). After this glorious moment, Jesus will subject all the enemies of God to Himself (1 Cor 15:24-28):

> 15:24 Then comes the end, when he delivers the kingdom to God the Father after destroying every rule and every authority and power.
>
> 25 For he must reign until he has put all his enemies under his feet.
>
> 26 The last enemy to be destroyed is death.
>
> 27 For "God has put all things in subjection under his feet." But when it says, "all things are put in subjection," it is plain that he is excepted who put all things in subjection under him.
>
> 28 When all things are subjected to him, then the Son himself will also be subjected to him who put all things in subjection under him, that God may be all in all.

After the general resurrection (1 Cor 15:23), Jesus puts all things in subjection to Himself: all authority and power, specifically all His

---

134 See Rom 8:20-25; Heb 2:6-8; and Eph 1:20-23.

enemies and death itself. Then Jesus, the Son of God, subjects Himself to God the Father. In this new creation, God is "all in all": opposition to God's rule is no more. This final outcome dovetails with Daniel's visions about the defeat of Gentile kings and kingdoms and the advent of the eternal kingdom of God. Daniel, the consummate wise person, foresees his own involvement in these events of the end: the resurrection of the wise (*sakal*) (Dan 12:1-3). For the time being, he serves as a model for OT and NT saints alike as we seek to walk the path of wisdom.

3. Babylon and the 70 "Weeks"

Nebuchadnezzar king of Babylon and his kingdom play a central role in the historical events of the book of Daniel; however, in both the OT and the NT, "Babylon" also becomes shorthand for Israel's extended exile under any Gentile power.

Babylon appears in the NT presentation of the first and second comings of Christ; Matthew 1:17 explains the timing of the coming of the Messiah in Jesus' genealogy:

> 1:17 So all the generations from Abraham to David were fourteen generations,
>
> and from David to the deportation to Babylon fourteen generations,
>
> and from the deportation to Babylon to the Christ fourteen generations.

For Matthew, the Babylonian exile serves as a marker in the events leading to the first coming of Jesus the Messiah. Matthew's language also indicates that at the time of Jesus' birth, exilic conditions still exist; when recording Herod's slaughter of the babies in Bethlehem, Matthew 2:17-18 quotes from Jeremiah 31:15's mourning for Babylon's slaughter of the children of Judah (see also Lam 2:11-12, 19-22). Matthew portrays the Roman context of Jesus' first coming as the extension of Israel's Babylonian exile into the subsequent Gentile kingdoms predicted in Daniel 2, 7, and 9.

As NT readers find out, Jesus' first coming does not end Gentile dominion and persecution. Babylon resurfaces as the emblem of Gentile rule in Revelation 14-18. In language saturated with references to the book of Daniel, Jesus extends the times of the Gentiles into the future beyond His first coming (Luke 21:24). Paralleling the angelic interpreter's explanation of the "weeks" in Daniel 9, Jesus indicates that because of Israel's rejection of her Messiah, the temple and city of Jerusalem will be made desolate again (Matt 23:37-24:3; Dan 9:26). In Matthew 24:15, Jesus also refers to the abomination of desolation, specifically referencing Daniel 9:27. Matthew even highlights this prophecy by interrupting Jesus' words with "let the reader understand" (Matt 24:15). "After the tribulation of those days" (Matt 24:29), the Son of Man comes triumphant on the clouds with power and glory (Matt 24:30; Dan 7:13, Luke 21:27).

Further Reading

Brasil de Souza, Elias. "Wisdom in Daniel." *The End from the Beginning: Festschrift Honoring Merling Alomia*. Benjamín Rojas et al, Eds. Lima: Universidad Peruana Unión, 2015: 265-282.

Goswell, Greg (Gregory Ross). "The Ethics of the Book of Daniel." *Restoration Quarterly* 57 (3): 129–42.

-----. "The Canonical Position(s) of the Book of Daniel." *Restoration Quarterly* 59 (3): 129–40.

Hamilton, James M., Jr. *With the Clouds of Heaven: The Book of Daniel in Biblical Theology*. Westmont, IL: IVP Academic, 2014.

Klein, Ralph W. "Reading Daniel as Part of the Writings." Donn F. Morgan, Ed. *The Oxford Handbook of the Writings of the Hebrew Bible*, New York, NY: Oxford Handbooks, 2018.

Scheetz, Jordan M. *The Concept of Canonical Intertextuality and the Book of Daniel*. 1st ed. Cambridge: The Lutterworth Press, 2011.

Segal, Michael. *Dreams, Riddles, and Visions: Textual, Contextual, and Intertextual Approaches to the Book of Daniel*. Boston, MA: De Gruyter, 2016.

Ezra-Nehemiah: Israel's Return – Wisdom and Folly

Old Testament Background to Ezra-Nehemiah

- The design and construction of the tabernacle: Ex 25-31, 35-40
- Laws regarding making covenants with the Canaanites: Ex 34:10-16; Deut 7:1-6, 23:3-6
- Teachings on divorce: Deut 24:1-4; Jer 3:6-10; Mal 2:10-17
- Ruth the Moabitess and Boaz: the book of Ruth
- Establishment of the temple liturgy by David: 1 Chron 25
- The foreign, strange, or adulteress woman: Prov 1-9
- Solomon's construction of the temple: 2 Chron 1-7
- Solomon and his foreign wives: 1 Kings 11:1-13
- Jeremiah's prophecies of the 70-year exile and return: Jer 25, 29-33
- Post-exilic prophets: Haggai, Zechariah, Malachi

Creation and Ezra-Nehemiah: Beginning Again

A number of OT texts, mostly psalms, summarize parts of the story of Israel, highlighting her relationship with the Lord. For example, Psalm 78 begins with the Exodus and concludes with the coming of David; Psalm 105 traces Israel's story from Abraham through Joshua's conquest of the land. One of the few historical psalms to begin with creation is Nehemiah 9:[135]

> 9:6   You are the Lord, You alone.
>
> You have made heaven,

---

[135] Jeremiah 32, Psalms 89 and 135-136 also begin with creation.

> The heaven of heavens, with all their host,
>
> The earth and all that is on it,
>
> The seas and all that is in them;
>
> And You preserve all of them;
>
> And the host of heaven worships You.

After this beginning, the singing Levites walk Israel through God's choosing of Abraham, several highlights from Moses' time, Israel taking possession of the land, the era of the Judges, the people's unfaithfulness, the exile, and finally Israel's situation in the post-exile.

In the same way Chronicles begins with Adam and therefore the Creator, this prayer in Nehemiah 9 situates the entire story of Israel within a creational framework. God's choice of Abraham and their ensuing covenant lay the foundation for the fulfillment of God's creation decrees: the Lord will multiply Abraham's seed, give them the promised land, and Israel will be a blessing to all nations (Neh 9:7-8). God's covenant with Abraham in Genesis 12:1-3 echoes the Lord's commands to creation in the Garden—to enjoy His blessing by multiplying and filling the earth. When the Jews return to the land in Ezra-Nehemiah, they are given the opportunity to begin again, to re-establish their lives before their Creator God.

As do so many OT historical reviews, the story in Nehemiah 9 develops two themes: Israel's unfaithfulness and the Lord's compassion. In this prayer, the Levites petition the Lord only once: "let not all the hardship seem little to you" (Neh 9:32). The prayer ends with a description of the Jews' distress: they live as slaves to the Persians on their own land (Neh 9:36-37). For God's creational plan to be realized, the Lord needs to take note of His people's current situation and change it. Only when the Lord restores Israel can Israel extend that creational blessing to all the families of the earth.

Ezra-Nehemiah: An Outline

The Cyrus decree recorded in Ezra 1:2-3 provides the outline of the book of Ezra-Nehemiah, a single book in the Hebrew OT. The words in bold predict the section headings in the outline below:

> 1:2 Thus says Cyrus king of Persia: "The Lord, the God of heaven, has given me all the kingdoms of the earth, and **he has charged me to build Him a house at Jerusalem, which is in Judah.**
>
> 3 **Whoever is among you of all His people**, may his God be with him, and let **him go up to Jerusalem**, which is in Judah, and **rebuild the house of the Lord**, the God of Israel—He is the God who is in Jerusalem."

Following these key features of Cyrus' directive, the book narrates three separate returns to the land, each in turn focusing on the temple, the people, and the city. The book ends with a picture of Israel's continuing folly:

I. Ezra 1-6: Return to rebuild the temple (538 BCE)

> Under Zerubbabel, the first return rebuilds the temple amidst local opposition.

II. Ezra 7-10: Return to rebuild the people under the *Torah* (458 BCE)

> The second return under Ezra the priest, intended to strengthen and rebuild the people according to the Law, ends in failure.

III. Nehemiah 1-7: Return to rebuild the walls of Jerusalem (444 BCE)

> Under Nehemiah, the third return rebuilds the walls of Jerusalem, again amidst local opposition.

Ending. Nehemiah 8-13: Dedication of the temple paired with moral failures

> Having rebuilt the temple, the people, and the walls of the city,

the Jews receive wisdom from the Law, confess their sins, and dedicate the temple. Nonetheless, the book ends with Israel's sin of intermingling with the people of the land.

In tandem with the faithfulness of the people in the face of opposition, the Ezra-Nehemiah narrative highlights Israel's ultimate moral failure: their intermingling and intermarriage with foreigners. This repeated sin stains the return from exile and the people's faithfulness to their God; the reader ends Ezra-Nehemiah with little hope that Israel's heart will change.

Major Themes: City-People-Temple, Intermingling with Idolatrous Foreigners, and a Bad Ending

1. City, People, Temple

City, people, and temple form the basic elements of Israel's covenant with the Lord (Dan 9). To restore or renew His covenant with His people after their exile, the Lord must rule from His house in Jerusalem, the Davidic king must sit on the Lord's throne in Jerusalem, and Israel must dwell in the promised land, walking wisely according to the word of the Lord.[136] Ezra-Nehemiah features a few small but necessary steps in this restoration.

The book narrates both successful and unsuccessful aspects of the people's return. Some Jews return to the land, obey the Lord by rebuilding the temple, confess their sin, and humbly receive instruction from the Law. On the other hand, the text returns three times to the people's sin of intermingling with idolatrous foreigners (Ezra 9; Neh 9, 13). Israel's historical pattern of rebellion and idolatry—one of the main reasons for the exile in the first place—continues into the post-exile.

Israel does successfully rebuild the temple, re-establish temple worship and the liturgy of David, and rebuild the walls of the city. Yet these accomplishments fail to meet Israel's hopes for restoration.

---

[136] See the Lord's promise to David in 1 Chronicles 17:4-15. The Prophets also address this topic—Isaiah: Jerusalem/Judah; Jeremiah: covenant; Ezekiel: temple; and the 12 minor prophets: people/land.

Unlike the tabernacle and Solomon's temple, this new temple does not house the glorious presence of the Lord (Ex 40:34-35; 2 Chron 7:1-3).[137] Though the walls are rebuilt, Jerusalem sits almost empty, containing no houses yet (Neh 7:4): only a remnant returned to the land, not enough to sustain the city. And finally, no Davidic king sits on the Lord's throne. Heirs of David, such as Zerubbabel son of Shealtiel (1 Chron 3:17; Hag 2:23), lived during this time and occasionally lead the people, but Gentile dominion over the land remains firmly in place.

Despite these weaknesses, the people's return from exile does mark a major event in the life of Israel: the Lord has not forgotten His people in exile. Ezra addresses this mix of success and failure in Ezra 9:8:

> 9:8   But now for a brief moment grace has been shown from the Lord our God, to leave us an escaped remnant and to give us a peg in His holy place, that our God may enlighten our eyes and grant us a little reviving in our bondage. (NASB)

Ever the realist, Ezra acknowledges both the significance of Israel's restoration and its smallness. His words describe the return as a first step, the first fruits of a larger harvest still in Israel's future. Though lacking the glory the prophets imagined (Jer 30-33), temple, city, and people are now in place to prepare for the coming Messianic king (Mal 3:1).

2. Intermingling with Idolatrous Foreigners

Israel's exile came about because of her unfaithfulness to the covenant between her and the Lord. After Israel suffered for her sins, as chronicled in Lamentations, the people return to the land. Sadly, Israel returns with the same propensity for unbelief, rebellion, and disobedience she had before the exile. In Ezra-Nehemiah, the people

---

[137] Additionally, the building of the first temple featured a wise craftsman, Huram-abi (2 Chron 2:13), and a wise king, Solomon (2 Chron 1-2, 9). It does appear that the people who rebuilt the temple were inspired by God (Ezra 1:5) and acted in response to Haggai and Zechariah's preaching (Ezra 5:1-2), but this new temple building does not reflect the wisdom of God the way Solomon's did.

demonstrate their continued unfaithfulness through their repeated intermingling and intermarriage with idolatrous foreigners. As will be discussed later in this chapter, these actions present a direct threat to the people's devotion to the Lord and their future as His chosen people: if the Jews acculturate to the peoples of the land, they are no longer set apart as the Lord's people.

Ezra 9, Nehemiah 9, and Nehemiah 13 narrate this sin. These passages make clear references to Mosaic laws, particularly Exodus 34:12-17 and Deuteronomy 7:1-6; Moses warns of the spiritual dangers involved in making a covenant, including marriage, with Canaanites: "they would turn away your sons from following me, to serve other gods" (Deut 7:4). In each of these three instances, the people respond differently:

- **Ezra 9-10:** After learning of Israel's sin, Ezra prays a prayer of confession. The people themselves resolve the situation by divorcing their unbelieving wives under Ezra's oversight.

- **Nehemiah 9-10:** Apparently in response to Ezra's reading of the *Torah*, the people repent, confess their sin of intermarriage, and "separate" from all unbelieving foreigners. The text does not specify exactly what this means. The Levites then offer a prayer chronicling the history of Israel and the Lord from creation to the post-exile. The people respond with promises to change their ways.

- **Nehemiah 13:** Again after a reading of the Law of Moses, the people repent and "separate" from foreigners (Neh 13:1-3). Upon returning to Jerusalem from an extended absence, Nehemiah learns of their failure to fulfill the covenantal promises of Nehemiah 10. The Jews had so acculturated that many children do not understand the language of Judah. Nehemiah curses the people and makes them swear to stop intermarrying with foreigners, citing Scripture and Solomon's negative example of this same sin. The book ends on this note of repeated failure with Nehemiah asking the Lord to "Remember me, O my God, for good" (Neh 13:31).

This scene of sin and failure concludes both Ezra-Nehemiah and the collection of the Writings. In his confession to the Lord, Ezra wonders how long the Lord will keep forgiving His people, asking (Ezra 9:14):

> 9:14   Would you not be angry with us until you consumed us, so that there should be no remnant, nor any to escape?

Readers end the book expecting Israel to intermingle again, continuing to dilute their identity by mixing with idolatrous peoples. Will the Messiah find any righteous remnant left when He comes? Faced with the choice between wisdom and folly, Israel has repeatedly chosen to embrace Lady Folly. God's program to bless all the nations through His chosen people appears on the verge of implosion.

3. A Bad Ending

"A bad ending" does not constitute a true theme, but the end of Ezra-Nehemiah leaves readers with loud questions about Israel's future.[138] In Nehemiah 10, the people took "an oath to walk in God's law" (Neh 10:29). When Nehemiah returns to Jerusalem, he finds the people have committed the exact sins they had forsworn. His last chapter catalogs these egregious choices:

- The people intermarry with and acculturate to the people of the land (Neh 13:1-3).

- They allow Tobiah the Ammonite to move into the temple: a foreigner lives in the house of God (Neh 13:4-5).

- They do not tithe; the Levites are forced to farm for their own food (Neh 13:10).

- They do not keep the sabbath (Neh 13:15-17).

---

[138] See Schnittjer, Gary Edward. "The Bad Ending of Ezra-Nehemiah." *Bibliotheca Sacra* 173:689 (2016): 32–56.

This list leaves readers wondering what the Jews were doing right. During Nehemiah's absence, the people follow their leaders into sin instead of into righteousness. With no properly functioning temple, no sabbath, and no distinction from the people of the land, Israel is ... not Israel. Given a little more time, the Jews will unite with the Canaanite people, becoming indistinguishable from the idolatrous peoples of the land. The text does mention wise, faithful, God-fearers such as Hananiah (Neh 7:2), but Israel's repeated sins, particularly of intermingling, leave readers echoing Ezra's question: will the Lord find any faith in the land when He returns?

Ezra-Nehemiah begins with Ezra's successful rebuilding of the temple, moves on to Nehemiah's rebuilding the walls of Jerusalem, but ultimately ends poorly. This pattern of beginning well and ending badly echoes Israel's journey to Sinai: Israel leaves Egypt in faith, experiences deliverance and joy at the crossing of the Red Sea, but soon commits idolatry with the Golden Calf. Hundreds of years later, post-exilic Israel repeats the same pattern: journey back to the land, promising beginning, sinful ending.

Compounding readers' disappointment, this bad ending serves as the last word in the Writings, ending not just one book but the entire Writings collection. Instead of providing a hope-filled, rousing climax like the Psalter's, Nehemiah 13 leaves readers deflated and desperate for answers about Israel's future. Israel's momentum is moving her in the wrong direction; will God-fearers bring the people back to the path of wisdom and blessing?

The Sages in Conversation

1. City, People, Temple

The Ezra-Nehemiah return to the land is simply disappointing. After hearing from the OT prophets, readers expect more than the difficulties and failures the text narrates; city, people, and temple each fall short of Israel's hopes for restoration. The glory of the Lord does not reside in the new temple, the people do not live in Jerusalem, and a son of

David does not sit on the throne. Throughout the text, Israel's behavior reveals a deeper problem: Israel's heart. The people have not learned from their destruction and exile; the *torah* of God is not written on their hearts, as the New Covenant promises (Deut 30:1-14; Jer 31:27-34). Disappointed and perplexed, the sage of Ezra-Nehemiah sits silently with his companions, downcast. The sages search their content for insight, ways to understand this turn of events. Daniel, Chronicles, and the Psalter respond.

The sage of the book of Daniel opens with a good news/bad news pairing. After reading Jeremiah, Daniel also expected the Babylonian exile to end with the restoration of the Davidic kingdom and the beginning of the New Covenant (Jer 29-33[139]). Instead, Daniel learns that the exile will be extended by seventy "weeks" to fully deal with sin and bring God's plan to conclusion (Dan 9:24). The angelic interpreter explains (Dan 9:25):

> 9:25 Know therefore and understand that **from the going out of the word to restore and build Jerusalem** to the coming of an anointed one, a prince, **there shall be seven weeks. Then for sixty-two weeks it shall be built again** with squares and moat, but in **a troubled time.**

The sages ponder this insight, agreeing that the events of Ezra-Nehemiah, above in bold, fall within the first sixty-nine "weeks" of the exile. This return, while lackluster, still marks a crucial milestone for Israel: the people restore and rebuild Jerusalem's temple and walls. Yet the sage of Daniel continues, pairing this good news with sadness: an anointed one will come and be cut off, and the city and sanctuary will be destroyed again (Dan 9:26). Only after this future destruction will the exile end and the kingdom of God come forever.

---

139 Jer 29, seventy-year exile; Jer 30:1-31:26, restoration of people; Jer 31:27-40, new covenant; Jer 32, Jeremiah purchases a field for the return; Jer 33, restoration of the people and Davidic kingdom.

Another long pause ensues—the circle's disappointment is palpable. The sage of the book of Daniel ends by reiterating his own directive: remain loyal to the Lord. The Writings teach that those walking the way of wisdom will inherit God's blessings in His kingdom. Full restoration of people, city, and temple will come. Surrounded by the folly of the nations and Israel, readers still face the same choice Israel has always faced: the wisdom of God or the folly of idolatry?

"With song," adds the sage of Chronicles. Surprising everyone, this sage speaks, drawing attention to the role of King David and the Davidic Kingdom in Ezra-Nehemiah.[140] The text refers to King David several times, calling Jerusalem the city of David (Neh 3:15, 12:37) and mentioning his establishment of the temple liturgy (Ezra 3:10; Neh 12:24, 36, 45-46). King David's influence on city, people, and temple permeates the celebration in Nehemiah 12:

- The people dedicate the wall of Jerusalem, the city of David, echoing David's own dedication celebrations.

- Choirs sing at the house of God, reviving David's psalmody.

- Levitical priests sing as instructed by David and Solomon.

- All Israel participates, as in the days of King David.

The puzzling part of this Davidic presence in Ezra-Nehemiah is the lack of any references to the restoration of the Davidic Kingdom. The people have returned to the land, devoting their lives to rebuilding the city and the temple, and yet the Ezra-Nehemiah record remains silent on the restoration of the Davidic Kingdom. When and how will the Lord restore the house of David to the throne? Compounding this silence, Ezra-Nehemiah closes out the Davidic Kingdom section of the Writings and the Writings as a whole, but leaves readers with no mention of the kingdom's restoration. Readers and scholars alike often puzzle over this ending.

---

140 See Ulrich, Dean R. "David in Ezra-Nehemiah." *The Westminster Theological Journal* 78 (1): 49–64. Also, Goswell, Greg (Gregory Ross). "The Absence of a Davidic Hope in Ezra-Nehemiah." *Trinity Journal* 33 (1): 19–31.

The sage of the book of Chronicles suggests a perspective on this narrative silence: perhaps Israel's hope for the coming Davidic King does not figure in the narrative but instead in the temple liturgy—in the song and sounds of the rebuilt temple. The reinstatement of temple liturgy brings the Lord's promise to David back to the center of Jewish life in the post-exile. Though the exact musical form of the temple liturgy in Chronicles and Ezra-Nehemiah is lost, the Psalter showcases the content of the Levites' songs: joy, sorrow, repentance, history, prophecy (1 Chron 25:1-3). Within these words coming from the temple, the past, present, and future of the Davidic covenant resonate in the returnees' daily life in the land. The message echoing throughout the city, from the rebuilt temple to anyone within the walls, points to the coming King and kingdom. The Ezra-Nehemiah narrative may be silent on the topic, but Jerusalem herself is not.

At this, the sage of the Psalter stands, spreads his arms wide, and sings (Ps 132:13-17):

> 132:13 For the Lord has chosen Zion;
>
> He has desired it for his dwelling place:
>
> 14 "This is my resting place forever;
>
> Here I will dwell, for I have desired it.
>
> 15 I will abundantly bless her provisions;
>
> I will satisfy her poor with bread.
>
> 16 Her priests I will clothe with salvation,
>
> And her saints will shout for joy.
>
> 17 There I will make a horn to sprout for David;
>
> I have prepared a lamp for my anointed."

Having lifted his companions' spirits, the Psalter illustrates Chronicles' earlier point with Psalms 132 and 126.[141] Book V's Songs of Ascents collection (Ps 120-134) focuses on Israel's redemption from her captivity to the nations. Echoing the people who "went up" (*'alah*) to Jerusalem in accordance with the Cyrus decree (Ezra 1:3, 5), the Psalms of Ascents (*ma'alah*) record the songs of the exiles as they "go up" to Jerusalem (Ps 122:4, 126:1-3). Underscoring this parallel, the collection covers the same ground as the Ezra-Nehemiah narrative, emphasizing the afflictions of the people and specifically focusing on city and temple.[142]

Partially sung above, Psalm 132 forms the apparent climax of the Ascents collection, looking back in time to see a picture of Israel's future restoration. The psalm's content links the past and future of Israel, addressing:

- David's afflictions (Ps 132:1)

- David's oath to build a house for the Lord (Ps 132:2-5)

- David and the people bringing the ark into Jerusalem with the priests (Ps 132:6-9)

- The Lord's promise that a son of David will sit on the throne forever (Ps 132:10-12)

- The Lord's choice of Zion as His eternal resting place with the seed of David and priests (Ps 132:13-18)

Solomon fittingly concludes his temple dedication prayer by quoting Psalm 132:8-9 (2 Chron 6:41). In that day, Psalm 132 appeared fulfilled: city, people, and temple prospered under a wise Davidic king. However, the rest of Chronicles narrates Israel's progressive decline from this high point of Solomon's reign; by the end of the book, all of David and Solomon's accomplishments have been undone. The kings of Judah and Israel played the fool—Jerusalem and the temple are destroyed,

---

141 Outside the Songs of Ascents, the so-called "royal psalms" proclaim God's promise to David to the temple worshippers: Psalms 2, 8, 18, 45, 72, 89, and 110, for example.

142 See Goulder, M. D. "The Songs of Ascents and Nehemiah." *Journal for the Study of the Old Testament* 22 (75): 43–58.

and king and people are exiled to Babylon (2 Chron 36:18-21). Yet in Psalm 132, Chronicles records a brief moment of the past glory of the kingdom of Israel's God under Solomon. When read in the post-exile, Psalm 132 provides a glimpse of the future. Israel's king will come again to reign in Zion, restoring the glory of the Davidic kingdom forever.

Complementing Psalm 132's look back to see the future, Psalm 126 sings of the future while looking at the present. The returning exiles experience a mixture of joy and ongoing suffering. Returned from captivity to the land, they sing (Ps 126:4-6):

> 126:4 Restore our fortunes, O Lord,
>
> Like streams in the Negeb!
>
> 5 Those who sow in tears
>
> Shall reap with shouts of joy!
>
> 6 He who goes out weeping,
>
> Bearing the seed for sowing,
>
> Shall come home with shouts of joy,
>
> Bringing his sheaves with him.

Even as the people rejoice that the Lord has brought them back from captivity (Ps 126:1-3; Ezra 3:10-13), they continue to petition the Lord to return them from captivity. Psalm 126 speaks to the difficulty of life in the post-exile: both Ezra and the priests describe life after the return from Babylon as bondage, slavery, and distress (Ezra 9:8-9; Neh 9:36-37). Psalm 126 validates the joys and disappointment of the Ezra-Nehemiah returns while continuing to petition the Lord to fulfill his promises to David. Israel waits in hope for another, greater return from captivity—this time with a Davidic king in Jerusalem, the Lord in His house, and all the people in the land at rest (Ps 132).

As Ezra-Nehemiah narrates, the Cyrus decree does not represent the fulfillment of the Davidic promises. Nonetheless, framed within Daniel's prophecies and the Psalms, Ezra-Nehemiah narrates the reinstatement of the voice of the people's hope: the temple liturgy pointing to the coming son of David. Even amidst the people's sinfulness, the book and the Writings close with city, people, and temple positioned for the future: at the appointed time, city, people, and temple will be fully restored.

2. Intermingling with Idolatrous Foreigners

Though the text of Ezra-Nehemiah rarely overtly speaks of wisdom, the narrative hinges on the OT principle that keeping the Law of the Lord is the path to wisdom. For instance, in Deuteronomy 4:6, Moses exhorts the people:

> 4:6 Keep [the statutes of the Lord] and do them, for that will be your wisdom and your understanding in the sight of the peoples, who, when they hear all these statutes, will say, "Surely this great nation is a wise and understanding people."

According to Moses, those who keep the statutes of the Lord are a wise and understanding nation. Ezra embodies this principle, even before he returns to the land (Ezra 7:10):

> 7:10 For Ezra had set his heart to study the Law of the Lord, and to do it and to teach His statutes and rules in Israel.

Knowing and keeping the Law of the Lord form a crucial part of the return to the land and Israel's identity as a people. The returnees know this; so does Artaxerxes King of Persia—talking to Ezra, he refers to the Law as "the wisdom (*hokmah*) of your God in your hand" (Ezra 7:25). One of several examples, Nehemiah 8 narrates Ezra, the Levites, and the people working together to restore the people to the *torah* of the Lord. Notice the wisdom language included in this chapter:

- Ezra brings the *Torah* before all so they can listen with **understanding** (*bin* – 8:2-3).

- The Levites give **understanding** (*bin*) of the *Torah* to the people (8:7).

- The Levites **explain** (*parash*) the *Torah*, providing **insight** (*sekel*) that the people might **understand** (*bin*) what is read (8:8).

- The people celebrate because they **understand** (*bin*) the words which were made known (*yada'*) to them (8:12).

- On the next day, the people gather around Ezra to gain **insight** (*sakal*) into the words of the *Torah* (8:13).

- When the people learn about the command to celebrate the feast of booths, they promptly obey. Ezra reads from the *Torah* each day during the feast (8:14-18).

As the scribe of the *Torah* (Ezra 7:21), Ezra fulfills a crucial role in Israel's restoration: he reads the *Torah* to the people, ensuring they understand (*bin*) the Law and gain insight (*sekel*) into its statutes. Israel appears to be in earnest, learning the Law and seeking to keep it.

Nonetheless, some in Israel break the Law by intermingling and intermarrying with the people of the land. Both before and after the exile (see Lam 1:2-3; 2 Kings 17:7-23), Israel sins against the Lord in this particular way. After a lively discussion of marriage in general, the sages of Ezra-Nehemiah, Proverbs, and Ruth discuss this issue of intermarriage with foreigners.

The Writings repeatedly cast marriage as a—perhaps the—wisdom decision, a constant influence in one's life either for good or ill. Every book in the Writings features or mentions marriage, usually emphasizing the role of the wife in the husband's life:

- **Chronicles:** References to wives and their influence both good and bad abound in this book. David took many wives (1 Chron 14:3), and Solomon removed his Egyptian wife from the city of David and the holy places (2 Chron 8:11). Jehoram, son of the good king Jehoshaphat, did evil in the sight of the Lord "for Ahab's daughter was his wife" (2 Chron 21:6).

- **The Psalms:** In Psalm 45, a song of love, the queen comes to the Davidic king. Psalm 128 describes the blessings of family life—a wife and children—on those who fear the Lord.

- **The book of Job:** Job's wife urges him to curse God (Job 2:9-10); he does not listen to her foolish (*nabal*) exhortations.

- **Proverbs:** Many proverbs praise a wise wife (Prov 12:4, 18:22, 19:14). Proverbs' foundational metaphor contrasts Lady Wisdom with the strange/foreign/adulteress woman (Prov 1-9). In Proverbs 31, the virtuous woman does good to her husband all the days of her life.

- **The book of Ruth:** Ruth the Moabitess actively seeks Boaz in marriage (Ruth 3); after Boaz redeems Ruth and Naomi, Ruth gives birth to Obed, King David's grandfather (Ruth 4).

- **Ecclesiastes:** The Preacher instructs the reader to enjoy life and love (*'ahab*) the wife of his youth during the days of his brief existence (Eccl 9:9).

- **Lamentations:** Jerusalem is personified as a foolish woman who has fruitlessly pursued her lovers (*'ahab*) and friends (Lam 1:2,19). Unfaithful Lady Jerusalem suffers the consequences of breaking the covenant bond between the Lord and His people Israel.

- **The book of Esther:** King Ahasuerus loves (*'ahab*) Esther more than all other women and makes her queen (Est 2:17). Haman's wife Zeresh stands out as a voice of wisdom alongside Haman's wise men (Est 6:13). She suggests building a gallows for Mordecai and later wisely predicts Haman's certain failure because Mordecai is a Jew (Est 5:14, 6:13).

- **The book of Daniel:** "The queen" advises Belshazzar to call upon wise Daniel to interpret the writing on the wall (Dan 5:10-12). Though the text is not explicit, this queen appears to be either Belshazzar's wife or the queen mother. Either way, Belshazzar's conundrum is resolved because of her advice.

- **Ezra-Nehemiah:** Israel's intermarriage with foreign women preoccupies much of the book (Ezra 9-10; Neh 9-10, 13:23-31). Nehemiah 13 explicitly links this behavior to the sin of Solomon, underscoring its wisdom implications.

Simply put, marriage is part of the fabric of human life, particularly in the ancient world. The sages exchange at length on the topic, eventually agreeing on several points:

- Marriage is a fundamental factor in the well-being of individuals, families, towns, and nation. The fact that the Lord established marriage at creation points to its importance for all humanity.

- Even outside the Garden and amidst human sinfulness, a good marriage is a blessing from God. A bad marriage causes long-term suffering.

- The texts present wives as wisdom figures, influencing their husbands, sons, and community toward either wisdom or folly.

In sum, marriage serves as the prime example of how relationships influence spouses to wisdom or folly. The Writings consistently paint marriage as a wisdom decision, emphasizing the effects of the union on the couple, the family, and the greater community. Perhaps the *Megilloth* collection (Ruth to Esther) highlights so many women to further underscore their influence.

This portrayal of marriage as central to walking the wisdom path forms the background for Ezra-Nehemiah's preoccupation with intermarriage. Israel's intermingling sets them up to violate the first and second commandments (Ex 20:3-6): after allowing idolatry into their marriages and families, Israel will inevitably forsake their covenantal faithfulness to their God and worship others.[143] Israel must keep separate from "foreigners" (*nokri*)[144] not because of their foreignness itself but because of their idolatry.[145] Nehemiah 10:28 confirms this distinction; when Israel takes an oath to walk in God's law, "all who have separated themselves from the peoples of the lands to the Law of God" are included in Israel's group (Neh 10:28, also Ezra 6:21). Having turned from their idolatry, these foreigners submit to the *Torah*. Their allegiance is now to the God of Israel.

Here the sage of the book of Ruth speaks up, offering a fuller narrative of a foreigner joining Israel. The Ruth story showcases Ruth the Moabitess' transformation from an idolater into a woman who fears the Lord (*YHWH*) and occupies a position of honor within Israel. Ruth is not just a foreigner—she is a Moabite, banned from joining Israel (Deut 23:3):

> 23:3 No Ammonite or Moabite may enter the assembly of the Lord. Even to the tenth generation, none of them may enter the assembly of the Lord forever.

Naomi's sons both took Moabite women as wives and subsequently died childless (Ruth 1:4-5). Without naming the specific reason, the narrative hints that the men of Naomi's household died because they sinned against the Lord. Ruth thus begins the story bearing her name in the same position as the idolatrous wives of Ezra-Nehemiah, the women condemned for diluting Israel's identity as set apart. Then, this Moabitess separates herself from her people, pledges her allegiance to

---

[143] Ezra-Nehemiah focuses on idolatrous influences from outside the covenant community. Foreigners were by no means the only source of other gods in Israel: without foreign aid, King Manasseh transformed Judah into an idolatrous people (2 Chron 33:1-9).

[144] The LXX translates the Hebrew word for "foreign" as *allotrios*: "belonging to another/other."

[145] Christopher J. H. Wright explains the problem thus: "So then, we need to understand that the underlying rationale for the prohibition on marrying the Canaanites (in the first place) was not racial but religious. It was not the foreignness of these wives that was the problem in itself, but that, being foreign, they were importing pagan gods and polluted practices into the heart of Israelite families." *Reading Ezra-Nehemiah Canonically*. Grand Rapids, MI: Eerdmans, 2018: 90.

Naomi,[146] and submits to the *Torah* of Naomi's God. Ruth is now in the position of the foreigners of Nehemiah 10:28, those who submit to the *Torah*. The text of Ruth constantly refers to "Ruth the Moabitess," making her assimilation into Israel that much more astounding. When she marries Boaz, "Ruth the Moabitess" is fully brought into the covenant community of Israel, influencing her family and town for good.

As discussed in the chapter on the book of Ruth, Ruth is Lady Wisdom of Proverbs 31, the wife of virtue (*hayil*), a great blessing to the house of Elimelech, Bethlehem, and all Israel. Ruth's turn to the Lord apparently overrides Deuteronomy's prohibition; instead of shunning this woman, Israel is to imitate her. Instead of posing a threat to the spiritual life of Bethlehem as the Ezra-Nehemiah marriages do, Ruth's presence and influence as a foreign God-fearer strengthen Israel's covenant relationship with the Lord. This woman serves as a real life example of Israel being a light and a blessing to the nations, drawing them to the Lord (Gen 12:1-3; Ex 19:5-6).

The sage of Proverbs interjects here with some comments on the word "foreign" (*nokri*), so significant in Ezra-Nehemiah. Proverbs also frequently uses *nokri* in the expression "foreign woman": the woman of Folly. Though Proverbs also warns against the influence of evil men (Prov 1:8-19, 2:12-15), the book primarily calls the royal son to embrace and love wisdom as he would a woman. The son's success or failure as a king and model for his people depends on his choosing Lady Wisdom over the woman of Folly. "Foreign" (*nokri*) occurs in parallel lines with "strange" (*zar*), "evil woman" (*'eshet ra'*), and "harlot" (*zonah*, Prov 5:20, 6:24, and 23:27 respectively). Such loaded vocabulary merits examination: *zar* and *zonah* each add a dimension to foreignness not readily visible in English translations. *Zar* suggests something illicit or that does not belong. For instance, Psalm 81:9-10a reads:

---

146 According to Deuteronomy 23:3, Moabites were not allowed in the assembly because they failed to show kindness (*hesed*) to the people of God. Ruth's labor in Boaz' fields for the good of Naomi adds another distinction between Ruth and unbelieving Moabites.

> 81:9 There shall be no strange (*zar*) god among you;
>
> You shall not bow down to a foreign (*nokri*) god.
>
> 10 I am the Lord your God.

These verses emphasize the centrality of the Lord in the life of His people: Israel must recognize, know, and shape her way of life around her God (*YHWH*), not other gods. The *zar* woman of Proverbs 5 and 7 is an illegitimate partner for the young man. Embracing the *zar* woman is akin to worshipping *zar* gods: neither belongs in the life of Israel. Such folly destroys life and leads to Sheol, the chambers of death (Prov 7:27). Though these texts certainly present the destructive consequences of committing adultery, the foundational choice facing the son—and by extension, the readers—is between pursuing folly and listening to wisdom, discretion, and knowledge (Prov 5:1-2, 7).

Further deepening the metaphor of the son embracing Lady Wisdom or the woman of Folly, Proverbs also uses *zonah*, "harlot/prostitute," to include the idea of unfaithfulness to a covenant. The *zonah*'s unfaithfulness can be both literal and metaphorical: she and the man actively, intentionally break their covenants with their marriage partners as well as with their God (Prov 7:10-20). Proverbs casts embracing the foreign, strange, adulteress as the greatest manifestation of folly.

The last word in Ezra-Nehemiah regarding mixed marriages highlights Solomon himself choosing between wisdom and folly. In his tirade against the men who married foreign women, Nehemiah wails (Neh 13:26):

> 13:26 Did not Solomon king of Israel sin on account of such women? Among the many nations there was no king like him, and he was beloved by his God, and God made him king over all Israel. Nevertheless, foreign (*nokri*) women made even him to sin. (CSV)

Even wise King Solomon, paragon of Israel, could not resist foreign women's influence on his life.[147] Instead of fearing the Lord to the end of his days, he worshipped his wives' foreign gods, setting his kingdom on the road to exile and death (2 Chron 36:14-17). Even after Moses warned that foreign, idolatrous women "will turn away your sons from following [the Lord], to serve other gods" (Deut 7:4; also Ex 34:16), Israel and her kings constantly wrestle with the temptation to embrace foreign women and their gods. As Solomon tells the son in Proverbs to choose Lady Wisdom, so the people in Ezra-Nehemiah must choose the Lord's *torah*. Only the statutes of the Lord protect the God-fearer and the nation of Israel from self-destruction.

Closing out this conversation, Proverbs connects with Ezra-Nehemiah over one last alarming dimension of the foreign women: their influence as mothers. Proverbs highlights the mother's role in teaching her children: the son should listen to his father's instruction and not forsake his mother's *torah* (Prov 1:8, 6:20, 31:26). Nehemiah 13:23-24 records the foreign women's guidance of their half-Jewish children:

> 13:23 In those days also I saw the Jews who had married women of Ashdod, Ammon, and Moab.
>
> 24 And half of their children spoke the language of Ashdod, and they could not speak the language of Judah, but only the language of each people.

The contrast is glaring. Not only are the foreign women failing to teach their children the *Torah*, but they are also not teaching the children the language of the Jews, the words needed to understand themselves, their people, the Law, and their God. In direct contrast with the wise path of King Lemuel's mother, the Proverbs 31 woman, and Lady Wisdom, these foreign women guide their children into ignorance and sin. In one quick generation, these children will be Israel no more.

---

147 Even though Nehemiah 13:26 uses causative language—the women "caused him to sin" (NASB), "led him to sin" (NIV), or "drew him into sin" (CSB)—this verse marks the only place in the book where foreign women are the subject of the sentence's verb. Elsewhere, the Jews are the active subjects and the foreign women the objects of the verb. This grammar puts the responsibility for Israel's sin squarely on Israel's shoulders.

Marriage thus provides fertile ground for the cultivation of wisdom or folly. Together, Ezra-Nehemiah, Ruth, and Proverbs outline Israel's options: embrace Lady Wisdom, life, and a future, or embrace the woman of Folly and the path to death. Israel's engagement with foreign women serves as a barometer of her spiritual priorities: unite with Ruth, the woman of virtue (*hayil*) who chooses the *torah* of God, or join the idolatrous woman on the path to Sheol.

3. Bad Endings

In the Hebrew Bible and MT order of Law, Prophets, and Writings, Ezra-Nehemiah concludes both the Writings and the Hebrew Old Testament. And what an ending! In the last chapter of the text, Nehemiah returns to Jerusalem only to find Israel forsaking the statutes of the Law: not only does a foreigner live in the temple, but the people of Israel are also breaking the Sabbath, withholding their tithe from the Levites, failing to ensure the temple sacrifices, and once again intermingling with idolatrous foreigners of the land. Though Nehemiah corrects these wrongs, readers end the Writings expecting Israel and Jerusalem to return to her sins at their next opportunity. Echoing Ezra and Lamentations, readers wonder whether the Lord's anger will destroy the people completely, leaving no remnant (Ezra 9:14; Lam 5:22). Given this ending, does Israel have a future? Will the Lord honor His promises to Abraham? Seeking hope, the sage of Ezra-Nehemiah compares endings with the Law and the Prophets, and then engages the sages of the Writings about their respective endings.

The endings of the Law and the Prophets collections differ from the Writings in that amidst their record of Israel's sin, they both include hope. Deuteronomy 34 closes the Law with the death of Moses. As Adam was exiled from the Garden because of one sin, so Moses' sin at Kadesh bars him from entering the promised land (Num 20:8-22). However, the last verses of the Law honor Moses' role in the history of Israel, reminding readers of the Lord's promise in Deuteronomy 18:15-18 to raise up "a prophet like Moses." As Moses mediated the Sinai Covenant, this future prophet will bring about the New Covenant

(Deut 30:1-14). Even though Adam's and Moses' sins lead to exile, the Law closes with the Lord's promise of another great act of salvation.

In turn, the Prophets collection ends with three post-exilic prophets, each addressing Israel's continued sinfulness after the exile: Haggai, Zechariah, and Malachi. For example, Malachi condemns Israel for:

- lacking respect for the Lord (Mal 1:6-14).
- the priests' teaching causing the people to stumble into sin (Mal 2:1-9).
- dealing treacherously with one other (Mal 2:10).
- profaning the Lord's sanctuary with idolatry (Mal 2:11).
- divorcing their wives (Mal 2:14-15).
- robbing God by bringing Him unacceptable offerings (Mal 3:8-15).

Yet after this disheartening list, Malachi's last words speak of the coming of "Elijah the prophet" to turn the hearts of Israel to the Lord: this prophet will restore Israel and avoid the Lord's wrath against them (Mal 4:4-6). Both the Law and the Prophets collections end with clear hope amidst sin: the Lord has not forgotten His people. A great prophet is coming to save Israel once again.

The Writings end with no such positivity. Ezra-Nehemiah offers glimmers of hope: the Lord's fulfillment of His promise to bring the people back to the land after the Babylonian exile and the people's confession in Nehemiah 9. However, the ending of the book returns to none of these hopeful moments. In fact, Nehemiah ends the book imploring the Lord to remember his attempts to bring the people back to their God. Any hope from earlier chapters is apparently snuffed out.

The conversation now turns to the other sages in the Writings, probing their content for insights less readily apparent if the collection is read in a rigidly serial order. Chronicles, Lamentations, and Daniel begin by echoing Ezra-Nehemiah's questioning ending:

- Chronicles presents the Lord's promise of an eternal kingdom to David but ends with the Cyrus decree. Cyrus, a Gentile, cannot be the messiah, the new *'adam*, yet he reigns securely over Israel.

- Several verses in the center of Lamentations speak of the Lord's lovingkindness, mercy, and faithfulness, but the people end the book wondering if the Lord has utterly forsaken them.

- After a series of visions about the coming eternal kingdom of God, the book of Daniel ends with instructions to wise Daniel to "go his way until the end," implying that difficult days still lie ahead for him.

These sages only confirm Ezra-Nehemiah's dilemma: does Israel have a future? The Song of Songs and Ecclesiastes speak next, each addressing the present instead of the future. The Song ends still preoccupied with its passionate longing, and Ecclesiastes urges readers to fear the Lord and keep His commandments all the days of their short life.

Heads turn to the remaining sages, still looking for concluding words of hope and blessing. With joy, they oblige:

- The Psalter begins with the afflictions of the Lord's Son and Messiah but ends with hope for the reign of the Messiah and a crescendo of praise (Pss 146-150).

- Job, the God-fearer, is restored (lit. "returned from captivity"), and the Lord blesses him two-fold.

- After opening by calling the son to embrace Lady Wisdom, the book of Proverbs ends with a portrait of the wife of virtue (*hayil*). The son appears to have chosen wisely and embraced Lady Wisdom.

- In the book of Ruth, Boaz and Ruth's son, Obed, fills Naomi's emptiness, linking the man and woman of virtue (*hayil*) to King David.
- In the book of Esther, the Jews are saved from annihilation and feast joyfully.

These uplifting messages of redemption and joy speak hope into the Writings' conversation, reminding the sages and the people of the Lord's *hesed*. As a collection yet also as individual texts, the Writings repeatedly hold two truths simultaneously; Israel's current situation of distress and slavery to Gentiles lives in tension with Israel's hope in the Lord and His faithfulness. The Writings as a whole could be considered a long form lament: repeatedly, the texts search for the Lord amidst suffering and tribulation. Psalm 13 provides the same juxtaposition on a small scale: first, abandonment and suffering, then hope (Ps 13:1-2, 5-6):

13:1		How long, O Lord? Will you forget me forever?
		How long will you hide your face from me?
2		How long must I take counsel in my soul
		And have sorrow in my heart all the day?
		How long shall my enemy be exalted over me?
5		But I have trusted in your steadfast love (*hesed*);
		My heart shall rejoice in your salvation.
6		I will sing to the Lord,
		Because he has dealt bountifully with me.

As Psalm 13 moves from suffering to hope, in conversation with one another, the Writings follow the same trajectory. Some texts depict sinful Israel's present afflictions; the Lord appears far away, unconcerned with their plight. Others provide great comfort: as in the past, so the Lord's lovingkindness will continue into the future. When readers consider the texts of the Writings in conversation with one another, the circle of sages points them back to the hopeful high points of the collection.

In contrast to the explicitly hopeful endings of the Law and the Prophets, the Writings prompt readers to reflect and meditate on a variety of texts and their interactions in search of wisdom. Such is the nature of wisdom. Thus, the Hebrew Bible finishes with an open-ended "ending": readers are to seek the wisdom of God as they wait for the coming Messiah, the One to redeem all of humanity ('adam).

Toward the New Testament

1. City, People, Temple

The Ezra-Nehemiah restoration of city, people, and temple prepares for the coming of the Messiah. Jesus' Triumphal Entry also brings together these three key elements: the people escort Jesus up the hill to the city of Jerusalem, heralding Him as the Son of David, come in the name of the Lord (Matt 21:9; Ps 118:25-26). When He arrives, He immediately enters the temple (Matt 21:1-11; Mark 11:1-10; Luke 19:29-38) and clears it out as one does a den of robbers (Matt 21:13; Jer 7:11). Yet instead of rallying around King Jesus and enthroning Him, Israel fails to recognize her Messiah. Jesus then curses the fig tree as a sign of the people's lack of faith and fruit (Matt 21:18-22). The Jews of Jesus' day harbor the same rebellion and stubbornness as their ancestors; they refuse to listen in faith and so kill God's chosen one. Just as Ezra-Nehemiah requires another future return to the Lord in the New Covenant, so the NT anticipates a second coming for Jesus to sit upon the throne of God in the temple-like New Jerusalem, surrounded by His faithful and wise followers (Rev 21:1-9).

2. Intermingling with Foreigners

As explained above, Israel's intermingling with foreigners brought idolatry and abominations into their homes, families, and culture.

The NT letters treat this same issue using terms of worldliness. Paul introduces and summarizes his instruction using wisdom language (Eph 4:17-18):

> 4:17 Now this I say and testify in the Lord, that you must no longer **walk** as the Gentiles do, in the **futility** of their minds.
>
> 18 They are **darkened in their understanding**, alienated from the life of God because of the **ignorance** that is in them, due to their hardness of **heart**.

Christians must lay aside the folly of the old Adam—their former worldly life—and put on the new Adam, Christ Himself: righteousness, holiness, and truth. Paul repeatedly emphasizes the severity of worldliness; Christians must cease thinking and acting like the world (Rom 12:2; Col 2:8; Gal 6:14; Tit 2:11-12). Similarly, John teaches that Christians cannot love the world or the things in the world (1 John 2:15-17). James goes so far as to call friendship with the world hostility toward God (James 4:4). Much like post-exilic Israel, Christians also struggle with worldliness; full resolution requires a total transformation of body, soul, and spirit in the resurrection. In the meantime, like Daniel and Job, Christians are instructed to seek wisdom, turning away from evil and avoiding the world's foolish path.

3. Bad Endings

In Jesus Christ, there are no bad endings; He comes to make all things new (Rev 21:4). Certainly, at the crucifixion, the life and times of Jesus of Nazareth appeared to end badly. In Luke 24, Jesus meets two of His disciples on the road to Emmaus; they recount to Him the events of the last few days. The One they hoped would redeem Israel was crucified and is now dead (Luke 24:19-21). For them, Jesus' life ended badly, on history's worst Friday. All hope is lost. Only once Jesus breaks bread before them at dinner are their eyes finally opened— they believe and rush back to Jerusalem to declare the good news to the other disciples (Luke 24:31-35). Jesus then explains to them all the suffering and resurrection of the Messiah through the Law, Prophets, and Psalms (Luke 24:44-47). The resurrection transforms the worst Friday into Good Friday.

Jesus Christ's resurrection takes every bad ending in Scripture and the human experience and turns them into good endings. Death, mourning, pain, and all the first things will pass away; Jesus will make all things new for the wise. To the sound of the Psalter's crescendo of praise from all creation, Jesus the Messiah will usher in eternal goodness and joy for all creation. This is the end!

Further Reading

Blenkinsopp, Joseph. "The Social Context of the 'Outsider Woman' in Proverbs 1-9." *Biblica* 72 (1991): 457–73.

Brown, A. Philip, II. "The Problem of Mixed Marriages in Ezra 9-10." *Bibliotheca Sacra*, 162:648 (2005): 437–58.

Goswell, Greg (Gregory Ross). "Having the Last Say: The End of the OT." *Journal of the Evangelical Theological Society*, 58 (1): 15–30.

Jackson, Bernard. "Ezra-Nehemiah." *The Dynamics of Early Judaean Law: Studies in the Diversity of Ancient Social and Communal Legislation.* Sandra Jacobs, Ed. Boston, MA: De Gruyter, 2024.

Knowles, Melody D. "Reimagining Community Past and Present in Ezra and Nehemiah." Donn F. Morgan, Ed. *The Oxford Handbook of the Writings of the Hebrew Bible*, Oxford Handbooks, Online Edition, 2018.

Shepherd, David. *Ezra and Nehemiah*. Christopher J. H. Wright, Ed. Grand Rapids, MI: Eerdmans Publishing Company, 2018.

Sprinkle, Joe M. "Old Testament Perspectives on Divorce and Remarriage." *Journal of the Evangelical Theological Society* 40: 529–50.

Reflections for Today

The conversation now falls silent. Each sage sits there, reflecting on the discussions recorded in this book. Slowly, each one turns to look at ... the reader of *Voices of the Sages*. After seeking wisdom in conversation with one another, the sages direct their attention to you.

As laid out in the Introduction, the Writings instruct the afflicted people of God to seek Wisdom during His apparent absence, as we wait for the coming David and His kingdom. The Psalter encapsulates these ideas in the *torah*-wisdom of Psalms 1 and 2. Psalm 1 presents two people: the one who meditates on the *torah* of the Lord and the wicked sinner. The Lord's path leads to a flourishing life; in the end, this person stands blessed in the assembly of the righteous. Psalm 2 presents the Lord's King, Son, and Messiah reigning from Zion in spite of foolish kings' attempts to eliminate Him. The wise choose the Lord, "kiss" the son, and live. Together, these psalms offer the reader a focus for their life, regardless of time or location: meditating on the *torah*-wisdom of the Lord and taking refuge in the Son, His Messiah, the Lord Jesus Christ.

"I've gathered that," you say. "But applying wisdom is tricky. How do I link these abstract concepts of wisdom to an actual action?" The sages nod, murmur, agree; that is the next question. Somehow, it's also still the wrong question. Since the application of wisdom is so situation-specific, wisdom can be taught but not prescribed. The wise learn to use knowledge and insight to reflect and discern how to apply wisdom principles well within their own life circumstances. To hone this skill, the sages exhort you: in affliction, seek the Lord and wait for the King.

1. In Affliction

The life of the Jews in the post-exile matches the NT and church history's picture of the life of the church: moments of joy, lots of suffering, affliction, conflict. A person's life under the sun contains a wide array of experiences and emotions, but life's most formative times usually involve suffering. Sickness, death, trials, sorrow, injustice, violence, fear: these all mark every human life. In suffering, people turn to God. The Writings welcome those who suffer, offering validation and consolation.

Times of trouble and tribulation call for the wise to trust in the Lord and not their own understanding (Prov 3:5-6). Psalm 73 recounts Asaph's struggle to keep his faith in the Lord as he sees the wicked flourishing and the righteous suffering. It is indeed difficult to cling to the Lord and His way when doing so brings no relief and the wicked seem to enjoy the good life. Job, too, experienced deep despair and suffering, even though he was blameless. In vain he sought to know why the Lord was afflicting him. When God does speak to Job, He does not answer his question. Instead, the Lord teaches Job a bit of His wisdom, and Job's newfound perspective puts him at peace (*shalom*)—peace with God and peace within his afflictions. Both Asaph and Job illustrate that in times of suffering, even God-fearers usually seek to resolve their situation on their own, with their own understanding. This is not the way of wisdom. Only the wisdom of the Lord provides the right perspective on adversity and affliction. Humans cannot find this perspective on our own. The Writings point us to the Lord to see our situation in a new light—the light of God's wisdom.

In contrast to Job and Asaph, who both cling to their faith, Naomi illustrates how God-fearers sometimes draw the wrong conclusions in their trials. After losing her whole family in Moab, Naomi tells the women of Bethlehem the Lord had embittered her life and afflicted her. Unlike Asaph and Job, she does not turn to the Lord but wallows in her affliction. Her perspective changes when she learns Ruth has gleaned in the field of Boaz, a potential kinsman-redeemer. Even in her misery and bitterness, Naomi recognizes the Lord's kindness (*hesed*) to her. Sometimes, the Lord, our good Shepherd, demonstrates His faithfulness to us in our trials, offering strength and hope, encouraging us to stay on the Wisdom path, avoiding folly.

Though still suffering, the wise learn to recognize the *hesed* of the Lord, correct their perspective, and enjoy His comfort.

Nonetheless, trials and troubles can force God-fearers to choose the wisdom path in the face of difficulty and danger. When King Darius banned prayer to anyone other than himself for 30 days, Daniel chose to face the lions' den rather than give up his prayers (the Psalms?). Similarly, Shadrach, Meshach, and Abednego refused to bow down to the image of King Nebuchadnezzar, choosing the fiery furnace in a simple but damning decision. In such situations, the wisdom path leads not to deliverance, but to more suffering, sometimes even death. Daniel and his friends model for us that God-fearers stay on the path of wisdom even in the absence of a promise of rescue. We are to choose the Lord at all costs.

The Writings offer the reader a variety of examples to follow, according to the circumstances of one's own life. Yet amidst their differences in time and space, these OT characters demonstrate that ultimately, the wise find refuge in the Lord. Troubles may ease or remain, but *shalom* is found only in the Lord, His perspective, and His wisdom.

2. Seek the Lord

The Writings consistently urge us to seek the Lord and thereby avoid folly. The sage of Chronicles offers David as an example here: David's first act as king was to seek out the Ark of the Covenant, the symbol of the Lord's presence and kingship over Israel. When David brings the ark into Jerusalem, he illustrates his submission to the authority of the Lord, the Great King. Then, under David's musical leadership, Asaph celebrates this event with a psalm, exhorting all Israel to seek the Lord (1 Chron 16:10-11):

> 16:10 Glory in His holy name;
>
> Let the hearts of those who seek the Lord rejoice!

11	Seek the Lord and His strength;
	Seek His presence continually!

David's own psalms also reflect his seeking the Lord (Ps 63:1):

63:1	O God, You are my God; earnestly I seek You;
	My soul thirsts for you;
	My flesh faints for you,
	As in a dry and weary land where there is no water.

David teaches us that seeking the Lord means directing our hearts to Him in worship and prayer. These active pursuits reflect and respond to His Word. Confession, praise, petition, prayer, and acts of obedience all serve to bring the reader closer to the Lord and his *torah*-wisdom.

The sage of Proverbs speaks next. First, he urges the reader to embrace Lady Wisdom. More valuable than gold, silver, and any treasure (Prov 2:4), her wisdom is the Lord's. Though seeking wisdom involves acquiring knowledge, the wise must embrace and love wisdom as a man loves and embraces a woman (Prov 4:4-9). Solomon's building of the temple, Daniel's interpretation of dreams, and the description of the Proverbs 31 woman all illustrate this principle: the words of the wise are Lady Wisdom's words, their deeds are her deeds. You, reader, need to pursue and embrace Wisdom. The sage of Proverbs continues, turning the discussion to the source of one's deeds and actions: our heart, "for from it flow the springs of life" (Prov 4:23b). Proverbs 4:23a exhorts God-fearers to "watch over their heart with all diligence (*shahar*)." As a noun, *shahar* means "dawn," the very first part of the day. God-fearers must seek the Lord as the first priority of our lives, directing our hearts to Him "above all else" (CSB).

The Psalter and Ezra-Nehemiah speak next, offering concrete direction: God-fearers are to listen to Scripture. Psalm 119:1-8, the great *torah* psalm, urges readers to walk in the way of the Lord, in His *torah*, seeking Him and keeping His word. The Lord paves the way for the righteous with His very words. The reader should pay careful attention to Scripture, reflecting on it day and night (Ps 1:2). The word of the Lord created everything (Ps 33:4-9); His word also recreates, restores, and renews us when we seek Him (Ps 19:7-10). As Nehemiah 8 recounts, hearing and understanding the *torah* of the Lord powerfully affects the people of God. In a scene reminiscent of the best church services, the people of Israel rejoice in their obedience to the proclaimed word of God: joy in the Lord was their strength and is still ours today (Neh 8:10). By seeking the Lord, God-fearers understand their place before the Lord, the King of Heaven, finding in His words joy and a refuge from the storms of life.

Yet amidst all this seeking the Lord, we humans still wander off the path of wisdom. The Psalter closes this directive with a petition. After the psalmist proclaims his love for the Lord and His word, he ends Psalm 119 with "I have gone astray like a lost sheep; seek your servant" (Ps 119:176). Even when we fail to seek the Lord in obedience to His word, the psalms guide us to ask Him to seek us, bringing us back to Him. This is the role of our Good Shepherd.

3. Wait for the King

Seeing through the Lord's perspective, seeking Him, the reader is to wait for the future King. The promise of His coming fills the pages of the Writings. Chronicles and the Psalter foretell a son of David who will suffer but also rule the Lord's kingdom forever (1 Chron 17; Ps 132). After all her folly and exile, Israel waits in hope for a wise son of David to come and usher in eternal blessing for God's people, Jew and Gentile together. Our King is coming!

During this time between promise and fulfillment, the mighty man of Lamentations calls us to hope (Lam 3:21-26):

3:21   But this I call to mind,

And therefore **I have hope** (*yahal*):

22	The steadfast love (*hesed*) of the Lord never ceases;
	His mercies (*rahamim*) never come to an end;
23	They are new every morning;
	Great is your faithfulness (*'emunah*).
24	"The Lord is my portion," says my soul,
	"Therefore **I will hope** (*yahal*) in him."
25	The Lord is good to those who **wait** (*qawah*) for him,
	To the soul who seeks him.
26	It is good that one should **wait** (*yahal*) quietly
	For the salvation of the Lord.

The OT uses hope (*yahal*) and waiting (*qawah*) synonymously. Living between promise and fulfillment drives us to hope as we wait for the Lord to accomplish His promises for Israel, for us, and for all creation. Reflecting on His character gives us strength to endure as we wait in hope for His Kingdom to come: because of His *hesed*, His promise is sound. He will bring about what He has promised. Even in the most distressing circumstances, such as the total destruction this mighty man experienced, we know daily that the Lord's faithfulness remains.

Psalm 78:65-72 describes the coming of David as the Lord "awakening from sleep." From a human perspective, David's arrival to shepherd Israel from Zion changed the whole narrative of Israel. Similar to the role Obed plays in the life of Naomi, David redeems Israel from the bitterness of the Lord's judgment for her sin. The genealogy at the end of the book of Ruth points to a time when the Lord awakens again, bringing the seed of Judah and David to redeem His people: the Lord Jesus. Christians today live in a blessed hope that Redeemer Jesus will one day return to establish the Lord's eternal kingdom. With those in Lamentations, we cry "How long, Oh Lord? How long?" When will the Lord awake again to complete His plans for us and all creation? When will the wise rejoice, go up, and kiss the Son in Zion?

We do not know. We Christians are to seek the Lord, most importantly in trials, with the hope that the wisdom path leads to the King in His kingdom. The sages sit quietly, gently looking at you. There is, at this time, nothing more to say. The sage of the book of Daniel stands, looks you right in the eye, and says, "Now go your way in wisdom to the end!"

Appendix: Conversations in *Voices of the Sages*

Listed by Chapter & Topic

Chapter 1: Introduction

- Purpose of *Voices of the Sages*
- What is Wisdom?
- The Books in the Writings: Dates, Authors, Order
- Themes in the Writings
- A Primer on Hebrew Poetry

Chapter 2: Chronicles

1. The House of the Lord
    - The Psalms
    - Lamentations
    - Ezra-Nehemiah
    - The Book of Daniel

2. The House of David
    - The Psalms

3. The Two Ways
    - Proverbs

Chapter 3: The Psalms

1. *Torah*-Wisdom

- Ezra-Nehemiah

- Proverbs

2. Suffering to Glory

- The Book of Job

- Lamentations

3. The Lord and His Son Reign in Zion with the Wise

- Chronicles

- Lamentations

- The Book of Daniel

Chapter 4: The Book of Job

1. The Fear of the Lord

- Proverbs

- Ecclesiastes

- The Psalms

2. Wisdom Manifest in Creation

- The Psalms

- Ecclesiastes

3. Actions and their Consequences

- The Psalms

- Proverbs
- Ecclesiastes

Chapter 5: Proverbs

1. The Fundamentals of Wisdom
   - The Psalms
   - The Book of Job

2. Lady Wisdom and Woman of Folly
   - Ecclesiastes
   - The Book of Ruth

3. Wisdom with Wisdom
   - Ecclesiastes

Chapter 6: The Book of Ruth

1. Naomi's Redemption
   - The Psalms
   - The Book of Job
   - Ezra-Nehemiah

2. Lovingkindness
   - Proverbs

3. Woman of Excellence
   - Proverbs

Chapter 7: The Song of Songs

1. The Passionate Pursuit of Love

- Proverbs
- The Book of Ruth

2. The Consummation of Love

- Proverbs
- The Psalms

3. Human Love, Love Divine

- The Psalms
- God in the Writings

Chapter 8: Ecclesiastes

1. *Hebel*

- The Psalms
- Lamentations
- Chronicles

2. The Good Life

- The Book of Job
- The Psalms
- The Book of Ruth

- Proverbs

3. The Limitations of Human Knowledge
    - The Book of Job
    - Proverbs
    - The Book of Daniel

Chapter 9: Lamentations

1. Lady Jerusalem
    - The Psalms
    - Proverbs

2. The Lord's Judgment
    - The Psalms
    - Ecclesiastes
    - The Book of Esther
    - The Book of Daniel
    - Ezra-Nehemiah

3. The Hope of the Afflicted Man
    - The Book of Job
    - The Psalms
    - The Book of Daniel
    - Chronicles

Chapter 10: The Book of Esther

1. Kings and Kingdoms

- The Psalms

- The Book of Daniel

- Lamentations

2. Esther: Woman of Wisdom

- Proverbs

- The Book of Daniel

3. The Absence of God

- Ezra-Nehemiah

- The Psalms

- The Book of Ruth

- Proverbs

- The Song of Songs

Chapter 11: The Book of Daniel

1. Daniel the Wise

- Proverbs

- The Psalms

2. God's Creation Decrees Realized

- Chronicles

- The Psalms

3. 70 "Weeks" of Exile

- Chronicles

- Ezra-Nehemiah

- The Book of Job

Chapter 12: Ezra-Nehemiah

1. City, People, Temple

    - The Book of Daniel

    - Chronicles

    - The Psalms

2. Intermingling with Idolatrous Foreigners

    - Marriage in the Writings

    - Proverbs

    - Ruth

3. Bad Endings

    - Endings in the Writings

Afterword: Reflections for Today

www.ingramcontent.com/pod-product-compliance
Lightning Source LLC
LaVergne TN
LVHW012033070526
838202LV00056B/5486